surrounded by
narcissists

surrounded by
narcissists

Or, How to Stop
Other People's Egos
Ruining Your Life

• • • •

thomas erikson

Vermilion

1

Vermilion, an imprint of Ebury Publishing,
20 Vauxhall Bridge Road,
London SW1V 2SA

Vermilion is part of the Penguin Random House group of companies
whose addresses can be found at global.penguinrandomhouse.com

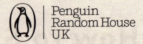

Penguin
Random House
UK

First published in Great Britain by Vermilion in 2022
First published in the United States by St. Martin's Essentials,
an imprint of St. Martin's Publishing Group in 2022
First published in Sweden by Bokförlaget Forum in 2021

www.penguin.co.uk

A CIP catalogue record for this book is available from the British Library

ISBN 9781785043673

Printed and bound in Great Britain by Clays Ltd, Elcograf S.p.A.

The authorised representative in the EEA is Penguin Random House Ireland,
Morrison Chambers, 32 Nassau Street, Dublin D02 YH68

Penguin Random House is committed to a sustainable future
for our business, our readers and our planet. This book is made
from Forest Stewardship Council® certified paper.

MIX
Paper from
responsible sources
FSC® C018179

Contents

Introduction

Love is a serious mental disease.

—PLATO

I

Love can be the most beautiful experience a human being has in their lifetime. True, genuine, requited love that's strong enough to shake the core of your being. It makes your heart race and your legs wobblier than usual. I'm talking about the kind of love where you find yourself dreamily gazing off into the horizon, brimming over with longing for the object of your desire. A love that makes you want to protect your partner from any threat that appears.

Normally, it takes two people to produce this kind of infinite, larger-than-life adulation. But sometimes it's a different story.

A few years ago, I wrote *Surrounded by Psychopaths*. Since its publication, I've had an astonishing number of people suggest to me that I should also write a book about narcissists. At first, the subject triggered no curiosity in me at all. This was mainly because of the close ties between narcissism and psychopathy; it felt difficult to add anything substantially novel or different to the subject.

As time went on, and I worked away on other projects, I began to notice a series of odd phenomena that are occurring in our society today. These were developments that honestly made very little sense to me. I found myself discussing a bunch of rather unusual questions with a whole crowd of people who had made similar observations themselves. Phenomena we hadn't observed before were becoming increasingly common right in front of our eyes.

Meanwhile, the inquiries kept coming from various interested parties: *When are you going to write a book about narcissism?* In the end, this question was posed to me by somebody I couldn't say no to—you know who you are—and I began, somewhat unwillingly, I might add, to research the subject. After some thorough investigations into the subject of narcissism, however, it dawned on me that I had stumbled across the explanation to a whole series of peculiarities that are making their way around the world.

Narcissism, in the sense of the personality disorder defined by psychiatrists, takes its name from the character Narcissus from Greek mythology. This youth, who was famous for his beauty, was the son of the river god Cephissus. Narcissus was so incredibly handsome that anybody who saw him would immediately fall in love with him. The trouble was that he rejected everyone, including the young girl Echo—and was thus fated to fall in love with his own reflection.

In one version of the myth—there are more competing versions out there than seems entirely necessary—Narcissus simply starves to death as he sits there by the pond, gazing at his reflection. Eventually, he transformed into a white-and-yellow flower, which has since been named after him—the *Narcissus* genus of flowers includes the daffodil.

Whichever version of the myth we decide to believe, poor Narcissus was the first person ever, as far as we know, to fall victim to this powerful kind of self-love. But then again, being that he is a mythical figure, it seems likely that the problem was a familiar one even before the story was first told. Myths usually describe and explain things that people have already made note of.

We've all come across them.

The people who talk about themselves incessantly, announcing their incredible knowledge, skills, experience, and credentials to the world; who feel entitled to the best of whatever life has to offer; who feel better, more attractive, and more successful than their peers; who take selfies by the hundreds, painstakingly pore over them to single out the best one, and then fly into a violent rage if it doesn't receive as many likes as they feel it deserves. These are the people who go to great lengths to be trendy, who put great value in being seen, and who seem to be prepared to do almost anything to stand out. They get upset when the success they're expecting fails to materialize, and succumb to needy whining whenever things don't go their way.

Perhaps you're thinking to yourself that people like this are nothing new. We used to just think to ourselves, *What a jerk!* Nowadays, people hardly even raise an eyebrow at this kind of thing. It's the new normal.

Families accumulating massive debt just so they can keep up with the Joneses. Parents convincing their children that they can be anything they want because of how naturally fantastic they are. Influencers whose only real achievement is appearing in social media in trendy outfits. How long has it been this way?

School kids who feel they don't need to study because they reckon they already know everything. Grade averages dropping in our schools, despite the constant dumbing down of the grading criteria. Families being run by members who have insufficient or no real-life experience. Teenagers choosing the family's holiday destination. Mothers buying their teenagers cars that cost more than the ones they drive themselves.

University students who, rather than engaging with their ideological opponents in debate, form mobs to shout and cause enough ruckus to make sure that speakers they disapprove of won't be able to make themselves heard. Individuals who openly admit that they would do anything—literally *anything*—in order to be successful. Successful at *what?* one wonders.

Perhaps at participating in reality shows on TV, shows that feature aspects of human anatomy and behavior that would have been incredibly shocking just a few decades ago.

What we think of as normal has taken on a very different face. The connections between the preceding descriptions and narcissism are as evident as they are disquieting. All of those descriptions include significant signs of narcissistic behavior. Sometimes, though, you need to take a few steps back to be able to detect the pattern. But as soon as you do, you see it as clear as day.

II

Psychologists are more or less in agreement: Clinical narcissism occurs in somewhere between 1 and 2 percent of the population. However, there is no absolute consensus on the subject, and different researchers quote different sets of figures. Disagreement and argument over these issues is rife in the field. But for our purposes, 1 or 2 percent will be accurate enough. You might think that doesn't sound like too many. One percent is a very small ratio. Like a tiny glitch in the system. But then again, that would mean that Sweden, my own country of residence, would be home to somewhere between one hundred thousand and two hundred thousand narcissists.

Applying the same percentage globally gives us a population of between 70 and 140 million narcissists. But there is a significant difference between the clinical term "narcissistic personality disorder," or "NPD," and what we call narcissistic *behavior*. The latter is exhibited by people who display obvious narcissistic tendencies without having received a clinical diagnosis. Later in this book, I'll be giving you a series of examples of what I have come to refer to as narcissistic culture. This is when narcissistic behaviors become increasingly prevalent in various levels of society. One example of this would be an increased emphasis on the self. International research suggests that in Western culture *this* is exhibited by closer to 10 percent of the population, maybe even more than that. Some have even suggested 15 to 20 percent.

Just the thought of applying this percentage to the global population is enough to make me feel like I need to lie down.

If we take a look at what clinical narcissism actually is, we'll soon find that among other characteristics, these individuals tend to entertain unrealistic self-images, indulge in self-obsession, consider themselves unique, speak only about themselves, deflect all criticism and negative feedback, feel that the rules don't apply to them, and basically strive for nothing but external rewards and social recognition. "Everybody else—*everybody*—should get out of the way, because *here I come!*"

Narcissists do genuinely strive for perfection, particularly in the eyes of others. They want everybody to view and think of them as the most beautiful, most intelligent, most informed, fittest, best dressed, wealthiest, most successful, and happiest people in the entire world. However, there is an obvious problem here: That goal is both irrational and completely unattainable.

Basically, we can't expect any good to come of narcissism becoming more widespread in society. However, if we're to approach this issue in a more serious way, we'll need to figure out what's actually going on first. In addition, we have to give some thought to the practical consequences we all stand to suffer if we allow narcissism to run rampant. What I'm getting at here is that we need to be aware of *the severity of the challenge*. If you don't know which problem you're supposed to be solving, you won't even see any need for a solution.

Once, long ago, there was no such thing as an SUV. Then, one day, SUVs became a thing. Some people bought them and reaped the benefits of a high, safe perch with a good view of traffic (at the expense of everybody else's), and enjoyed the sense of security that came from knowing that they would be quite safe if they were to collide with an ordinary car. However, anybody who wasn't driving an SUV was suddenly in greater danger, because they were now at risk of colliding with one. The most significant cost related to the creation of SUVs was paid by all the other drivers, basically.

More and more people bought SUVs. They wanted to feel safe and have that great view of the surrounding traffic, too. But what were the consequences? Fuel consumption spiked; the planet's resources were more carelessly exploited than ever; emissions increased . . . If everybody were to drive an SUV, many of the original benefits would simply be gone. It's like a trap, in a way.

Narcissism functions very similarly. The behavior of a narcissist comes at a cost to others, just like the invasion of the SUVs happened mainly at the expense of other drivers. Narcissists can maintain their sense of pride by lashing out at somebody who has somehow insulted them. Similarly, they can maintain their sense of personal fabulousness by taking credit for the achievements of their peers. They can cultivate a cool *player* image for themselves by dating countless potential mates who never even learn of one another's existence. Narcissists can go on feeling wonderful and amazing, while they make everyone around them suffer.

Some people claim that there is a limit to how many self-infatuated narcissists we can cope with, collectively. That's an interesting thought: How much narcissism can society actually tolerate? Assuming the phenomenon really is becoming more common, that is.

III

Of course, the question of how we ended up here is incredibly interesting, and it's unlikely that it can be answered simply.

Some blame the Internet and social media, while others point to the omnipresence of the message that we must all cultivate our self-esteem and be the best we can be. Social media companies were originally created by people who genuinely wanted to do good in the world and connect people to one another to help them share their lives online. Others suggest that this narcissistic strain has actually been there all along and that what has changed is simply that we now have the tools to express it.

Little mention is ever given to the fact that parents who encourage their little darlings to believe that they are princesses or world champions from the moment they are born, admittedly with the best of intentions, are inadvertently producing a sluggish armada of egomaniacal underachievers. Later in this book, I'll be sharing examples from schools in which comparisons were made between the performances of students with varying degrees of self-esteem. The results can only be described as . . . interesting.

Imagining that you're amazing and successful before your work has even begun is one approach, of course. Admittedly, too, we don't know for sure that people aren't striving to feel successful rather than actually be successful.

What I will be reflecting on is whether we *might actually* have reached the point of diminishing returns when it comes to the benefits of egocentricity. At what point does good, healthy self-esteem turn into vanity and self-obsession and settle into a pattern of pathological egoism?

Even those who only risk developing narcissistic traits rather than becoming full-on narcissists, should take warning here. Although narcissists are invariably able to own a room, a conversation, or even an entire organization, they inevitably end up giving themselves away, eventually. The people around them start to genuinely dislike them. If the narcissist doesn't abandon their overt self-centeredness, it will eventually trigger feelings of loathing in others. This is the very opposite of what the narcissist is actually trying to achieve, i.e., unwavering dedication.

IV

Before I move on to addressing the narcissistic culture we're seeing emerge, I'll describe and offer examples of NPD—which is a truly disturbed state.

I also have a challenge for you and everyone else: Think, very carefully, about what we as a society ought to be striving to become. What kind of people do we want to be? Who do *you* want to be? What do you want to have control your life and your personal growth? How would you like others to view you, starting today?

We could opt for the distinctively narcissistic path, which is paved with vanity, self-centeredness, superficial relationships, greed, social isolation, guilt, and chaos.

Or we could choose another path, which leads us away from all those things.

That approach is a pursuit of a far greater truth and freedom, but also the acceptance of a far-reaching sense of responsibility— for ourselves, our families, our kids, and all the people we care the most about. However, this responsibility also extends to the society in which we live.

This path is admittedly a more demanding one, but unlike the narcissist's approach, which is largely based on an illusion, it is gen- uine. Rather than some vain pursuit of a utopian idea of personal perfection, we can strive for a state of continuous improvement. While this is in a sense a journey with no real destination, it is at least an authentic one, which will allow you to remain truer to your- self.

However, there is one requirement: We have to allow ourselves to pause and reflect on these things. We need to slam on the brakes here, and reflect deeply on issues that could impact us for the rest of our lives. Thinking a little less about ourselves and a little more about one another is the road to true success and happiness.

That's what this book is about.

PART I

Narcissism: A Brief Introduction

. . . .

1

What Is Narcissism?

We love ourselves more than other people
but care more about
their opinions than our own.

—MARCUS AURELIUS

Narcissism, like psychopathy, has always existed. It is part of the species *Homo sapiens*. Just as there are quiet and loud people, early birds and night owls, cat people and dog people, and so on, there are narcissists. Evolution has produced the phenomenon of narcissism, and there probably isn't much point in our asking why. Perhaps it's all a cruel joke that our creator came up with back at the dawn of time. "Check this out: I'm giving them an interesting challenge! Why don't I send them a human-shaped Trojan horse?"

Why not, indeed? As a species, the human race has struggled in the face of a bewildering variety of problems and disruptions. Narcissism is just one example among many.

One thing that you'll have to bear in mind when it comes to narcissism is that it isn't a disease—it's not really an aspect of mental health as such. You can't treat it with medication or learn to live with it. Narcissism is a personality disorder. It's important to realize this, so that you can immediately lay to rest any ideas you have of curing or treating the condition. I'll touch on the methods that tend to be used, but narcissism seems to be no more curable than color blindness or the unfortunate affliction that causes some people to enjoy listening to the Rolling Stones. It is, as they say, what it is.

Wikipedia says: "Narcissistic personality disorder (NPD) or megalomania is a personality disorder characterized by a long-term pattern of exaggerated feelings of self-importance, an excessive craving for admiration, and struggles with empathy."

The Mayo Clinic offers this description of narcissistic personality disorder: ". . . a mental condition in which people have an inflated sense of their own importance, a deep need for excessive attention and admiration, troubled relationships, and a lack of empathy for others."

Just like many other diagnoses, this one is frequently used rather imprecisely in everyday conversation. Sometimes all it takes for somebody to be labeled the office narcissist is that they tend to get a little carried away when they talk about themself. Self-centered people can certainly be irritating, and it's definitely one of the signs of narcissism, but it isn't the only one.

COMMON CHARACTERISTICS OF NARCISSISM
- Unrealistic, grandiose self-image
- Incredibly self-centered
- Speak only about themselves
- Feeling special and unique
- Arrogance and haughtiness
- Quick to criticize and judge others
- Highly sensitive to criticism
- Think the rules don't apply to them
- *Constant* self-promotion

- Feeling entitled to the best of everything
- Value power and fame
- Demand constant acknowledgment
- Will respond with aggression when questioned
- Deceitful and manipulative

All these separate points can be broken down into smaller components, and studying the various points in depth is worthwhile, as it can often help you find the explanation for what might otherwise have remained just a feeling. I'm sure you've met people who would be diagnosed as narcissists, even if you never knew it at the time. You've probably thought things like, *This feels odd,* or, *Why is this conversation making me uncomfortable? Is there something wrong with me?* Perhaps this description will help clear these things up for you.

In addition, if you've been incorrectly told that somebody is a narcissist, this chapter will give you the tools you need to figure it out. You'll learn to detect the patterns, even if you're not a qualified psychologist.

AN IN-DEPTH LOOK AT EACH CHARACTERISTIC

If we take a brief look at each characteristic, we'll soon see that they all actually fit together rather well. Some of them even overlap without being identical.

UNREALISTIC SELF-IMAGE

This is sometimes called a grandiose self-image. Having an unrealistic self-image is exactly what you'd expect: It involves having a self-image that doesn't match up with reality. "Unrealistic" seems to be open to two different interpretations, however: Wouldn't a highly successful individual who felt like an utter failure also have an *unrealistic* self-image? All "realistic" means in this context is that it matches up well with reality, after all. In this case, though, I'm only discussing the inverse relationship: people who overestimate their achievements, so that even those who are moderate failures might see themselves as true winners.

One particular kind of narcissist (who, unlike other narcissists, actually often end up seeking help, partly because of the depressions they suffer and partly for the recognition it affords them) tends to think of themselves as failures. However, they make a point of pointing out that their failure is the direct result of their unfair treatment at the hands of the world, and that their talents would surely have set them apart from the masses if it hadn't been for that. They're usually jealous of other people and often suspect that their successes must have been achieved by nefarious means, rather than genuine talent or merit, like those of the narcissist.

Narcissists' unrealistic self-images will often hinge on their failure to acknowledge their own limitations. They take jobs they aren't qualified for and then experience genuine surprise at how challenging they find them. They get involved in discussions about subjects they know next to nothing about and then have a difficult time accepting it when their ignorance is exposed and they lose the argument.

INCREDIBLY SELF-CENTERED

Merriam-Webster's online dictionary defines self-centeredness as self-sufficiency on the one hand and being concerned solely with one's own desires, needs, or interests on the other. The former has nothing to do with narcissism—on the contrary, narcissists tend to be utterly dependent on others for satisfying their psychological needs. Narcissists essentially think only about themselves, their own experiences, their preferences, and their needs. Other people? Well, they do exist, certainly, but mainly to be exploited by the narcissist for their own benefit.

Basically, everything else orbits the narcissist. Their view of the world is the only one that matters, and everyone else had better adjust. Anything that happens in the vicinity of a narcissist will be judged based on their own opinions. If they see an angle that might allow them to benefit from a situation, that's a positive—even if it has negative consequences for ten other people. If it's bad for the narcissist but good for one hundred others, it's a bad thing overall.

SPEAK ONLY ABOUT THEMSELVES

Any conversation will inevitably end up being about the narcissist. The topic doesn't really matter much. Nothing comes more naturally to narcissists than inserting themselves into everything. That's what interests them the most, after all. Narcissists want to be involved in every story and announce their experience of something or other. Since other people aren't too interesting, it only makes sense to change the subject to something more exciting. And if a narcissist should fail to make the particular subject of conversation about them, they will simply change the subject to make it more directly about them.

I'm sure you know the old joke:

That's enough about me. Let's talk about you. What do you think about me?

FEELING SPECIAL AND UNIQUE

Narcissists feel that they are highly unique and genuinely special. Naturally, every human being is unique in their own way, but to a narcissist, what this means is that they genuinely possess abilities that almost nobody else has. They have different, better talents than everyone else.

They look better, are smarter, or are more successful. These are individuals who think of themselves as God's gift to humanity. They consider themselves to be fully and completely fabulous, and if anybody claims otherwise there will be trouble. On top of this, people who tend towards narcissism will often imagine that people appreciate or even love them to a very great extent. They seriously believe that they are highly popular among many people—perhaps more popular than anybody else—but the truth is that they are more likely to be popular with a particular group of people and far less so in other circles.

Narcissists believe themselves to be on top of the world even when everyone else can see they aren't even close.

QUICK TO CRITICIZE AND JUDGE OTHERS

Since a narcissist is already the best at everything, and shares this fact freely with anyone they meet, they also know that everyone else is far worse at everything. They don't mind sharing this fact, either, often in a rather judgmental fashion. Since a narcissist feels entitled to think and say whatever they want to, they often do just that. And, as a result of their obvious contempt for everyone else, they can't help but put people down. Basically, putting others down makes narcissists feel better, because it makes them feel more important. Like winners—more or less.

Since narcissists tend to exhibit arrogance and haughtiness in their behavior and attitudes, there are only a few people whom they will be prepared to spend their time and attention on. The little people aren't really worthy of their attention.

A narcissist who possesses developed social skills can cause tremendous harm to unwitting victims. An example of this is the tremendous increase we've seen in hate speech online in recent years. Attacking people you don't like for some reason or another is a particular specialty of narcissists. It doesn't matter if the victim is guilty or innocent. Since narcissists are unhindered by moral laws, believe they are entitled to do what they want, and feel that putting others down somehow elevates them, they're prepared to spend huge amounts of time picking people apart. Sometimes they're basically just bullies.

HIGHLY SENSITIVE TO CRITICISM

Some people are quick to criticize because they prefer an open and frank conversation, but when it comes to narcissists, this is always a one-way street. They feel entitled to criticize and tear down others, but they are far too sensitive to be prepared to listen to what people think of them. Since they will invariably take any criticism as a sign that the world around them is failing to perceive their greatness, they will react quickly, often with forceful, sudden rage. And along with that, a thirst for vengeance.

Criticism can be interpreted in a variety of ways. On the one hand, it could be genuine criticism, that is, a negative assessment of the narcissist's performance, for example. However, it could also be a case of insufficient praise, or not cheering loud enough about how wonderful their achievements are. If what you give the narcissist fails to live up to their expectations, they can erupt at any moment.

THINK THE RULES DON'T APPLY TO THEM

The previous point frequently results in the following. Because narcissists think of themselves as incredibly special and unique, an interesting effect occurs: The rules and regulations that the rest of society has agreed on don't apply to them. It could be anything from sticking to the speed limit to taking responsibility at work. If you genuinely believe that the ordinary rules of society don't apply to you, that will set you apart. Making an effort to be nice and acting polite and welcoming are within a narcissist's repertoire, of course, but since they feel no genuine compulsion to conform to these norms, they are able to drop the pretense with surprising speed if provoked.

This is one of the reasons why other people seldom have any genuine appreciation for narcissists. They can certainly attract a coterie of admirers to orbit them, but nobody genuinely likes them. Their lack of respect for the rules makes them too unpredictable. Most people find this exhausting in the long run. Narcissists' relationships are actually much more superficial than they may realize.

CONSTANT SELF-PROMOTION

The first word, of every sentence, is "I." "*I* think, *I* feel, *I* believe, *I* wish, *I* want, *I* demand . . ." Because narcissists think of themselves as the best at everything, they will always emphasize their own qualities. They are also bound to inform everybody about their popularity, important acquaintances, and unrivaled network. This is a variant of the grandiose self-image, and it can produce an odd effect when a narcissist keeps emphasizing their contributions to the world. This goes beyond simply talking about yourself, too.

Narcissists might well donate money to charities—they just won't do it unless they can somehow tell the rest of the world that they did it. The reason for this is very simple: They want to receive credit for their huge hearts. Donating one hundred dollars to Save the Children isn't enough for them; to ensure that they will receive the ovations they deserve from their imagined fans, they have to post about it on Instagram and Facebook.

Alarmingly enough, narcissists are overrepresented within the hierarchies of global charities such as Save the Children or UNICEF. They do the minimum amount of work required of them but make a point of trying to climb the rungs of the organization at the expense of colleagues who have actually dedicated their lives to charity work. Yes, this has been studied, too.

FEELING ENTITLED TO THE BEST OF EVERYTHING

Narcissists feel entitled to the best the world has to offer. This is an important drive for them, a constant striving for perfection and need to have the very best. Just like a little child imagines that they can get away with doing anything they feel like, narcissists do the same because they feel entitled to it. Claiming space, insulting or stepping on others, receiving maximal compensation for minimal effort— narcissists feel naturally entitled to all that stuff.

In addition, it's also their essential birthright to live in the most elegant house in the best neighborhood, drive the most expensive car, and wear only the finest clothes. The list goes on. Whenever a narcissist wants something, this feeling hinges on the sense that they are entitled to it. No further arguments are necessary. However illogical this may sound, it seems perfectly rational to them. And since they prefer their rewards to be instant, they won't hesitate to take a shortcut.

VALUE POWER AND FAME

Power and fame are highly valued attributes in the eyes of a narcissist. They are evidence of the narcissist's worth, which is something everybody should be acknowledging. Attention matters. Amusingly enough, narcissists don't insist that the attention they receive be positive. Negative attention is better than no attention at all. In this regard, narcissists are just like little children.

The consequence of this is that narcissists, like psychopaths, are drawn to any place in which power and attention tend to concentrate. However, problems will soon arise if people fail to acknowledge narcissists' importance. They may even exhibit signs of mild depression if they don't receive the attention they crave.

DEMAND CONSTANT ACKNOWLEDGMENT

Many people work hard and enjoy basking in the recognition they receive from the world for the successes they achieve. But that's it for them. The acceptance they've been given actually satisfies them. Not so for narcissists.

These people live for constant recognition. And since they believe themselves to be entitled to it, they are always looking to get more, too. This could be an employee who always runs errands for the boss in exchange for praise. But it could also be a boss who keeps buying the team cake in order to hear how popular they are.

Narcissists' need for recognition requires constant refilling, and this can seem incomprehensible to the people around them. How could anybody need to be told how handsome, well-dressed, skilled, successful, and popular they are—every single day?

DECEITFUL AND MANIPULATIVE

Narcissists are often highly efficient when it comes to detecting people's weaknesses. They also tend to be prepared to exploit these weaknesses to deceive and defraud their victims. Exploiting others comes naturally to them. They are often indifferent to the emotions of others, which makes them skilled at manipulating the people around them. Since they are reasonably indifferent to the danger of being exposed, they will take risks and behave with such boldness that it can often be difficult to believe that they are being deceitful.

WHAT CONCLUSIONS CAN WE DRAW SO FAR?

These are the basic features of narcissism. There are psychological tools we can use to measure these characteristics quite accurately, and I will be discussing one of these later on. If you score high enough for each area, you might actually be a narcissist in the clinical sense. However, the diagnosis can only be made by qualified experts, who specialize in this particular area. Not just any psychologist is qualified to do this, because many within the field believe that narcissism and even psychopathy are treatable conditions. They are approaching the whole problem from the wrong direction, basically.

Plenty of ordinary people exhibit distinct narcissistic traits without ever being diagnosed. There is no doubt, either, that our society promotes and rewards these kinds of behavior. I'm going to take a closer look at some of these behaviors and identify the risks involved. I'll also be looking into whether there might be any benefits to being a narcissist.

2

Being a Cut Above the Rest

Always remember that you are absolutely unique.
Just like everyone else.
—MARGARET MEAD

Are you unique? I'd have to say you are, because evidently all human beings are given a unique blueprint by nature.

Every human being has their own unique DNA sequence. In each living individual, the DNA strands are different. Large portions of them will actually be identical, but let's not delve too deep into the scientific considerations here. In any case, all that is just a small part of what makes you a unique being. There's plenty more unique stuff to be found if you examine other factors, too. Your personality is probably nearly unique, if not fully.

It's actually less than obvious what parts of an individual's personality we can consider unique.

HOW UNIQUE CAN SOMEBODY GET, EXACTLY?

If we consider your sex, you'll differ from close to half the population based on that alone. Your age? Only a tiny minority of people are exactly your age. How many people on the planet have the exact same education as you? Your same background and income? Do you adhere to any particular faith? What are your opinions on climate change? What political camp are you in? Are you married? Single? Cohabiting? Do you have children? Why is that? No kids, eh? How come?

What about your hobbies and interests? What kind of food do you like, and what dishes do you hate? How tall are you? Are you good at your job? How much of your workday is actually spent doing productive work? Would you say you're a reliable person who practically always keeps your promises?

Are you organized or messy? What about your temper? On a scale from 1 to 23 million, where 23 million is the most advanced computer in the world and 1 is practically dead: How quickly do you make decisions? Are you an early bird or a night owl? If someone holds a gun to your head and asks you to choose between cats and dogs, which is it?

If we were to make a list of every single factor that might have an impact on a particular individual's personality, we'd soon realize that there's far more than just your DNA to set you apart from the other 7 billion of us.

It's often suggested that we ought to focus on our similarities, rather than on our differences. While I understand the intentions behind this comment, I also think that it's based on a misunderstanding of the whole point of emphasizing uniqueness. Considering all the differences between us that I've just been discussing, pretending that we're all the same is more than a little naïve.

BEING UNIQUE AND INCREDIBLY SPECIAL

We've arrived at an interesting conclusion. Claiming to be unique seems like it would be a waste of time in a world where everybody else is unique, too. If we're all unique, the word itself seems to lose all meaning. Unique means *one of a kind*. There's nothing special about that.

But okay, let's agree to emphasize how unique we are and avoid evaluating any differences we might observe in others. The challenge lies in accepting our differences without judgment. Suggesting that one of them might be better or worse than another seems problematic to me.

Perhaps you're beginning to wonder where I'm going with all of this?

Defining yourself as unique simply means that you're claiming nobody else is *exactly like you*.

However, defining yourself as *special* is a whole different matter. To claim to be special is to suggest that you possess something specific that most other people do not. It means you're a cut above the rest. You're not simply unique; you possess some special ability or gift or spirit, which we're about to highlight.

You're special, amazing, wonderful, and you can do anything you want by virtue of being . . . you.

I'm sorry to have to tell you this, but statistically, chances are you're not particularly special. Only a very small minority of the people on this planet are actually special.

This is precisely where narcissists have found their angle.

The Dangers of Being Special

Perhaps that's not the right heading. Sometimes there is no risk at all in being truly special. I don't just mean unique; I mean having something in you that can create value for millions of people on this planet. There have been many people like that. Isaac Newton. Mother Teresa. Albert Einstein. Nelson Mandela. Marie Curie. Michelle Obama, Bill Gates, William Shakespeare, Beyoncé.

Being special is a good thing, of course. On one condition, that is: You have to be *genuinely* special.

Let's be honest: Most of us have no obvious, unrivaled, hero-level talents. I know for certain that I'm not naturally gifted at any single discipline I can think of right now. There are things I'm not too bad at. I'd even say I'm pretty good at some things. But none of it came naturally to me. I've had to learn every skill I have.

This is where we notice a bit of a problem. Although I haven't met a large number of remarkably special people in my lifetime, I've met a few truly exceptional individuals. You know the type: the kind of person you wish you could be like but who also makes you painfully aware that you'll never measure up to them in any way.

However, I've met plenty of people who *acted like they were special*.

The main danger of being special, I think, is that it's something others want to be. Special, as in possessing qualities that set them apart from others. They are *better* than the rest of us, somehow. Special, then, basically means *better*.

So, How Do You Get to Be Special?

The answer to this probably lies hidden deep within the concept of heredity, underneath countless layers of incredibly complex assumptions about how certain individuals are obviously born with traits that almost nobody else shares with them. We know that we become the individuals we are through an interplay of nature and nurture. The precise mechanics of this are still being debated by the world's leading experts in biology, psychology, and a few adjacent fields. I'm in no way claiming to have a grasp of anything beyond the fundamentals of this.

But I do know something else: Simply *telling* yourself that you're special won't actually make you special. You also won't become special as a result of somebody else claiming that you are. If your mother told you that you're truly special, it might be a good idea to ask her what, exactly, she meant.

Perhaps 99.9 percent of us will have to face the fact that while we may be unique, we are in no way special. Maybe that's not a problem. If you're not a narcissist, it probably won't be. But if you are, you'll find the very idea unthinkable.

3

The Rest of the Dark Triad

Hell is empty and
all the devils are here.
—WILLIAM SHAKESPEARE

Narcissism isn't the only troubling personality disorder around. There are actually other, even more serious, variants of this less than charming disposition. The dark triad is a disquieting set of three major personality disorders that can each make an individual pose a threat to other people. There are no clear boundaries between these three disorders, and they have some characteristics in common.

Self-centeredness and a grandiose self-image, combined with manipulative behavior towards others, are the common denominators here.

These three personality disorders make up the dark triad: psychopathy, Machiavellianism, and *narcissism*.

In discussing these disorders, I've left the realm of annoying but essentially harmless behavior well and truly behind. This is no longer a matter of little ego boosts, but of dangerous, pathological behavior that can pose a threat to anybody who encounters it. These individuals are bad company, sometimes even dangerous company.

Unfortunately, misconceptions about these disorders abound, and there are all kinds of ideas about the meanings of these concepts in circulation on social media and the rest of the Internet. Sometimes it all seems to blend into a jumble of concepts, so I'd like to clear up some of the differences between, say, psychopathy and narcissism. Because although they are connected, they are not the same thing.

PSYCHOPATHY

Since I dedicated an entire book to psychopaths a few years ago, I'll limit myself to a brief account here. A psychopath is a person who looks like you, and who often speaks and generally behaves much like you. But deep down, they are actually nothing like you. Under the surface, there is stuff going on that you could never even imagine.

Psychopaths are one of the most troubling influences on our society. They have no inhibitions when it comes to trying to reach their goals. If somebody is in their way, they will stop at nothing to get past them. Psychopaths can hide among us, in plain sight, but they always give themselves away in the end. When they do, it's usually too late.

They can be extremely manipulative and can convince almost anybody of almost anything. And yes, that includes you and me. They have a knack for identifying other people's weaknesses and exploiting them for their own personal benefit.

There are several competing checklists in use as measures of psychopathy, but the following one is the most common. It was developed by Robert Hare, a psychologist who has spent decades researching psychopathy.

ROBERT HARE'S PSYCHOPATHY CHECKLIST, REVISED PCL-R 2016:
1. Glib and superficial charm
2. Grandiose (exaggerated) estimation of self

3. Lack of remorse or guilt
4. Callousness and lack of empathy
5. Cunning and manipulativeness
6. Shallow affect (superficial emotional responsiveness)
7. Impulsivity
8. Poor behavioral controls
9. Need for stimulation
10. Irresponsibility
11. Early behavior problems
12. Antisocial behavior as an adult
13. Pathological lying
14. Parasitic lifestyle
15. Sexual promiscuity
16. Lack of realistic long-term goals
17. Failure to accept responsibility for own actions
18. Juvenile delinquency
19. Breaking parole
20. Criminal versatility

This checklist will, in theory, produce a score ranging from 0 (not even you or I would score this low; we've all lied, for example) to a maximum of 40 points. Each of the mentioned behaviors is examined, and the frequency with which it is exhibited is assessed. If it's almost never, the score is 0 points. If it's occasional, that's 1 point, and if it's a regular occurrence, you score 2 points. If a large enough number of these behaviors is exhibited with sufficient frequency, an individual can be given the diagnosis of psychopathy.

However, this requires a clinical assessment by qualified personnel and can't be done in a single, quick session. Observing patterns can require time, particularly since many of the more intelligent psychopaths learn how to blend in with the crowd.

What is the required score for a diagnosis of psychopathy? That depends slightly on where in the world you live. For example, Great Britain has set a limit of 25 points. In the United States, they draw the line at 30 points. Why is this? I honestly don't know. I've not been able to identify the different motives involved in the creation of these standards. Basically, they made different judgment calls. Although the requirements for psychopathy are more stringent in the USA, it is still said that the ratio of psychopaths to the general population is higher there than in Europe. I haven't found any data to explain the reasons for this, either.

However, people should tread carefully even when with anyone whose score is around 15 points. A score that high spells trouble.

Generally speaking, we could say that a psychopath is everything a narcissist is plus more. A psychopath is prepared to do anything to achieve their goals. Breaking the law means nothing to them. They rarely consider the consequences. Of course, they prefer to live in freedom, but regardless of the risks, they are going to go ahead and do whatever they feel like. They tend to have difficulties with impulse control, and this frequently causes them problems. The systems that regulate their emotions are mute, which means that they never experience fear, stress, anxiety, empathy, love, or any other of the emotions that the rest of us tangle with on a daily basis. Using other people causes them no more discomfort than ordering dinner at their local restaurant. Lying is nothing to them. They could be pulled over by the police with a body in the trunk of their car without the slightest elevation of their heart rate.

Less intelligent psychopaths are often incarcerated. The criminal justice system in Sweden estimates that 25 percent of all prisoners in the country are clinical psychopaths. That alone is a good reason for anybody to stay well clear of prisons.

For smarter psychopaths, it's a very different story. Other popular data suggest that 10 percent of all people in upper managerial positions are psychopaths. This goes for all kinds of organizations, from drug cartels to religious movements. It's hard to verify this data, but it's obvious that the higher up in an organizational hierarchy you look, the greater the ratio of psychopaths will be. The reason for this is simple: Psychopaths crave power and attention. They believe that they belong at the top of the food chain, and that makes it only natural for them to seek to rise in the ranks. As is usually the case, they will utilize any acceptable means, and a few more besides, to get what they want.

Opinions vary on how large a percentage of the overall population can be categorized as psychopaths. In Sweden, where I live, psychologists usually claim that it is about 1 percent. I've discussed this with many of them, but nobody has been able to explain what this estimation is based on. Quite a lot of research is being done in this field globally, and worldwide the ratio is often said to be 2 to 4 percent.

The challenging thing about psychopaths is more or less the same as the challenging thing about cats: They can't be studied because they refuse to participate in studies.

Psychopathy can't be cured. It can't be treated. Therapy doesn't work. In fact, it only makes them worse because it teaches them more about how people function. It adds new weapons to their arsenals.

It's estimated that about 50 percent of the psychopathy trait is hereditary.

There are more male psychopaths than female ones.

Psychopathic behavior tends to make its initial appearance in the early teens, but it can also be evident earlier. If you want to learn more about psychopathy, there are quite a lot of books on the topic in addition to my own, *Surrounded by Psychopaths*.

MACHIAVELLIANISM

You hardly ever hear about this disorder, and maybe that's for the best. Machiavellianism is the second leg of the triad, and a person who exhibits it will be so focused on their own interests that they will manipulate, lie, and exploit others to achieve their goals. This is a genuinely unnerving behavioral pattern, which is largely reminiscent of psychopathy but may actually even seem worse on a closer look. Some people claim that Machiavellianism should be treated as a part of the psychopathy spectrum, but others feel that this disorder is distinct enough to merit a separate classification.

While narcissists just can't help but put themselves center stage and psychopaths can't help scamming the people they encounter, individuals with Machiavellianism are always in full control of their actions.

The term "Machiavellianism" is derived from the infamous Niccolò Machiavelli, an Italian Renaissance diplomat and philosopher whose most famous achievement was his book *The Prince*. This notorious work proposed that strong rulers ought to treat their subjects and enemies with severity, and that honor and survival could legitimize any means, including those otherwise thought amoral or excessively brutal.

At the close of the sixteenth century, "Machiavellianism" became a popular term used to denote the art of using deception to further your ambitions. It didn't become a psychological term until the 1970s.

Machiavellianism, like psychopathy, has proven to be more prevalent among men than among women. It can occur in anybody, though—including children.

Machiavellians usually exhibit the following behaviors:

- Focus only on their own ambitions and interests
- Prioritize power and money over relationships
- Exploit and manipulate others to get ahead
- Frequently use flattery
- Lack principles and values
- Are hard to truly get to know

- Exhibit cynicism, a lack of appreciation for goodness or morals
- Are evasive in terms of commitment and emotional relationships
- Are capable of great patience as a result of their calculating nature
- Seldom reveal their true intentions
- Have frequent new sexual encounters
- Are good at decoding social situations and other people
- Lack warmth in social interactions

This disorder is easily conflated with psychopathy, but there are several important distinctions between the two. The most significant of these has to do with the difficulties psychopaths experience in resisting their impulses: They see something they want, and they act more or less immediately to make it theirs. Psychopaths are always looking to manipulate and deceive others, largely because of the excitement they experience from seeing how far they can push things. Machiavellians, on the other hand, are always in full control of their actions. They might be incredibly generous to certain people and absolutely ruthless to others. They know exactly what they're doing, and they are highly skilled at keeping their plans under wraps. Psychopaths will always expose their true nature eventually, but a Machiavellian personality disorder can take many years to detect.

Machiavellianism is ultimately focused on one's own well-being. Individuals who exhibit these traits believe that they need to be deceptive and manipulative to get anywhere in life. They don't trust in human kindness, and they find it frightfully naïve to place faith in others. They prioritize power over love or connections with others. For some reason, there is almost no literature at all on Machiavellianism. For a good overview of the background, I recommend you read Machiavelli's own *The Prince*.

Each part of the dark triad—psychopathy, Machiavellianism, and narcissism—can pose complex challenges to the people who encounter it.

Psychopathy mostly involves being cold, unempathic, and insensitive to the needs of others.

Machiavellianism mostly involves manipulating people for personal gain.

Narcissism mostly involves feeling deserving of praise and special treatment that others don't receive.

Somebody who exhibits all three of these disorders will pose a genuine danger to the mental well-being of other people. Now, imagine somebody like that who also happens to lack inhibitions when it comes to violence. Could that be the definition of pure evil, perhaps?

Despite the seemingly obvious connections between the three parts of the dark triad, and the existence of a trait that usually occurs in conjunction with the other two, researchers have yet to discover clear evidence of a true correlation.

4

Is It Normal to Think About Yourself All the Time?

More the knowledge, lesser the ego.
Lesser the knowledge, more the ego . . .
—ALBERT EINSTEIN

Thinking about yourself isn't a very strange thing to do. It comes naturally to us, and we were probably all designed that way from the start. Some behavioral scientists claim that 95 percent of our thoughts are about ourselves, or about events related to ourselves. I've tried to test this and see if it's correct, but despite being prepared to accept the logic of the claim, I haven't been able to log the contents of my thoughts with much accuracy.

However, there's a difference between focusing on yourself on the one hand and focusing on yourself at the expense of everyone else on the other.

Most of the people we encounter are ultimately loyal to themselves, but they reflect on and factor in the effects their decisions will have on others in their deliberations. Since we live in a world where nobody can succeed entirely on their own, we have to take other people into consideration. We don't have to like it, but on an intellectual level we need to grasp that this is the way things are and adapt accordingly.

To simplify things, you could say that this is what separates a civilized person from, say, a narcissist. We all have that innate drive to focus on ourselves and treat ourselves as the number one priority. A narcissist does precisely this, without any hesitation. The rest of us regulate our urges and conform to the requirements of whatever circumstances we're in.

Although the instinct to put yourself first will always be there, various processes within us ensure that we factor the interests of others into our decisions. We don't want to embarrass ourselves; we don't want to hurt anybody; we also don't want to hurt ourselves by giving ourselves a guilty conscience for no good reason. We deal in long-term consequences.

What will everyone else think if I just grab as much cake as I want, without worrying about how many of us are supposed to be sharing it? Maybe nobody will say anything—that's how conflict-averse people are in this department—but I might find it difficult to win support from my coworkers in other situations if I've made everybody think I'm selfish.

How will Roger fare if I fudge the truth about his mistakes a little when the boss asks me about what happened? What if I exaggerated his errors a little, to make myself look better in comparison? Do I really want to make a complete fool of Roger over a single little mistake he made? Perhaps what I should really be doing is offering to help him clean up the mess he's made.

If I lie to my wife about what I did last Thursday, I'll gain short-term relief from having to deal with her reaction if she were to discover the truth. But when she does figure out where I was, her rage will be all the fiercer for it. Not to mention the guilty conscience I'll have to carry around until then.

All these considerations, which all of us make from time to time, are entirely normal. We weigh the short-term gain against the long-term risk. Sometimes we make the right choice.

Narcissists don't function anything like this. They simply go ahead and do whatever they feel like in the moment and wager on the short-term rewards of amoral behavior. They do this despite realizing that others might be sad, hurt, angered, or otherwise negatively affected as a result of their decision; it matters little to them. They are entitled to behave amorally, as it happens. It's somewhere in this vicinity that we make the transition from normal behavior to something very different. Using other people as stepping-stones to your own ends should be considered an aberration.

THE BASICS OF HUMAN BEHAVIOR ACCORDING TO THE DISC THEORY

If you've read any of my other books, you'll no doubt be aware that we will at some point be discussing the DISC (Dominance, Influence, Steadiness, Compliance) system of behavior analysis and the four colors associated with it: Red, Yellow, Green, and Blue. This book is no exception to that rule. Now, although the DISC model is not required in order to explain narcissism, it can still be helpful to remind ourselves about our own natural behavior. The DISC method can help explain some of the reactions you may experience while reading. It can even make it easier to sift out stuff that's actually quite normal—however incomprehensible it might seem—and allow us to better focus on the topic at hand: narcissism. I use the well-established DISC model to explain variations in behavioral patterns. There are countless other methods out there, but this model covers most of what you need to know at this juncture. If you prefer to use the five-factor model or Myers-Briggs, that's also a useful tool. I'll stick with this one, though, because it's the one I know best.

There are many things that might influence how a person functions—countless, in fact—and I'm going to be discussing two of these next: a person's behavioral profile and their level of personal growth.

I should mention at this point that this system is based on the analysis of subjective reports, and that it is thus not intended to give a comprehensive account of the inner workings of human beings. However, it can provide a basic insight into our most common reactions.

So, here is a brief introduction. If you feel you're an expert at the four colors by now, feel free to skip this section—but my advice is that you check it out either way. Repetition, as they say, is the mother of learning. Let's go!

Reds, who are fact-oriented and extroverted, are driven to solve problems and take on difficult challenges. The more demanding a task is, the better. If something works better than expected, their suspicion is aroused. "What's the catch here? Why is this so easy? It's supposed to be hard; it's supposed to be difficult. No pain, no gain. Sometimes more pain is better than less. Pain makes you stronger." They like a quick pace, plenty of action, and wild times.

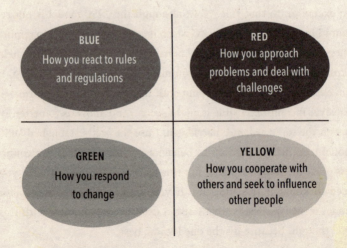

BLUE
How you react to rules and regulations

RED
How you approach problems and deal with challenges

GREEN
How you respond to change

YELLOW
How you cooperate with others and seek to influence other people

If Reds are all about action, then Yellows, who are relationship-oriented extroverts, are all about interaction. These are the people who can't resist trying to convince everybody else about the validity of their own thoughts and opinions. They can't leave the room until consensus has been reached. They are optimists, able to see a glimmer of sunshine in the most violent of rainstorms. Yellows, too, enjoy a quick pace.

Greens, who are relationship-oriented and introverted, are change-averse to the core. A lot of Green in a personality profile signals the person will have no interest in changing anything. Change is viewed with suspicion, even when it is entirely and obviously necessary. These are the people who talk about the good old days, who say you know what you've got but not what you'll get, or that the grass is never greener on the other side. Any new idea is immediately dismissed in favor of the status quo, thank you very much.

Finally, Blues, who are introverted and fact-oriented, enjoy rules and regulations. They are sticklers for protocol and always know what the correct procedure is. These people read the assembly manual before they even unpack their new IKEA shelves. Ideally, they read it in three different languages.

These four attitudes, along with the differences between introversion and extroversion, or between being fact- or people-oriented, give rise to certain behaviors.

WHAT ARE THESE BEHAVIORS, MORE SPECIFICALLY?

If we look at what these behavior profiles lead to, we'll start to see obvious differences in all sorts of contexts. Following this section is a list of different specific attributes that are correlated with different colors. At this point, I should tell you that there are exceptions to these rules. There are always exceptions. Understanding people is a complex challenge. However, each characteristic is specific to the color in question.

It also feels important to add that we all have some of all the colors in us. We are all able to behave in a variety of ways, but there are definite behavioral patterns that each of us will be more or less comfortable with and that we will display to the world around us. Statistically, the most common pattern—which accounts for about 80 percent of the population—is a combination of two colors. Common combinations include: Red-Yellow, Yellow-Green, Green-Blue, and Blue-Red. Less common are: Yellow-Blue and Red-Green. We don't know what causes this distribution. Around 15 percent of the population exhibit three colors, making them even more difficult to interpret, and a mere 5 percent of the population stick to a single color. These statistics were taken from a sample of about 50 million respondents from all over the world.

AN ATTEMPT AT A SCALE OF SELF-CENTEREDNESS

Narcissism is largely a matter of self-centeredness, but this doesn't mean that everybody who is self-centered is a narcissist. As usual in the field of psychology, it's hard to draw sharp distinctions here. If I were to try to design a scale for a concept as multifaceted as self-centeredness, it would probably be something along the following lines:

All people take the greatest interest in themselves and in their own needs. This is just human nature. The same is true of most animals we know about. Most individuals would be prepared to fight for their own survival.

Some people don't *display* much of this side of themselves. That doesn't mean it's absent! It only indicates that they've learned to suppress the less attractive aspects of their nature.

	RED	YELLOW	GREEN	BLUE
BEHAVIOR	Driven, direct	Optimistic and spontaneous	Caring and considerate	Thoughtful and conscientious
DEMEANOR	Businesslike	Forthcoming	Discrete	Formal
APPROACH TO WORK	Meticulous Ambitious Formal Efficient Precise	Inspiring Personal Flexible Stimulating Eloquent	Personal Relaxed Friendly Informal Low-key	Structured Organized Specialized Methodical Laconic
WORK PACE	Quick and decisive	Quick and spontaneous	Slow and solid	Slow and methodical
PRIORITIES	The task and the results	Relationships and influence	Maintaining good relations	The task and how to approach it
FEARS	Losing control	Losing face	Confrontation	Making a fool of themselves
BEHAVES UNDER PRESSURE	Dictates terms and asserts themselves	Attacks and uses irony	Gives way and acquiesces	Withdraws and avoids
WANTS	Results	Inspiration	Stability	Methodology
WANTS YOU TO BE	Direct	Stimulating	Nice	Precise
WANTS TO BE	In charge	Admired	Liked	Right
TRIGGERED BY	Inefficiencies and indecisiveness	Passivity and routines	Insensitivity and impatience	Surprises and whims
WANTS TO HAVE	Success and control	Status and flexibility	Peace and quiet and close relationships	Credibility and time to prepare

	RED	YELLOW	GREEN	BLUE
DEMEANOR	Businesslike	Elegant	Friendly	Law-abiding
LIVES IN	The present	The future	The past (the "good old days")	Their mind
RELIES ON	Gut feeling	Recognition	Themselves	Specialists
CAN'T STAND	Sitting still	Being alone	Unpredictability	Rushing things

When it comes to the *introverts*, the Greens and Blues generally seem calmer and quieter, and they recover more energy when they don't need to interact with too many people. They're quite content to be their own sources of recognition, rather than seeking it from others. They don't talk much, unless they're very comfortable with the company they're in. Being the center of attention in public situations is not their favorite thing in the world. They prefer to stand to one side, observing or watching. Preservation is more important than change. Introverts will often be fully content to spend time inside their own minds. In terms of the DISC theory, this makes them Green and Blue. They're less noisy, and other people tend not to perceive them as particularly self-centered, although, of course, they still belong to the overall category of human beings in general.

Next, we have their opposites—the *extroverts,* who enjoy action, bustle, and for things to be happening. Fast-paced situations energize them, and they move around in the world at a much quicker pace than introverts do. They don't mind being the center of attention one bit; some of them would even say they enjoy it. Any change is like a burst of fresh air, and they like it when things unfold quickly. The old days are over and gone. According to the DISC theory, again, these individuals are Red and Yellow.

While *Reds* do have rather large, powerful egos (*ego* is Greek for "self"), they don't always care what everybody else thinks about them, because they aren't relationship-oriented. They can definitely be self-centered, but usually not in any of the more annoying ways. They simply have a way of pointing out how they happen to be right and everyone else is wrong.

The behavior of *Yellows* is perceived as particularly attention seeking. If you're at a dinner or party of some kind, look for crowds. More often than not, you'll find Yellows at the center of them. They'll be telling jokes or amusing anecdotes—or just being entertaining in general. They are good at making whatever they say sound interesting and important, and they have a natural knack for holding other people's attention. In other words, they are professional-level speakers. Many of us have fallen for charming Yellows and their well-communicated visions.

It's not necessarily a case of having great social skills, but it's definitely a social activity. Yellows love attention and are unusually receptive to positive feedback. They will happily lap up any praise, recognition, or acknowledgment that comes their way, while making a big show of saying it was really nothing.

Many Yellows you encounter will be prepared to go to some lengths to entertain their fellow human beings. Sometimes it can feel like everyone is part of an audience in their mind. This can cause them to take up more space than is strictly necessary, which can attract some ire. "Why don't you let someone else get a word in, dude?"

Much of this behavior actually happens subconsciously. Yellows tend not to have more than a vague idea that they are being loud. They probably don't mean to claim every molecule of oxygen in the room. It just happens. They simply act on their natural instinct—which is to open their mouths and see what happens next. This will not uncommonly end up resulting in another few sentences starting with "I."

Although a fair number of people, particularly Greens and Blues, can get quite irritated at Yellows and their behavior, I'd still say that most Yellows are actually fairly harmless. There's nothing evil about them; they simply lack self-awareness. So, when somebody eventually, inevitably, shouts at them, "Will you *never* stop talking?" the Yellow will respond with genuine surprise. "What just happened? I thought we were having such a nice time?"

One of the biggest fears a Yellow knows is that of being ostracized. Being denied the acceptance of your peers and ejected from the group is a terrible form of punishment. Yellows feel that judging them solely on the basis of their less charming traits would be unfair. They can also get a little indignant when they notice that the people around them aren't responding well to their childish antics. Sometimes they can even get upset. Tempers have been known to flare.

Fortunately, they are just as quick to forget all about being angry. And the sun is bound to be back out again soon.

If there's any color that's more often accused of being narcissistic than the others, I'd wager it's the Yellows. However, that's not the kind of narcissism I'm discussing here.

Now, what happens if we shift our gaze from Yellow behavior and instead take a look at something we'd have to agree is less normal? Is it possible to be even more self-centered than a Yellow without being a clinical narcissist?

HISTRIONIC PERSONALITY DISORDER

Beyond the Yellow, moderately annoying self-obsession, we enter the territory of a concept that is little discussed: histrionic personality disorder, or HPD. This is characterized by a pattern of excessive attention seeking, uninhibited and seductive behavior, and an exaggerated desire to be accepted. People who have been diagnosed with

HPD are often described as lively, dramatic, animated, enthusiastic, and flirtatious. Women are diagnosed with HPD about four times as often as men. Why? Because it's true? Because of bias from psychologists? Who could say?

HPD is nested within a cluster of more dramatic personality disorders. People with HPD are *very* keen on attention and often make loud, occasionally even inappropriate, comments. Their behavior can often seem rather exaggerated, and they crave constant stimulation. They can be sexually provocative and express powerful emotions—anything they need to make a strong impression on the people they encounter. They can be highly egotistical, and can sometimes be deeply manipulative in seeking to satisfy their own needs.

Individuals with HPD tend to be quite highly functioning, in both social and professional terms. They will usually possess average social skills, which they will at times put to use to manipulate people and ensure they will be the center of attention. However, HPD can also have consequences for social and close relationships, which will be further exacerbated by these people's inability to process defeat or failure. HPD individuals won't always have realistic views of their own situation, and tend instead to overdramatize and exaggerate their everyday challenges.

They change jobs often because they are quick to grow bored. Their strong preference for thrills and excitement can get them into some sticky situations. If they aren't permitted to live the slightly crazy life they want, or are denied the adulation of an audience, they could even develop depression.

There is a useful mnemonic that can help you learn the basics about HPD:

Provocative behavior
Relationships are considered more intimate than they actu-
    ally are

Attention seeking

Influenced easily by others or circumstances

Speech (style) wants to impress; lacks detail

Emotional lability; shallowness

Makeup; physical appearance is used to draw attention to
   self

Exaggerated emotions; theatrical

PRAISE ME

It's simple, but I like it. But how does the transition from regular to moderately excessive self-centeredness to pathological self-infatuation happen?

To put it bluntly: Do we succumb to narcissism as a result of getting too much of a good thing?

5

A First Encounter with Linda

We are each our own devil
and we make this world
our own hell.

—OSCAR WILDE

Please let me introduce you to a fictional person: Linda. In this book, I'll use her as an aid to illustrate how narcissistic behavior will often express itself in real life.

AN EXAMPLE OF EVERYDAY NARCISSISM

Linda's twenty-second birthday was in 2020. She is a business student in college. She feels that she's worked hard, but her teachers don't think she's done everything that could be expected of her. They consider her performance average.

Linda has a very large social circle. She's constantly interacting with an endless supply of attractive, smiling people on social media. She publishes at least one post every day, often more than that. Her posts offer a wealth of information on how amazingly exciting her days and nights are. You could say she has lots of superficial relationships but only one or two genuine close friends. This is actually quite strange considering her open attitude, good looks, upbringing in a nice family in a good neighborhood, passable people skills, seeming popularity, and promising prospects.

She lives in a small apartment that's fairly centrally located in a medium-sized Swedish town. Her parents bought the apartment for her because she didn't want to have to get up so early in the morning to make it to her lectures on time. After complaining loudly and repeatedly about this to her parents, with increasingly obvious insinuations that they would do something about it if they still cared about her, they reluctantly opened their wallets. The apartment cost almost as much as the suburban house her parents live in.

While Linda studies, her mother—who also has a part-time job—cleans her apartment and even does Linda's dirty laundry for her. Her mother has tried to get out of this arrangement on a couple of occasions, suggesting gently that an adult ought to be able to take care of their own laundry. Each time, Linda broke down in the face of the pressure of having to study and keep a home all at once. Her mother has never dared to ask Linda how many hours she spends studying each day. She hasn't shown them any exam results.

Truth be told, she doesn't spend that many hours on schoolwork. Actually studying for an exam would restrict Linda's social life far too much. Linda's studies aren't as interesting as she had hoped they would be, so she spends more of her time partying or hanging out online.

She isn't unintelligent or poorly educated. She has every opportunity to succeed, really. The reason why she won't apply herself to her studies isn't entirely clear. Her own explanation is that life can't be all work. You need to make some time for yourself, too. Grow into your future self. Feel things out. Since she considers it her inviolable right to receive a passing grade, she isn't even that concerned. Other students passed the exams, so why shouldn't she?

It actually looks like she should be able to graduate if she does a couple of repeat exams in core subjects.

Before she enrolled in the business program, she took a year off to travel. Now she feels like she needs another year off after having to deal with all this pressure for the last four years. So, she goes to her parents and asks them to fund her lifestyle for another few years, since she can't quite decide what to dedicate the rest of her life to. Maybe she'll look for work in a field related to her studies, or maybe she'll go back to school for a while. She'll have to see how things play out. She's young, and she's in no rush to make her mind up. Those things always work themselves out in the end.

SO, WHAT'S THE PROBLEM HERE—REALLY?

Okay, Linda is a bit spoiled. Her parents are perhaps too generous with their time and money. On the other hand, as a parent, you love your kids even after they've grown up. Of course you would do anything to help them get off the ground in their lives. What parent wouldn't?

The problem is Linda's methods for getting all the things she currently has.

To get an apartment in the city, which is worth as much as her parents' house, she manipulated them by threatening to commit suicide if they didn't do what she asked.

To coax her mother into cleaning for her and doing her laundry, she cried, screamed, and complained that her mother didn't love her anymore.

To ensure she'll be able to graduate despite her lackluster performance, Linda has accused one of her professors of discriminatory treatment. This scared him straight in a hurry, and he soon gave her a passing grade.

To secure a supply of new clothes and pretty shoes—not to mention enough makeup to keep an opera production up and running—she's made a point of bringing her dad to heel. He never could say no to her. Even when her monthly clothing budget is greater than his own yearly one, he keeps shelling out.

None of this is obvious on the surface. These are simply the methods that Linda has found to be particularly effective for getting her way. Neither of her parents has ever really pushed back. Since Linda genuinely feels entitled to all these privileges, she can't see anything wrong with the way she's behaved. She's going to get the things she needs to have a good life, and nobody is going to stop her.

However, there are a number of clues here. For somebody who only has one or two real friends but many superficial acquaintances, Linda has done a good job of stabbing people she doesn't like in the back. If somebody criticized her, she paid them back threefold. If somebody failed to give her the attention she felt she was due, she would slander the person in question and spread malicious rumors about them. Social media is a wonderful tool for spreading lies about people who have failed to be sufficiently respectful or fawning.

Maybe you're thinking to yourself that this all sounds like sheer idiocy. You're not all wrong, in that case. It *is* idiocy.

But the question you should ask yourself as you read on is this: If it were up to you, would you classify Linda as a very strong-willed Yellow-Red person, as somebody with HPD, or as a narcissist?

PART II

Narcissism: An In-Depth Look

. . . .

6

Surveying the Depths of Complex Souls

There is always some madness in love.
But there is also some reason in madness.
—FRIEDRICH NIETZSCHE

Apart from wanting the same things as everyone else, i.e., a good life that progresses as smoothly as possible, narcissists specifically want certain things that the rest of us might not be prepared to accept.

WHAT DO NARCISSISTS WANT?

Deep down, what narcissists want is control. They prefer to be in the driver's seat because it makes them feel better. Better than what? Everybody else, basically. Anything that can produce this feeling of superiority or brilliance will seem desirable to a narcissist. Anything that can make them feel like they are the center of attention will be hugely important to them. Anything that allows them to live in a fantasy world in which everything genuinely revolves around them is worth striving for.

They want things that will make them feel like they come first;

they even actively enjoy being favored over others, regardless of the context. A child with narcissistic tendencies will have no time for any concept of justice that also considers the rights of their siblings. Arguments to the effect that a certain arrangement would be unfair to the narcissist's brother are a total waste of air. Narcissistic children don't want justice for anybody but themselves. When they can't have more of something, or the better something, or all of something, this is all deeply unfair.

It's not enough just to get a lot. A narcissist wants reassurance that what they are getting really is more. They need to see and be convinced that they are being given more respect and admiration than the next person. If the people around them fail to signal how important they are *in comparison with everybody else,* this speaks to some fundamental flaw in those people. This means, then, that if your partner is a narcissist, you can't simply say, "Gosh, don't you look handsome!" Just to be safe, you should probably add this: "compared to everybody I have ever met."

Power, as I mentioned earlier, is another important component. This could be power over yourself, over others, over a situation, over an encounter, or over the decisions that are being made. Another word for this is "control."

Appreciation or, rather, *admiration.* The greater the number of people bowing or applauding, the better.

However, I should also mention *sympathy.* Many narcissists are very good at playing the victim, since this is a surefire way to gain a lot of sympathy. Sympathy also happens to be synonymous with attention. If you think about it, you'll find that lots of people are currently defining themselves or the group they belong to as victims. I have a hunch that narcissism might be the culprit here, too. More on this later, though.

Compassion is disturbing to most people; if other people feel compassion for you, that just goes to prove that you must be in a miserable state. However, for a narcissist, it fits in perfectly with the overall pattern.

Prestige and *status*. An elevated position within their social hierarchy is definitely something most narcissists crave. They want it not just for the power that comes with it, but rather for the attention, admiration, and maybe even fear it brings.

Influence can be associated with power. A narcissist wants to feel that they exert some degree of influence over the events and people in their life.

Service is another important ingredient for narcissists. This could mean anything from being particularly pampered in a restaurant to having a significant other who magics away all the boring household chores. We could actually just as well call this category servitude. Not having to spend time on depressing household chores makes a narcissist feel particularly important.

Appreciation and *praise*. Of course. There's simply no way you could ever praise a narcissist enough. They will lap it all up, including any obvious exaggerations or lies in their favor—and then gesture at you to keep it coming. "There's more? Really? Okay, bring it on!"

Submission. Others must obey and ideally surrender all their agency in the face of the greatness of the narcissist. This suits the narcissist perfectly, as it gives them absolute power to play with us as though we were pieces on a chessboard.

Absolute loyalty is the end result. Everyone simply must obey. Nobody gets to talk back. More submissive individuals, who think of themselves as followers, are more likely to be enthralled by narcissists.

It's not always too clear what interest a narcissist takes in these things, though. They are good at concealing their true selves, because they realize that their need for public adulation would not always be perceived as a sympathetic trait by the public.

HOW DO YOU SATISFY A NARCISSIST?

It's also worth noting at this point that even if a narcissist were to be given all the things I listed earlier, they still wouldn't be happy. They will always harbor some suspicion that they might have been cheated out of something they're actually entitled to. Even if they were to receive everything the world has to offer, they would still experience discomfort or even anger rather than satisfaction over what they had.

Once you've come to know a narcissist and learned to detect this pattern, you'll soon find that there really is no pleasing them. Anybody who has ever felt a lump of anxiety in their throat over giving their partner the best, most expensive, and most thoughtful gift ever deserves to know where that lump came from. Often, its source will be earlier birthdays, when despite their best efforts to get a good gift, they ended up being told that so-and-so actually has a slightly better one of these and how life is very unfair, actually.

The reason for this unappealing reaction is not simply that the person in question is childish; it also reflects the truth that expensive gifts are not viewed as the fulfillment of some deep wish. They are better viewed as reparations for perceived injustices. Things were supposed to have been this way all along, so it's about time this was remedied.

Anyone seeing a child snort indifferently before tossing incredibly expensive gifts aside at Christmas or on a birthday is bound to think to themself that the child in question is insufferably rude. But this could also be a case of narcissistic tendencies that shouldn't be encouraged. The same behavior would be absolutely intolerable in an adult.

It's got nothing to do with the actual gifts themselves. Humble or expensive—it doesn't matter. You could wrap up a Bentley or a ring fitted with the biggest diamond in the world and hand it over to a narcissist; they would simply place it in their pile of swag with every-thing else. There would be no sign at all of any genuine gratitude.

There's simply no way to satisfy a narcissist. Even King Midas himself could never produce enough gold to get a genuine narcissist to shut up. They usually feel unfairly treated by life because their wishes never come true. This often leads them on to a series of unfor-tunate behaviors, such as bossing people around and making others work even harder in their futile attempts to satisfy the narcissist.

7

Do I Love Myself? It's Complicated.

No tree can grow to heaven
unless its roots reach down to hell.

—CARL JUNG

Narcissus fell in love with himself, and this ultimately became his downfall. But that's just a Greek myth, right? Falling in love with yourself surely can't be a problem—things must be far worse for all the people who don't appreciate themselves at all, right?

A significant portion of the population has truly terrible self-esteem. These people can barely stand their own company, and if anybody offers them a word of praise they soon dismiss it and point out that they are actually completely useless.

One way of ending up like that is to fall victim to a psychopath. Psychopaths have a particular knack for tearing people down, piece by piece. Psychopath survivors frequently end up going through a full-on life crisis and often go on to struggle with shattered illusions and post-traumatic stress disorder. These individuals badly need to find a way to accept themselves again.

They could also be the grown-up children of addicts, who often have to live with the memories of decades of physical and psychological abuse. Their entire lives were organized around the needs of their substance-addicted mother or their violent dad, to the point where they hardly know who they are. They might have spent their entire childhoods hiding in corners, not knowing when the next slap would come.

Teaching an individual like this the value of self-love is absolutely vital. They'll be starting out from a place of abject self-loathing, and I know from experience how difficult it can be to make somebody like that even attain the most basic degree of self-acceptance.

This is where *love yourself* is actually an important message. Lots of people in the self-help industry do this kind of thing, often with impressive effects.

LOVING YOURSELF

But what about people who already love themselves from the start? What happens if we keep telling them that they should commit fully and go all in on self-esteem?

This is a tricky subject, I'm the first to admit that. It's probably impossible to draw a clear line between healthy self-appreciation and self-esteem and unsympathetic, self-promoting egotism. Or narcissism, for that matter. But that line must be somewhere.

The media, as usual, is having fun frightening everyone. Sometimes it seems like young people are feeling worse than ever. It's certainly true that many young people have difficulties processing the things they experience on social media. Once upon a time, the only people you had to worry about were your classmates at school. Now it's the whole world. It's not easy to always be comparing yourself to the best of the best. We're also seeing alarming reports of an increase in suicide attempts among young people because of online bullying. Those bullies aren't appearing out of thin air—but where do they come from?

It might be helpful for you to know that young people today are more satisfied with themselves than their grandparents were. There is a clear difference between these generations. Extensive psychological studies have shown that there is a clear correlation between one's age and one's self-esteem. This is a significant difference, too. In an American study from a few years ago, it was found that self-esteem among college students had increased by more than 80 percent between the 1960s and the 2010s. In primary school children, the increase was 93 percent over the last fifty years.

Those are impressive numbers. Who could possibly find anything objectionable about that?

During a study of the mothers of three-year-olds, the mothers were asked if they felt that it was important for their children to have a strong self-esteem. Naturally, all the mothers wanted their kids to have good self-esteem.

The grandmothers were asked the same question, too. They, too, felt that strong self-esteem was preferable to weak self-esteem.

When the mothers were asked if a child could have too much self-esteem, they all agreed that they couldn't. The interesting thing was what happened when the grandmothers were asked this question. They were in agreement, too—only they claimed that you can absolutely get too much of a good thing in this case. According to them, excessive self-esteem could easily be mistaken for arrogance, self-centeredness, and entitlement.

This study was an American one, so if you live elsewhere it may not say too much about the place where you live. Naturally, there are some cultural differences between the United States and, say, my own country of Sweden. However, I also know that anything that catches on in America is bound to make its way here over the next five to ten years or so.

By the way, the study I just mentioned was from 2010.

At this point, I should note that some people feel strongly that we're actually seeing the opposite development. Young people are increas-

ingly struggling with mental health, they claim. The truth is probably that well-being varies between different groups. Large swathes of
society are feeling better than ever while a portion of young people
are having a difficult time. On the other hand, things have probably
always been this way.

GOOGLE'S TAKE ON HOW TO LOVE YOURSELF

At this point, you might be thinking to yourself that this means the
necessary changes have already been made. Perhaps things, for some
unknown reason, were nudged just far enough, in just the right direction. Maybe the youth of the world are finally enjoying a comfortable
state of healthy self-respect and self-esteem, all correctly calibrated
and tuned? Maybe we're not in danger of causing an outbreak of narcissistic behavior after all? Well.

A few months ago, I read a book about a different subject in which
it was stated that a Google search of the string "how to love yourself"
would get 191,000 hits. That's quite impressive. The authors were
amazed at how many hits it got.

I took a look at the inside cover; the book was published in 2013.
Okay.

Just for fun, I ran my own search for "how to love yourself" while
I was writing this, in the winter of 2020–21.

Are you sitting down?

Number of hits: 2,450,000,000.

Almost *two and a half billion* hits on the question of how to learn
to love yourself.

That only makes sense, though. There are plenty of titles in the
literature that claim that if you can just love yourself, your problems
will be solved. If you start out with this one thing, there's no limit to
what you might achieve.

WHEN YOU LIKE YOURSELF MORE THAN YOU SHOULD

Self-admiration is perhaps not an unexpected side effect of having strong self-esteem. They are tightly connected to each other, although the latter is positive while the former is not. We should like ourselves, certainly, but self-admiration frequently produces negative effects; the danger of being viewed as a narcissist and all the harmful behavior associated with this is just one of these.

"Narcissism" is a psychological term, but that doesn't mean you need a psychology degree to be able to recognize the signs: arrogance, hedonism, vanity, self-promotion, grandiosity, and self-centeredness. Narcissists are completely preoccupied with themselves, think mostly about themselves, and adore the sound of their own voices. A great number of egotistical jerks are narcissists, but there are also superficially charming and charismatic individuals who clearly present narcissistic traits. The boundary isn't perfectly defined here.

The trait they have in common is their excessively positive self-images. These people go beyond confidence; they are self-obsessed and smug. They are firmly convinced that they are not only unique but also very, very special. There's nobody else like them in the world.

However, all of this comes with a special challenge.

You see, narcissists are faced with a dramatic psychological paradox: How do you maintain your sense that you're special and important when you're not *really too different from anybody else*? One way, of course, might be to find some partners in crime to further inflate your dangerously oversized ego. If you manage to convince yourself and everybody else that you're actually as great as you think you are, you really could be a winner. However, all you'd be winning at is self-admiration.

So, Does This Mean that Strong Self-Esteem Is the Same Thing as Narcissism?

No, of course not—and I hope I've been clear on this so far. Narcissism and self-esteem differ in a number of important ways.

People with strong self-esteem definitely have a positive self-image—that's the whole point, after all—but they are also able to think of the bigger picture. They don't only consider their own benefit, and because they feel so secure in themselves, they don't mind helping others. They think of themselves as moral agents and strive to make ethical decisions.

Narcissists think highly of themselves but spend most of their time bragging about their abilities. They don't promote themselves for being thoughtful or friendly or humble. No, they think of themselves as winners, and they announce this to anybody who is prepared to listen. They don't even try to hide the fact that they think they are the best. Why should they?

Sometimes you hear of sore losers—people who get into arguments because they hate to lose so badly. Did you know there are sore winners, too? I knew a guy like that once. If he ever won anything—it could be a game of Ping-Pong, a round of Trivial Pursuit, or just getting to the front of the restroom line at the local bar—he would taunt his opponent with a victory dance and be generally rude to them. He had entirely missed the whole sportsmanship ethos. And, as you might expect, he soon became the target of some rather serious criticism. People really hated that guy.

Aha! So It's People with *Weak* Self-Esteem Who Become Narcissists?

Well . . . There is a fairly popular idea that narcissists actually hate themselves and that just looking in the mirror fills them with dread.

Their behavior is actually all a ruse designed to hide this fact. Underneath the surface, deep down inside, they're terribly insecure.

We've all heard this more times than we care to recall. Back when I was in school, they were already suggesting to us that the big bad bullies in the schoolyard who didn't mind kicking or punching somebody if the teachers weren't looking were actually "very insecure deep down." That annoyed me then, and it still annoys me now. Why is that guy harassing me if he's so insecure?

I was as insecure as anyone, but I never picked on other kids. Everybody was insecure, come to think of it—so how was that idea even supposed to work?

Some psychologists call this behavior masking. The idea is that we're supposed to believe that while the narcissist is standing before us, giggling smugly, full of self-importance, it's all really a cry for help. Poor thing. But it's all hidden away, as I said.

This is probably too generous and an oversimplification. The vast majority of people who have endured difficult childhoods and major life trauma don't end up spending their time making everybody else's lives difficult. Certainly, some people do struggle with their past. There are, without any doubt, individuals who feel genuinely insecure. But they aren't the ones I'm talking about. The people I'm talking about are the ones who exhibit narcissistic characteristics.

Years ago, I used to work for a large company. We had a guy in my department who got up to some pretty strange stuff. To put it bluntly, he was a blatant bully. Rather than transfer him, or even remove him from the company entirely, the HR department decided to offer him therapy. His victims were asked to overlook his slights. Or, if they couldn't do that, it was suggested they might seek employment elsewhere. The bully might be going through a difficult time.

A REVEALING STUDY OF REAL-WORLD NARCISSISTS

Narcissists are commonly divided into two subcategories: Grandiose narcissists are the extroverted types we all recognize. But there is also a smaller group, which is referred to as vulnerable narcissists. These are the ones who have poor self-esteem and who don't attract as much attention. There is no evidence that grandiose narcissists—the variety this book mainly deals with—are actually insecure underneath the surface. On the contrary, there are lots of studies that show that adults who score highly for narcissism also tend to score highly for self-esteem. In fact, these individuals tend to be more content with themselves than the general population. The same is true of sociopaths and psychopaths, who often think very highly of themselves.

The statements in the questionnaires used are usually along these lines: "I feel that I possess some value, at least as much as other people" and "I feel that I possess a number of good qualities."

If you feel entitled to the best of what life has to offer, you won't find much to argue with there. To a true narcissist, these statements would actually seem too vague.

"You bet I possess some value—more than most people, actually! And I don't just have *a number* of good qualities—I have all of them!"

Researchers have devised fairly accurate tools for measuring this. One system, IAT (Implicit Association Test), is based on the idea that you respond "me"/"not me" in relation to a sequence of positive and negative words. Among other things, the tool considers how quickly you respond to certain questions an indicator of how convinced you are of your response.

People who have good self-esteem tend to associate themselves with words like "good" or "wonderful." However, they associate themselves less with words like "awful" or "wrong." Researchers have used this method to find out how narcissists really feel—deep down inside.

The results speak volumes.

It turns out that deep inside, the majority of all narcissists feel anything but miserable. On the contrary, they find themselves to be completely *exceptional*.

It's much easier—easier than for non-narcissists, that is—for narcissists to select words like "good," "wonderful," "great," "brilliant," and "right" as descriptors for themselves. They find it equally easy to distance themselves from words like bad," "terrible," "awful," and "wrong."

If we simplified things slightly, we could refer to this as "explicit self-esteem." However, implicit self-esteem can also be measured.

Narcissists perform better even for words like "assertive," "active," "energetic," "outspoken," "dominant," and "enthusiastic" (rather than "quiet," "reserved," "withdrawn," "submissive," and "inhibited").

However, when it comes to terms like "kind," "friendly," "generous," "cooperative," "pleasant," and "affectionate" (rather than "mean," "rude," "stingy," "quarrelsome," "grouchy," and "cruel"), they mess up. Narcissists don't score anywhere near as highly here.

How should we interpret this? Narcissists have a highly cohesive self-image, on the surface as well as at *any* depth we choose to look at. We could go as deep as we like. They are the same, all the way through.

Narcissists think of themselves as natural winners, but caring about others isn't anywhere near their list of priorities. The difference is glaringly obvious here. Non-narcissists with strong self-esteem are glad to help others. Narcissists are not.

The next time you hear somebody expressing sympathy for a schoolyard bully—or workplace bully, for that matter—you mustn't let anybody suggest that you need to help build their confidence up even more. If the bully isn't already a narcissist, they might very well develop narcissistic traits if somebody were to, say, decide to give them self-respect training. It's not a lack of self-respect that's the problem; it's a lack of respect for others.

DON'T BE SO NEGATIVE; WHAT'S THE HARM IN A LITTLE NARCISSISM?

Well, maybe there's no harm. The world can be an uncaring place, there's no denying that. Demands are high, and the competition is deadly. Maybe it would be for the best if we were to toughen up a little, so we could be more assertive. Could a touch of narcissism actually be a healthy thing?

This begs the question: Healthy for *whom*?

If you're more selfish, a single person will benefit: you. Grabbing an oversized piece of cake for yourself may benefit you in the moment, but it might also mean you won't be invited back to this particular party.

I'm fully aware that these questions are difficult ones; we're constantly in danger of ending up in complex philosophical discussions about Darwin's theories of who survives in nature. The answer, unfortunately, is not the nicest, but the most adaptable. The ones who can see where things are headed and position themselves accordingly. These folks won't necessarily be the friendliest crowd.

Who gets into the lifeboats first when the ship starts sinking? You can bet your life it's the narcissists. That's adaptability for you. But if they took that spot from a child, would that really be okay?

My own opinion is that harming others is wrong. It would surprise me if you feel very differently. Narcissistic traits mainly harm other people. For this reason, then, I don't consider narcissism to be preferable in any context of any kind.

But this is all just a small part of the truth.

If you were a narcissist, you would not see anything wrong with the preceding descriptions. You would think it entirely logical that you should get a seat on the lifeboat. But please, think again.

In the long run, narcissism is harmful to the narcissist, too. Failing an exam because you were too overconfident is hardly beneficial to anybody. Asserting yourself so forcefully that the other person actively distances themself from you—where's the good in that? Being secretly hated because the people around you have seen through your lies—is that what you wanted?

If you feel good, and are content with yourself, and if you feel like you're on top of the world, then by all means. As long as it helps your performance *without having a negative impact on anyone else,* it's all good!

The problem is it rarely stays at that.

8

Emotions and Narcissists—Like Oil and Water?

When you love someone, you love the person
as they are, and not as you'd like them to be.

—LEO TOLSTOY

It might seem natural to claim that the opposite of love is hate, but I'm not entirely convinced that's true. Love and hate are both strong emotions, and hate is probably the stronger of the two. The opposite of love is more likely to be apathy.

THE UNWANTED REACTION

Regardless of whether narcissists are able to feel true love for anybody but themselves, they definitely seem to have access to the emotion of hatred. A social media researcher I spoke to claimed that the reason why arguments can get so heated online is, without any doubt, the fact that so many people genuinely hate the people they attack. It's not a case of mere attention seeking; they seriously want to destroy certain individuals. The reasons why will vary, but the underlying disdain is very real.

Ignoring a narcissist is the optimal way of becoming the object of their unbridled rage. They hate not being seen, missing out on the action, or not being considered important. Being ostracized can be frustrating to all kinds of people, of course, but narcissists genuinely despise feeling invisible. Considering how important narcissists think they are and how much good they think they could do for every last group of people on the planet, it's an absolute mystery how anybody could even consider ignoring them. Retribution can come quickly, in the form of a vicious assault on whoever had the nerve.

The same thing happens if narcissists are questioned. They hate to be challenged, and this might sound a little odd when you consider that many narcissists don't really experience much in the way of fear. Many of them are even outright aggressive. Why wouldn't they look forward to some verbal sparring, assuming it's a subject worth debating?

To understand this reaction, you need to look at the narcissistic psyche. Differences of opinion are one thing. They can actually be opportunities to sharpen your arguments and then ask for a rematch when you meet again. However, the narcissist is enraged by the very act of questioning *them*. "How could anybody have the gall to contradict me? *Me?*" If this perceived offense continues, their rage and frustration will turn into verbal assaults before you can say "antisocial personality disorder."

Again, the same thing goes for being disobeyed. There are some people, after all, who don't really appreciate being given too much direction on what to do or not do. Narcissists occasionally issue long lists of more or less ridiculous demands to the people around them, and usually they consider it their birthright to be obeyed. If somebody fails to acknowledge this, their rage will once again be ignited. The rest of us should do as we're told, basically.

Bosses with narcissistic tendencies tend to give themselves away quite quickly in this regard. They don't hesitate to ignore the inappropriateness of their reaction: If their coworker doesn't do as he's told, all hell might break loose.

If we study the reverse relationship, we'll find that narcissists also hate being criticized. Any manager who has had to lead a team that includes a narcissist will know how hard it can be to reach them. They simply refuse to listen. Since everything they've ever done was great, probably some of the best work ever done, they will respond aggressively if somebody points out their errors or mistakes or even speaks poorly of the narcissist's efforts in public. If you're convinced that you're the best at everything, criticism can come as something of a shock.

Instant counteroffensives are very common. They give in to an animalistic instinct to seek to destroy the enemy—that is, the source of the unjustified criticism in this case. Usually, their actual performance has nothing to do with anything. Narcissists will not infrequently feel that they would do a better job as managers of their workplaces. Why aren't they the ones handing out the criticism? It's not as though there's a shortage of reasons to criticize other people.

While none of this is really too surprising, there are other, more subtle things that can be harder to grasp, like a refusal to respect other people's boundaries.

Narcissists are essentially uninhibited, but they demand that others comply with their rules. As always, this is a one-way street. Occasionally, just like psychopaths do, narcissists will deliberately overstep other people's boundaries and then sit down and wait for a reaction. All they really want is to show us they can do it. It could be a matter of punctuality, or performing a task in a certain way, or taking other people's belongings.

A PECULIAR EXAMPLE

Not too long ago, I heard of a landlord who made a habit of using his master key to enter his tenants' apartments while they were away. He didn't steal anything or get up to any other kind of mischief. Not much of anything happened, really. However, when one of the tenants grew suspicious, she hid a camera in her home. The whole affair was soon uncovered. The landlord was entering the apartments to take a look around, basically. He saw the camera, too. How do we know that? Well, he waved to the tenant in the footage. Then he left the room. When confronted with this evidence of his transgressions, all he could offer by way of explanation was that he did it because he could. He didn't like the idea that something was forbidden to him. He had to show the world that he could do as he liked.

That's another thing narcissists can't stand: not being allowed to do something. Even if this is just a case of workplace regulations that apply to everybody and that everybody follows, that won't sit right with a narcissist. They feel they really ought to be afforded a little more freedom than everybody else, on account of being, well . . . better. Serious conflicts can arise from this, and if the narcissist's boss is a strong enough leader to keep the situation under control, that will just be another reason for the narcissist to hate them.

What else? Being denied special privileges would be bad, of course. Not getting your way is an immense slight, as we all know. Not receiving good enough service is also a problem, as this indicates that somebody is failing to give them the respect they deserve by virtue of their mere existence. It might imply that somebody is paying them less attention than they are due. A serious infraction indeed.

After all this, it may come as a surprise that they also hate it when they feel insufficiently appreciated by others.

I'm sure the paradox here isn't lost on you—it certainly can be challenging to comprehend the contradictory nature of a narcissist.

Behaving like an immature, whiney child is not going to win you any friends, basically. Nobody likes people who are always in a bad mood over some unique, special treatment they imagine they deserve just for being themselves.

ARE NARCISSISTS CAPABLE OF LOVING?

That's actually a trick question; mainly, they love themselves. The question is complex to put it lightly, because this particular love is more of a love/hate kind of deal. On the one hand, they love themselves, but on the other hand, they hate that they aren't even better, more attractive, wealthier, more popular, or whatever it is they feel they need.

There's no way we could produce a definition of love that everybody would agree to. However, one that I like personally is goodness. Being good, doing good deeds. Not good as in enjoyable—that's too basic—I mean good as in ethically good.

What does it mean to be good? Could it be to do something for another person without expecting anything in return? The philosophical question of whether truly unselfish acts are even rationally possible has not yet been put to bed.

Despite this, it seems reasonable to say that how you behave towards somebody who can't reciprocate your behavior reveals the values you hold.

It's also a context in which narcissists never prosper. The concept of goodness can't do anything for them unless they direct it at themselves. They don't mind giving some change to a homeless person as long as somebody is present to acknowledge them for it. Announcing on social media that you give money to panhandlers whenever you can is not necessarily an unselfish deed. It might also be intended as a subtle suggestion to others that the giver is good and generous on a personal level. If the giver is popular and has a large fan base, the praise will be deafening. However, most people who see a post like that know what's up. And they are not too likely to be impressed.

So, what about that question about love: Is a narcissist really able to love another person? Since narcissism, like many other personality disorders, is a rather broad spectrum, there's no one-size-fits-all response here. Generally, though, it will depend on what we mean by "love."

Is a narcissist, then, able to love another human being in the sense of longing for that specific person, not being able to stop thinking of them, and experiencing a physical temperature shift throughout their body whenever they see the person in question? Are narcissists able to experience the pain of not getting to be with the person they want to grow old with? Do narcissists feel their whole world get brighter when the person they're waiting for walks through the door?

Are narcissists able to feel the need to care for another person, significant other, child, parent, or friend that many people feel?

As usual, there is no consensus on this in the literature, but I'd still be prepared to guess that none of the above is the kind of thing a narcissist spends much thought on.

What does loving somebody mean, anyway? For most people, it could mean anything from "I enjoy spending time with you" to "I am prepared to give my life for you."

This isn't something you can sit down and have a discussion with a narcissist about. They will simply agree with your definition, whatever it may be. If you say it's important to you that you do things for others, the narcissist will inform you that they feel the same. If you claim that love is something that makes you smile when you think of somebody, the narcissist will nod knowingly. They will under no circumstances give you the truth; they know it's not too pretty.

A PHRASE BOOK OF LOVE

To a narcissist, love means "you make my life more comfortable." It could also mean "thank you for giving me what I need." Or "I love you because you make me look amazing." How you make a narcissist look to other people matters a great deal. If you're younger, more attractive, or have some cash hidden away for a rainy day, this will reflect well on the narcissist. Watch out! That's exactly the kind of person they want to be seen with.

It could also mean "I'm glad you acknowledge me and recognize my greatness." Or "thank you for sticking around even though there isn't much in it for you."

"I love you" really means:

"I love that you love me."

"I love you for making my life fantastic, for continuing to tolerate my little abuses, and for never calling my bluff."

"I love you for buying all my bull crap, day after day."

"I love you for taking all the responsibility for our relationship, and keeping it going—I don't have to do much, while you wear yourself out trying to get me to reciprocate your love."

In the worst case, "I love you" means "you're a bigger fool than I thought; you're lucky to even get to spend time with me."

Loving a narcissist is no walk in the park, basically. However, there are enough people struggling in life to ensure there will always be a steady supply of people who will put up with anything to avoid being alone. Narcissists know this, too. They are fully aware that they can get away with treating their partner quite badly without having to worry about consequences.

There is a wealth of testimonies from all over the world about what living with a narcissist can be like, and the reality they all describe is very different. Feel free to read more about this in chapter 15: "The Challenges of Being Close to a Narcissist" (see page 139).

It seems, then, that narcissists don't just have a hard time loving, but they frequently cause their partners to feel miserable and neglected. Some people describe feeling used, exploited, ignored, betrayed, and abandoned. And then, to top it off, intensely hated.

As one listens to some of these testimonies, the victims' denial is sometimes so obvious. "He told me he loved me, so this can't be happening." Unfortunately, it is happening. To my mind, this kind of mental abuse is actually worse than physical violence. It can harm people for life—especially good people.

9

The Secret Language of Narcissists

And once you are awake,
you shall remain awake eternally.
—FRIEDRICH NIETZSCHE

It's not easy to tell if somebody is a narcissist just by listening to them. Narcissists have a knack for making much of what they say sound appealing, or even tempting. Skilled manipulators often have the gift of the gab.

Early-warning signs, of course, include talking about themselves a great deal. But that's nowhere near enough. As we've seen, there are plenty of people who do that without being narcissists.

Another warning sign, which is more common in romantic relationships, is when somebody who has known you for all of three weeks announces that you are their soul mate. That can be nice to hear, especially if you've been thirsting for some human contact. But when you reconnect your hard drive and think about it, you'll realize that it might take more than a couple of dates to become soul mates. It's just a ruse they're using to manipulate you.

However, generally, that's the kind of thing you can expect to hear from a narcissist. Assuming they're in a good mood, that is. If a narcissist suffers a setback, violent rage will often follow.

One way of determining if somebody's a narcissist is to compare their words with their deeds. We all make promises we can't keep from time to time, but if this is a pathological pattern, it might be time to look around for some other company.

If, on the other hand, you already have a narcissist close by, it can be good to know what the real-world implications of their words will be. I've collected the following quotes from "survivor forums" (yep, there are several online communities dedicated to former victims of narcissists and psychopaths). Each of these examples is so common, it definitely seems like there is a pattern to them.

THE TRUTH BEHIND A NARCISSIST'S WORDS

Why not begin with the whole topic of soul mates? What does it mean when a narcissist calls you their soul mate?

Translation: Well, all available data suggest that this simply means "you are my latest supplier of everything I need. Thank you for being there for me."

He/she is just a friend.

Translation: You are my *main* supplier of sex, money, company, adulation, or whatever I happen to need. It's amusing to me that you'll put up with so much abuse.

My ex never reacted like that.

Translation: My ex reacted *exactly* like that, which is why they are now my ex. You're actually reacting much the same as all my other victims. Your reactions encourage me to continue behaving as I do, so I can make you feel bad and cause you grief.

You're being so dramatic and oversensitive. You're always overreacting.

Translation: I'd like to make you think the problem is you and your completely normal reactions, rather than my own rude behavior. If we're being honest, it's me who's causing the drama, and deep down, I love to provoke chaos in any given situation. I'm also highly sensitive when it comes to criticism, and I overreact whenever my perceived greatness is endangered. Besides, I've mastered the art of projecting my emotions onto others. Have you noticed that yet?

You're much better than my ex. He/she was completely insane.

Translation: If anyone was insane in my last relationship, it was probably me. However, there is no way I will admit to being to blame for the breakup.

Let's take a break.

Translation: I need some time to acquire new allies and benefactors or initiate new sexual relationships. Meanwhile, feel free to miss me and feel unwanted. Besides, it's quite a drain on me to have to feign empathy all the time. I need some time off to recharge my batteries.

We're just too different.

Translation: I lack all empathy, but you don't. In fact, somebody like me doesn't really match up very well with somebody normal. To be completely honest, I don't think I match up very well with anybody. I'm literally surrounded by idiots.

Where's your sense of humor?, or *You're taking my jokes far too seriously,* or *I was only kidding.*

Translation: I often use jokes as a subtle way of putting you down. If you can't take a joke, that's probably because you see it for what it really is: a way for me to get away with acting like a total jerk.

I want to have sex. Now.

Translation: I've just done something really bad. So let's have sex and strengthen our bond. That way, your attraction for me will be perpetuated by a strange biochemical cocktail that causes you to associate pleasure with pain. That way, you'll keep coming back for more.

I don't want sex. Sex is of no interest to me.

Translation: Withdrawing from you sexually and using other people to make you jealous allows me to coax you into believing that you're completely unwanted. I like the sense of power over you that I feel when you're insecure. It makes me feel even more superior.

We don't have enough sex, or *you don't agree to* (fill in the blank with any unthinkable act you've long since told the narcissist you will under no circumstances agree to perform), *like all my past partners did.*

Translation: In reality, none of my previous partners ever agreed to do any of these horrible things for me, even though I told them how my favorite porn stars do them all the time. None of them agreed to do what they found unacceptable, and they were all just as shocked as you are that I even dared to ask. However, by claiming that they did, I hope to convince you to agree to things you find absolutely detestable.

I'm sorry you feel that way.

Translation: I don't actually care one bit what you think. I'm pretending to care to shut you up. The problem isn't my recurring mental abuse; it's the way you react like a normal person with emotions when all I'm asking for is what I'm entitled to. How dare you?

I'll never do that again.

Translation: If you let me get away with this now, you can count on me to do it again. However, as I've just learned more about how you'll react, I will fine-tune my next transgression just a little, for maximum effect.

I'm a really nice guy/girl.

Translation: If I really were such a nice person, would I have to keep pointing it out? Wouldn't my actions just speak for themselves? That's right.

Let's be friends.

Translation: Please dial down your expectations, so it will be easier for me to keep using you until somebody better turns up.

I've had enough!

Translation: Yuck, you're a normal person with normal emotions and empathy and stuff—I can't deal with this!

You seem to think you're something else.

Translation: You *are* something else, but the fact that you're so secure about yourself is making me insecure, and I can't deal with that. Therefore, I've decided to explain to you that you're not as attractive or popular as you seem to think. Give me a few months and I'll crumble every bit of your confidence.

Nobody cares about you or your achievements in life.

Translation: Far too many people care. Therefore, I'm going to isolate you from your supporters and take you down a couple of notches. There's only room for one winner in this relationship.

You're nuts! You're such a narcissist!

Translation: I know very well that the narcissist here is probably me, but I'd prefer it if you felt as bad about it as I do.

This needs to be taken with a pinch of salt, of course. But a narcissist's stream of consciousness might actually look this confused. When you think you might be dealing with a narcissist you need to practice recognizing all these varieties of malarkey for what they are. The sooner the better.

10

When Did a Little Narcissism Ever Hurt Anyone?

People will do anything, no matter how absurd,
to avoid facing their own soul.

—CARL JUNG

At this point, we need to ask ourselves some questions. These include: Does it really matter to the rest of us that there are a few narcissists running around out there? What harm can it do if some people think about themselves a bit too much? These are relevant questions, because the world is facing a fair number of challenges of various kinds and various magnitudes, so somewhere along the line we're going to have to prioritize. Which problem do we take on first?

One way of determining whether a problem is even *worth* trying to solve might be to reflect on whether it *can* be solved in the first place. Many problems are readily solvable while others require gargantuan efforts. Climate change is a problem of the latter variety. Those who propose we do all we can are prepared to accept the costs. However, they are pitted against those who feel the problem doesn't even need solving, or can't be solved. Others still claim there isn't even a problem in the first place! This is a large part of the reason why the proponents of competing theories can never seem to agree: They're not working from a common definition of what the problem even is. In that situation, there's not going to be much point in discussing solutions until people have come to an agreement about the problem.

Maybe somebody's mother-in-law is a total nightmare. Maybe somebody's uncle goes on horrendous benders at the weekends. That's too bad, of course. But those are things that might be solvable, or might not be solvable, depending on who you ask. Either way, resolving these situations won't require the same kinds of efforts that tackling climate change and its consequences will.

THE STRENGTHS OF A NARCISSIST

So, what do narcissists do well? Besides lying, deceiving, and defrauding you, they're also very adept at identifying your weaknesses. They go about it the same way psychopaths do. In the initial stages of your relationship, they will spend a great deal of time figuring out who you are. Basically, they're studying you.

This is particularly common during the initial love-bombing phase, when they shower you with false promises, flowers, and chocolate. They will tell you fabricated secrets about themselves, to get you to open up and tell them things you might not have felt like telling them. The point of this activity is exactly what you'd expect: to learn everything they can about you, so that they can use it against you in the future.

A narcissist confides in you that they live in fear of becoming homeless. You tell them you sometimes freak out over the idea of losing your job and not being able to pay your bills. Good, they know that now. Might be useful at some point. Is the narcissist really scared of homelessness? Who can say? Probably not. But now they know something about you, something that might come in handy down the line.

It could be that you're afraid of going at high speeds. This might cause a particularly malicious narcissist to drive very fast in some situation where they want to unbalance you.

Perhaps you tell them that you're particularly uncomfortable around aggressive outbursts and raised voices. The narcissist will wait for the perfect moment to shout at you and make you submit.

Just as they put you on a pedestal by doing all the things they know you like, they can tear you down from there anytime they want, by doing all the things you *don't* like—sometimes in a very cruel way. It simply depends on what the narcissist wants on the occasion in question.

They know what triggers your insecurities, your traumas, your fears. Remember that narcissists have no inhibitions. They just go ahead and do whatever comes to mind. Since they lack empathy, there's nothing to prevent them from acting on some imagined reason or another to hurt you.

They also happen to be very good at maintaining a charming façade. Anybody who has tried to break up with a narcissist has heard this or something like it: "What? You're breaking up with so-and-so? Why? He/she is so nice!"

Narcissists spend a great deal of time cultivating this superficially perfect persona for themselves. Because most of the people who listen to them are more or less like yourself, they believe in that image. Because your friends don't live with narcissists, they won't believe you when you tell them what your partner actually did. Why should they? After all, they've already been told that you've changed beyond recognition.

One thing many people find to be a bit of a contradiction is the fact that most narcissists actually have a very good grasp of how people function. Although their own emotional lives are different, and although they lack empathy, they still *understand* what makes the rest of us tick. They've studied us up close, with zero emotional interference. This gives them an edge when it comes to analyzing what's actually going on.

One of the more important reasons for this is that they need to learn to mimic human emotions. And they have learned to do that. Don't you doubt it.

SURELY, THOUGH, THEY MUST HAVE WEAKNESSES, TOO?

Plenty. Naturally, they refuse to discuss most of them.

They hate apathy. Being overlooked is a narcissist's kryptonite. They can't take it when people don't pay attention to them. They prefer anger or hatred over apathy. Any kind of reaction is interpreted as evidence that they matter to somebody else. It's very frustrating if somebody refuses to respond to the narcissist's antics because this suggests that the narcissist has no power over the person in question. How do you provoke anguish and misery in somebody who doesn't seem to care?

Being loved in the early stages of a relationship is important. That's an obvious source of recognition. Apathy? No response equals no potential to sabotage the other party. How can you ruin somebody's day when they're not even listening to you? If the intended victim is able to just move on without so much as a glance in the narcissist's direction, this can trigger a total breakdown.

They can never truly belong to the world you and I live in. Their superficial emotions simply blind them to life's true potential. Once they realize this—remember, these aren't psychopaths, who would simply congratulate themselves over being free of the trouble emotions seem to bring—they can suffer deep depressions. A narcissist knows that there are parts of life that are inaccessible to them. This insight probably doesn't arrive until the individual grows older and learns to reflect on their own deeds and their life.

Some narcissists get this stuff, absolutely. It's a sliding scale, with the vulnerable narcissists who actually hate themselves at one of the extremes. They know that everybody hates them and that nothing they can do will change that. It's a complex blend of enjoying the privileges that come from not getting mixed up in messy emotions on the one hand and knowing that people detest you for that very same reason on the other.

In case you've ever thought to yourself that it might be nice to be more narcissistic, think again!

They're all rather apathetic inside. They will never experience true love; they know it exists, certainly, and they grasp the concept, but they are nonetheless forever shut out from it. It's not for them. And since narcissists hate to be denied anything, the whole situation can get very confusing.

CAN NARCISSISTS BE DANGEROUS?

Now we've returned to the question I posed at the start of this chapter: Does it really matter to the rest of us that there are a few narcissists running around out there? A relevant question here is what harm a narcissist can do to a fellow human being. Could they pose a genuine danger to you, or to your family, for example?

How do we define "danger" in this context? We could approach it from many points of view. We could discuss danger in terms of risk to individuals, which would be the simple example. This can in turn be divided into physical dangers versus psychological dangers.

Many people who are neither narcissists nor psychopaths are capable of violent behavior. Husbands who beat their wives are usually just cowards who would never dare strike another man. They wouldn't pick on anybody who might fight back. Unfortunately, bullies have been around forever. But we simply don't know if narcissism is correlated with violent behavior. It all seems to depend somewhat on whatever the narcissist's particular baggage happens to be.

Research has found that parents who abuse their children have often suffered similar abuses as children. However, this is shaky ground, seeing as many others with the same history behave very differently. They manage to break the chain of their parents' abuse and don't pass it on to their own kids.

But we still have no convincing evidence that narcissists are more likely to resort to violence than others. My own personal reflection is that if you live with somebody and find yourself entertaining the notion that your significant other might be dangerous, caution is very much advised. If I were you, I'd already be packing my bags. There's no point in waiting to see.

However, if the question is whether a narcissist might pose a psychological danger, the answer is definitely *yes*. Just like psychopaths do, they cause mental harm to others by their behavior. They manipulate, they lie, they cheat, they use, they indulge in *mind games,* and they can be so genuinely evil to their partners that it seems almost impossible that anybody could avoid being influenced by it.

We know that a large proportion of those afflicted with post-traumatic stress disorder have been exposed to a particularly venomous kind of relationship. These emotional abuses often go on for decades. Narcissists are sophisticated bullies, and although their methods are less brutal than those of psychopaths, they still tend to prey on people's emotions in ways that are bound to have far-reaching, if not permanent, negative effects on somebody's trust.

In summary, narcissists are bad news for your mental health.

However, narcissists can also pose a danger to groups of people. Take a company or a business, for example. When an individual behaves in a way that impairs the company's functions, they can cause a great deal of damage, of course. The worst-case scenario is when the boss is a narcissist. A person like that could exploit their position to pit their employees against one another—the old divide-and-conquer approach.

However, narcissists can cause a great deal of harm on other levels, too.

We can always think of narcissism as the psychological counterpart to secondhand smoke. Their behavior usually ends up harming the narcissists themselves, but it does equal harm, if not more, to the people around them. The effects are more immediate in this case than with secondhand smoke, however.

Narcissists can be deeply manipulative and can cause their victims a lot of trouble, just like psychopaths and Machiavellians. If you don't see it coming, it can become dangerous indeed.

So, in conclusion, I'd have to say narcissists do create problems for the rest of us. Also, the closer you happen to be to a narcissist, the greater the risk will be that you might experience something you'd rather not.

11

Manipulation

If you are an approval addict, your behavior is as easy to control
as that of any other junkie. All a manipulator need do is a simple
two-step process: Give you what you crave, and then
threaten to take it away.

Every drug dealer in the world plays this game.

—HARRIET B. BRAIKER, *WHO'S PULLING YOUR STRINGS*

Narcissists want to cut your social ties, to make you more pliable and
easier to manage. There are countless manipulation techniques. Imagine that a narcissist would use two, three, or why not all of these techniques on you at once. You could suffer devastating consequences.
The strange thing here is that a great number of narcissists and other
manipulative types are up to similar mischief. Sometimes I wonder if
there must be a secret manual out there somewhere.

ARBITRARY POSITIVE FEEDBACK

Giving an individual powerful, personal recognition at times—and
at times withholding it! Making a person dependent on the particular kind of acknowledgment they crave in order to feel good. We all
want recognition of some sort. Perhaps you're one of those people

who feel good when they're told they've done a good job. It feels nice to receive your boss's praise. Imagine that you just left a job where praise and positive feedback were in scarce supply. The most common reason for somebody to speak to you was to tell you what you had done wrong. As I discussed earlier, we all have flaws and weaknesses.

Many managers are terrible at acknowledging their team members' efforts. Perhaps they are quicker to criticize than to praise. Now, you've found a new job, and your new boss gives you a great welcome to the company. She immediately acknowledges your best qualities and praises you for being efficient, organized, helpful, competent, and a bunch of other things you're proud of yourself for.

What effect would this have on you? It would make you want to work even harder, to receive more positive feedback. In just two weeks, your boss has made you enjoy your work more than you ever have before in years of professional life. Things carry on this way for a few months.

But then, suddenly, your new boss falls silent. No further recognition is forthcoming. After finally getting the credit you deserve for your hard work, you're suddenly facing a wall of stifling silence. Whenever you and your boss meet in the hallway, she just looks right through you. She doesn't respond to your questions, doesn't even acknowledge your existence with a brief look your way. A long, endless month passes like this, in silence.

How would you react to this? You would work even harder to get your daily dose of appreciation.

But then, suddenly, your boss summons you to her office again. She's gushing with praise over something or other that you've done. Dumbstruck with gratitude, you stumble out of her office, ecstatic over suddenly receiving her attention again. Perhaps you'll even accuse yourself of being overly sensitive.

Maybe it's not ideal for you to be that desperate for attention. But praise does motivate. Recognition keeps you going. When it is withheld, you're bound to feel a bit hollow.

If your boss asks you for help again and you think there is some promise of personal recognition in it for you, you'll do whatever you're asked to do. Even if the task is one that you don't really enjoy. You'll do it, and again, you'll be praised for working so hard. You'll feel better, and everything will seem okay. Bit by bit, your boss will be able to get you to take on assignments you would never even have considered before.

Then she falls silent again. She makes a face in a meeting when you're speaking. Or maybe she ignores you entirely. This stratagem will allow your boss to send you off on an emotional roller coaster.

Perhaps she plans to ask you for something truly inappropriate later on, or simply to get you to work harder without asking for anything in return. Little by little, your behavior will change, and you'll find yourself crossing boundaries you would never have considered crossing before.

How Will You React?

Well, that depends on who you are. Feel free to take another look at the four colors in chapter 4 (page 27). If Red is dominant in your personality, this boss's behavior might enrage you. In general, you actually don't need as much recognition as the average person does. You know your abilities and your limits. You're not emotionless of course, but you're probably brave enough to confront your boss and ask what she's playing at. In this case, she'd be certain to deny everything, and you'll be free to decide what to do next.

If you're mostly Blue, it's very much the same story. You're capable of assessing your own workplace performance. You already know what constitutes quality work. You also happen to be naturally suspicious of praise. While this doesn't mean Blues are immune to this kind of manipulation, it does make it a lot harder to cultivate the kind of insecurity described in the preceding example. Since both Reds and Blues are fact-oriented, their relationship to their boss will matter less to them than it would to others.

If your profile is dominated by Yellow (Yellow-Green, Yellow-Red, or Yellow-Blue), you'll be vulnerable to this unfair tactic. You're dependent on recognition to begin with—public recognition, ideally—and receiving it makes you feel incredible.

Yellows will often deny this, as they feel it sounds too self-centered. But that doesn't make it any less true, of course. Be honest with yourself. You know that praise has an effect on you. And you know what it feels like to be suddenly banished into the cold. If you're denied recognition from the people you hold in high esteem, you will feel weak and vulnerable. It's like being invisible.

Praise—silence—praise—silence.

Yellows might even talk to their coworkers about it, although the appearance of being rejected by the boss might trouble them. Some will decide to keep it all to themselves.

Yellows won't quite have the courage to confront the boss about their behavior. This is particularly true of Yellow-Greens. For them, the risk of escalation is severe, and they will be very uncomfortable with the situation. Little by little, the Yellow will submit to the whims of the boss.

Green workers are quite sensitive about relationship issues, too, and they also tend to choose to suffer in silence. They will never confront the boss. It all comes down to how the positive acknowledgment was initially delivered. Perhaps the boss has celebrated the Green's endeavors in front of the whole team in the past. They hate that kind of attention.

Not having to endure that kind of public attention is always going to be good news for the Green. However, if the boss has realized that summoning the Green to their office to receive the praise in a more intimate setting is what the Green prefers, that is specifically what will be withheld. Greens have a glaring weakness in this sense.

Considering all of this, arbitrary positive feedback is a potent weapon. The trick is to get the victim accustomed to receiving positive feedback first. The effects really take hold once it's withheld.

ARBITRARY NEGATIVE FEEDBACK

When a manipulator uses negative feedback, they stop doing something *you* dislike when you start doing something *they* like. As a result, you end up doing what they want.

This is complicated from the outset in relationships. Maybe you want to go out with the guys on a Friday night, but your girlfriend is all grouchy about it and keeps making a scene until you call to cancel on your friends. Now she's suddenly all smiles again.

Or inversely: She wants to have a girls' night out, and you feel there's been a bit much of that lately. Why can't she spend Friday night with you for a change? When you express your request, she gets angry and complains about everything you ever did or didn't do. Soon, you give in and say, "Fine, go out with your friends." And just like that, everything is sunshine and rainbows again. Her mood seems to hinge on what you say.

This tactic is just as simple as it is effective. You get negative feedback, consistently, until you give in and concede the argument. Then everything returns to normal. It's an easy way to make you come to heel. Nothing to it.

Now, you need to see through the pattern here. Your manipulator knows that you are acquiescing in the hope it will bring relief from the negative behavior she's subjecting you to. The problem is, if you start backing down, you're very likely to keep going. And now your behavior is being determined by somebody else.

Next, imagine a skilled manipulator, who has learned to optimize the combined use of *both* positive *and* negative arbitrary feedback. You won't be able to make sense of them or predict their behavior. None of it has any real connection to your actions. No matter what you do, or don't do, you could receive any given reaction. You're entirely subjected to the whims of the manipulator. Can you imagine the stress?

COUNTERMEASURES

Your behavior is exactly the same as in the example of arbitrary positive feedback. You need to learn to see through it. Sometimes all it takes is indicating that you've seen what's going on. If you're dealing with a healthy individual who doesn't have any ill intent, you'll probably end up having a fruitful discussion, in which you resolve the issue and decide to move on.

It can be useful to know that manipulation often occurs subconsciously. If something works, you keep doing it. Many people don't even consider the harm they do their victims, but if it's pointed out to them, everything changes. As I noted at the start of this book, most of us mostly think of ourselves, after all.

That's how you can tell if you're dealing with a narcissist or some kind of subconscious manipulator.

Trust your gut instincts. If something feels wrong, chances are it is wrong. There's no need to apologize for your feelings in a situation like this. You have the right to do whatever you need to do to protect yourself.

Step off the train. Get on another one.

LOVE BOMBING

I'm sure you've heard of this technique before. (Note: Many men are prone to variations of this behavior in the early stages of a relationship, before the realities of everyday life take hold. This doesn't make them narcissists or psychopaths—just less charming and engaging members of their gender. Don't hate them for it. They may just not know any better.)

In any case, the term love bombing has been used to denote this despicable tactic for many years now.

The narcissist begins by announcing their unconditional love for you. They expose themself completely to you, perhaps opening up to you over dinner (which you're paying for, of course) about how they've never met somebody like you before. It's incredible. In all their life, you are the most exceptional person they've ever met, and they want to grow old with you. This ego pampering is kept up until you surrender, basically. All of this could happen within three weeks of getting to know the other person.

If you're a Red, you've always been told that you can be insensitive at times. And now here comes somebody who doesn't seem to have any problem with that. In fact, they even encourage your dominant alpha behavior. They appreciate it when somebody has the guts to take charge.

If you're a Yellow, you may know deep down that you have a way of claiming every last bit of oxygen in the room for yourself. However, your new soul mate wants nothing more than to hear more entertaining and amusing anecdotes from your interesting life. Finally, somebody who appreciates your greatness!

Narcissists will tell Greens that they've always admired the strong and silent type because of the stability and security they radiate. Finally, somebody with the sense to keep quiet and leave some space for their partner! Just think if everybody else could do it just as naturally and unpretentiously as you?

Blues, who have always suspected they may be a bit too square and dull, will be told that their enormous intellects are incredibly sexy. A full 12.36 percent sexier than the mean of all samples collected according to such-and-such principle, and so on.

Add the following to the equation: gifts, flowers, friendly gestures, warmth, kisses, 24/7 text messages with cute lovey-dovey messages from your admirer.

I know—it all looks ridiculously simple from the outside. How would it feel to be told you're the pinnacle of nature's creation by somebody you have strong feelings for? Can you honestly swear you'd be invulnerable to that?

The unfortunate truth here is that the narcissist is merely getting you into position for their inevitable ambush. Perhaps six months or a year from now—that all depends on how extensive their scheme is, which will in turn tend to depend on your financial resources—the love bombing will suddenly cease, as if by magic. Poof.

One fine day, your texts will go unanswered. The hand that is usually in yours when you go shopping stays in its pocket. Perhaps your betrothed is suddenly smiling at other people in a way that seems far too inviting. Sooner or later, they will start telling you about their past relationships. There are plenty of things you have no desire to know about. However, those might well be the precise things they are talking about.

Now, you might already be married, or expecting a child. All you can do is go along for the ride. Then *boom!* Suddenly, you're being criticized for the very same personality traits they used to praise you for.

If you're a Red, you're suddenly being told how you're far too dominant and that your need to call all the shots is stifling them. Yellows will be accused of being too flighty and immature and of never listening. Greens will be accused of stubbornly resisting any and all change and of never wanting to leave the house, and Blues will probably be chided for being so incredibly dull. Such sticklers for procedure. So hopeless.

Perhaps you'll be faced by a wall of silence. For a whole week, your partner refuses to respond when spoken to. Gets up before you. Goes to bed after you. Locks themselves in rooms. Leaves the house without explaining where they're going. This makes for an extremely draining combination. Can you imagine all the thoughts that will pass through your mind?

Slowly, gradually, things keep getting worse. Much worse. Nonetheless, there are moments when you get the attention you crave. All of a sudden, you find yourself enjoying a romantic weekend trip, with lots of wonderful moments to share. You breathe a sigh of relief. Whew! Your partner is back to being the loving person you once learned to love. There's still hope! You still mean something to them!

Until, that is, they withdraw again, and you've unwittingly sat back down on the emotional roller coaster from hell. Whatever they ask for you'll try to provide. You want to be happy, after all.

WHAT TO DO WHEN YOU'RE BEING LOVE BOMBED

How do you correctly handle a narcissist's love bombing?

Keep your cool. Remember this:

If it sounds too good to be true, it probably is.

Read that sentence at least three times. Write it down, and look at it whenever you have some time to spare.

It's actually incredibly simple. When it comes to romantic relationships, you should try to put your emotions to the side.

Yes, I know that this sounds like a contradiction. But think about it: If you were to tell everybody you know that you've finally met your soul mate and that you're about to move in together after knowing each other for just seven days, what would your well-meaning friends say to you? I can guarantee you they will question your mental state. "Seven days? Are you out of your mind?"

On the other hand, if you've been dating somebody for seven years without even moving in together . . . Who's fooling who, here?

So, we've established that a stable relationship takes more than seven days but less than seven years to form. How long does it take, exactly? I don't know. And neither do you. You can look at it statistically. How many relationships do you know of where the couple met, moved in together, and got married, all within a few weeks? Or, for that matter, a few months? How long did these relationships last?

If you need more than your left thumb to count them, I owe you lunch.

The objective of love bombing is for the manipulator to force themself onto you with such intense energy that you never have time to pay attention to who they really are. For heaven's sake, please don't fall for this. If it's genuine, this person will keep the love bombing up for at least a year. If they have the means and the commitment to do so, then perhaps they are right for you after all. But if not, you should be cautious about exposing yourself to emotional harm early on in the relationship. It's sad but true.

SMOKE SCREENS

This manipulation technique aims to confuse you—no more, no less. "You're overreacting again! You're so volatile! Can't you see how much trouble you're causing?"

A skilled manipulator can say just about anything to get you off guard. The objective here is to shift the focus from the genuine issue to a discussion about some serious flaw of yours. To get there, they'll have to push some of your emotional buttons.

If, for example, you have serious suspicions that your partner is cheating on you, you may want to have a talk about it. Perhaps you're completely calm. You just want to talk. All you are looking for is confirmation that your suspicions are unfounded. But rather than discuss the true issue—the potential cheating—your partner denies everything, and shifts the focus of the conversation to you. Your own flaws and weaknesses are suddenly more important. For example, there is the matter of your unflattering jealousy. How can you make such outrageous accusations? All this is intended to do is raise doubts about your relationship.

The infidelity may or may not have actually occurred. You may actually find real proof of it. It wouldn't be too surprising, either, considering how promiscuous narcissists tend to be. So, what do you do? Well, you confront them with your discoveries, of course.

Again, focus immediately shifts to something else: in this case, the fact that you've been snooping around in their car. A serious infraction indeed. Ironically, you end up the accused here, for being so untrusting. Considering how you behave, it would be little wonder if somebody cheated on you. Not that they did, of course.

A manipulator with strong narcissistic tendencies is capable of the most incomprehensible behavior, as long as it promises to shift your focus away from them.

Once you've been drawn into this confusing world, you need to bear in mind that the ordinary rules no longer apply.

HOW TO PROTECT YOURSELF

Now, it doesn't matter what color you are—everybody is vulnerable to this. I imagine Reds and Blues might find it a little less of a challenge to resist, but *nobody* is entirely immune to manipulation. Stay cool and stay rational. Note any deviations in your counterpart's behavior, and be prepared to confront them with what you discover.

Say things like: "I think you changed the subject there, right? Could we finish the conversation we were having first?"

Or "Of course we can discuss my shortcomings. But right now I am more interested to know why there is lipstick on your collar."

Or "My hearing is fine; there's no need to shout. It's not okay. Please stop immediately."

Or the simplest response of all: Leave the room, the house, or the county. Bring the subject up when there are other people around. For example, do it in a restaurant or in the company of somebody you trust. A mutual acquaintance, relative, or other person whose presence makes this technique too obvious to be used without the narcissist exposing themself completely. When others can see the bad behavior come out, the whole situation tends to change. As I've touched on previously, narcissists tend to be rather preoccupied with what everybody else thinks of them.

The problem here is that your narcissist is bound to have combined this technique with a whole load of other stuff, so that when they decide to call you out on whatever personality trait you happen to be the most ashamed of, you'll be quite likely to just back down instinctively. If you're like most people, you'll find the whole situation unbearable. But sometimes it's better to tough things out for a while and really get at the problem.

WHEN YOUR OWN EMOTIONS ARE USED AGAINST YOU

Another form of manipulation involves turning your own emotions against you. This tactic is designed to shift your attention away from the real problem. The idea is to apply pressure to sensitive points in your personality—aspects of yourself that you may be aware of, and perhaps don't even like. Emotions are tough to handle. Hard emotions are even worse.

Imagine a Red person with a characteristically confrontational mind-set. This might seem like a tough nut to crack. But then again, maybe not. Reds can behave in a very bristly fashion, sometimes even aggressively. Assuming they are relatively self-aware, they will know about the problem. Sometimes things can get out of hand.

It's easy for the manipulator to trigger anger in their victim. If there's smoke coming out of the fuse box, it's easy to exclaim, "There you go again! Yelling at me! You're always mad; it's not healthy!"

The consequences are readily predictable: From now on, you'll be discussing the aggressive behavior of the Red rather than whatever it was the manipulator did in the first place.

This also works the other way around, however. If the manipulator knows that their Red victim is uncomfortable with the outbursts and with the endless discussions of anything but the point that will follow if they lose their temper, they will say things like the following: "Are you about to throw one of your tantrums again? I guess you'll be screaming in my face as usual in just a second . . . I knew this was going to happen! Please stop shouting!"

The Red stifles their anger, to keep from falling for this ploy. It's quite a task for somebody with a fiery temper. If the Red has decided not to lose their cool, there will be some price to pay and it will take a lot of inner effort.

If the manipulator's victim is a Yellow, the situation is different. In this context, the initial tactic of eliciting a certain behavior would go something like this: "I suppose you're about to blabber on about God knows what, without making any sense. Why do you always have to talk about yourself? You never listen to me!"

This is definitely the weakness of Yellows: their aversion to putting themselves first. In response, the Yellow will begin to speak loudly, rapidly, and anxiously—and if we're being honest, they won't be making much sense. The groundwork is done, and the manipulator can lean back and say, "I told you so, didn't I? You only talk about yourself! You don't care about anybody else!"

The second version is similar to the Red example: "Could you be quiet for once and let me speak? Hello?" Throw some tears into the mix, and a Yellow will be at a loss for words. They'll grit their teeth and fight hard to resist their instincts. Everything will stay bottled up inside, and they'll end up feeling awful. The manipulator has silenced them effectively.

Greens are sensitive, and they respond in completely different ways. If a manipulator is living with a Green victim, they'll have a pretty easy time of things from the get-go. I wouldn't go so far as to say Greens are the most prone to being manipulated, but they are agreeable by nature, and they always aim to please. Unfortunately, this makes them ripe victims for nefarious characters.

Considering this, how is anybody able to be deliberately mean to a Green?

Sorry! I was thinking logically there. That won't do, of course. Naturally, narcissists don't care how anybody else feels. The Green is simply a tool to be used to gain some advantage or another.

The manipulator might divert the Green's attention by telling them, "You never speak, you're a coward, and you always back down. You're too damned afraid to discuss anything, ever! I'm so fed up with you!"

This is often closer to the truth than the Green would like, and so this statement can cause some emotional turmoil. The manipulator is trying to provoke this exact behavior. The Green withdraws and sits there with a lump in their throat. Beneath the surface, their frustration is raging. There's so much they would have liked to say. But how? They hate getting into arguments.

You can even get a Green to act in ways that directly contradict their own instincts. A truly skilled manipulator is able to get a Green sufficiently off-balance to trigger their rage. Everything gets vented, and lots of harsh language and negativity comes out. The Green will lay it on thick, mentioning every last injury they feel they have suffered over the last few years. The rage won't die down, either. These individuals hold grudges, so they will have plenty to work with.

The benefit for the manipulator here is the horrendous shame the Green will experience afterwards. Devastated, they will offer heartfelt apologies for their actions. The narcissist plays the victim expertly, quickly negotiating their way into further benefits as compensation for all the abuse they just endured. "How could you be so mean? Poor me!" This is going to end up costing the Green; you can count on that.

How does a manipulator exploit the behavior of Blues? It's simpler than you might imagine, actually. One way of pushing a Blue's buttons is to subject them to situations they aren't comfortable with. For instance, forcing them to join a team of all Yellows for a project. That could get really uncomfortable. The Blue would have a hard time formulating a single cohesive thought.

However, a Blue might be able to handle this. Their relationships with their coworkers and managers aren't as important to them as they would be to others, but in close relationships Blues are as vulnerable as anybody else.

Let's say a Blue's wife wants him to do something he doesn't want to do. She wants to go away for a weekend getaway. She's picked the best hotel, and she expects him to pay for it all. "Expensive" is an understatement. Also, some rather uninhibited shopping is to be expected— this is a special weekend, after all. It all depends on him. Again.

The first attack has him concerned. His wife has anticipated his response, so she bluntly demands that he refrain from getting the calculator out. She wants him to listen to her, for once. Since he loves his wife, he agrees (besides, he's good at mental math). He ultimately determines that it's too expensive—not within his means—and then the wife makes the move she's been planning all along: She accuses him of being uncaring. How can he be so cold to her? If he really loved her, he would do this for her, just this once.

If he persists in resisting, she breaks out the weapon that not even a Blue can resist: tears. Emotions run raw. The outburst doesn't die down until he begins to muse out loud whether he might take on some extra overtime to finance a trip he has no interest in taking.

COUNTERMEASURES

Emotions are a very messy subject, and there are no surefire solutions. Usually, your main priority is to stay calm. However, this can be quite challenging, particularly for extroverts. Both Reds and Yellows tend to react instinctively, and they may need some time to think things through.

My best advice, actually, is to call them out. State openly that you feel like they're trying to manipulate you, and ask how this makes them feel. In a later part of this book, I will give you a set of hands-on methods for escaping the clutches of a narcissist. Feel free to go over them in more detail.

Act Red. Let your true emotions out, and react forcefully and quickly. Save yourself from becoming a mere shadow of your former self. If you don't, that's what your partner will turn you into. They will dilute you until you're just a pale replica of who you used to be. Anytime you feel chronically unhappy, anxious, or hurt, you'll get caught up in the drama you're currently going through, and you'll have a very hard time picking up on the big picture and figuring out the details of the narcissist's far-reaching plans.

You need to remember something I've mentioned before in this book: Narcissists don't experience emotions the way you and I do; they often fake it, and when they drop the pretense you'll have all the information you need to make your decision. Don't forget that whoever is the most anxious to preserve the relationship will be the weakest.

Why should you give a narcissist a single minute more of your time? You deserve so much better.

GASLIGHTING

This method is all about confusing the victim and getting them off-balance. Let's say you live with a narcissist.

Now, they tell you they're working on a big surprise for you. You'd better make sure your bags are packed for next weekend. Excited, you wonder what this might be about. Naturally, you pack your bags, get your hair cut, and call all your friends to share the news: What do they think the surprise might be?

It's all so exciting!

You make sure to get everything ready for the big weekend, and when Friday arrives you're a little surprised that your partner doesn't mention anything. It's almost as though they'd forgotten all about what they said on Tuesday. On Saturday morning, when you cautiously broach the subject, they look nonplussed.

"What are you talking about? I'm playing golf with my friends today." And with that, they're gone. You're left alone with your confusion. You suppose there must have been some misunderstanding.

Reacting to this as though it were completely unthinkable is evidence that you're completely normal.

Or how about this?: Your girlfriend is getting ready to go out with her friends. She tells you she's going to meet up with Susan. Susan is going out with a friend of yours, so when it gets late and your girl-friend has neither returned home nor responded to your text messages you check with your friend to see if Susan made it back okay. He tells you Susan has been in all evening.

What's this? Is there something going on here? This could mean absolutely anything, but I suspect I know what most people would think.

When she finally gets home, in the middle of the night, you're upset, and you accuse her of lying. She wasn't out with Susan after all! Since your girlfriend is a narcissist, she will simply tell you that she said "Sandy," not "Susan." You are 100 percent certain you heard her say "Susan." There's no way it was Sandy—and who *is* Sandy, anyway?

At this point, your girlfriend will resort to some shenanigans. If you're a Red, you'll be told that you're an insensitive buffoon and a terrible listener; if you're a Yellow, she'll suggest that you only think about yourself and that you really should make the effort to learn the names of her friends; if you're a Green, she'll simply raise her voice and shout until you yield; and if you're a Blue, she might well question your mental capacity—perhaps you need to be evaluated for Alzheimer's?

Gaslighting is all about causing confusion. The narcissist says one thing on Monday, another on Tuesday, and denies ever having said either by the time Wednesday rolls around. You can keep up with this for a while, but a skilled narcissist will apply this approach step by step. They start out small, and then increase the volume gradu-ally. In the end, you won't have a clue what's going on.

Gaslighting is particularly effective because of the great ease with which a narcissist can lie. Without giving it more thought than you would in calling a taxi, they're able to say any falsehood that may suit their devious purposes. If anybody around you tries something like this on you and you pick up on the signs in time, run! I don't think I can make my advice any clearer than that.

A GENERAL ATTITUDE TO MANIPULATIVE MACHINATIONS

Trust. This might be the key to the whole situation. We need to understand *why* we should or shouldn't trust a person.

New acquaintances. It doesn't take us long to make up our minds. We're either in favor or opposed. The person either feels reliable or doesn't. Think about what makes you trust a certain person. If you've begun to trust somebody, you're going to be prepared to listen to them. Thus, you need to pay attention to what causes you to trust a person. Once you view this person as reliable, trustworthy, and deserving of your confidence, you've already stacked the deck against yourself ever so slightly. Anything that person says is going to be considered the truth. The messenger will become more important than the actual message.

However, if somebody does win your trust, this can't mean you suddenly take everything they say and do at face value from that point on. You need to consider *each separate action* in isolation, and you definitely need to question anything that feels off—even when you're dealing with somebody you essentially trust. A person's trustworthiness can be reconsidered regularly, if they act in ways that you're not okay with.

The advice I usually give to people who wonder how to determine if they can trust somebody is to compare their words to their deeds. If they match up well enough, that's excellent. You may have a future together! If their words seldom or even never match their actual deeds, there's no basis for trust. You can't rely on this person.

THE TERMS OF TRUST

Trust depends on three things: *predictability, reliability,* and *conviction.*

Predictability is a consequence of another's behavior. It contrasts with unpredictable behavior, such as positive feedback being offered and withheld at random, or loving and tender speech being suddenly replaced with silence and criticism over things that used to be lauded as positives. When somebody's behavior is highly variable, this might not necessarily be caused by an intention to manipulate you, but it is nonetheless a call for caution. A psychological diagnosis like bipolar disorder is one thing, but narcissism is something else entirely. The former can be treated; the latter cannot.

Reliability is what determines whether you can assume somebody will be honest and worthy of your trust in the long term. Can you rely on this individual? Have you caught them in the act of lying to you or withholding information from you? How much evidence have you seen of long-term trustworthiness? Did the honeymoon only last a few weeks before the truth was revealed? Not much point holding on to that, then. However, if this person has stayed by your side through thick and thin, and is still there to protect you from the evils of the world, you can feel quite secure.

Conviction, finally, is a matter of how convinced you are that this person will respond to your needs and behave like a loving, supporting partner—beyond the first month or so. Narcissists are quite impatient; they want their rewards to come quickly. They can't keep up appearances indefinitely.

Therefore, you could be making a huge mistake if you base your evaluation of somebody's trustworthiness on their past behavior alone.

Assess the predictability, reliability, and conviction of a person, and reflect on them right now. Not last year, not before you were married, and not that time at your parents' house. You should be considering what happened yesterday, or what is happening right now, in a conversation where the things the person says are making you almost physically sick.

Is the relationship worth putting up with this kind of behavior? Is what you just witnessed acceptable behavior? Is what you just heard the kind of thing people should be proud to say? Skilled manipulators are experts at winning your trust, but they can be bad at keeping it, unless you let them off the hook, of course.

Once you've seen through the manipulator's tricks, act immediately. This should be no different from domestic abuse. One strike and you're out. They will only hurt you again. All available research confirms it. Their bad behavior is just the tip of the iceberg. There's much more to come.

It's the same with psychological manipulation. If your partner exhibits this kind of behavior, you can be 100 percent certain they will do it again. Narcissists and people with narcissistic traits use proven methods. If they can make you back down again by manipulating you some more, why wouldn't they?

To simplify things even further: If a thief finds a hundred-dollar bill on the ground, puts it in his pocket, and then enjoys a great night out on someone else's money, why would he leave the next hundred-dollar bill he finds where it is?

MORE METHODS OF MANIPULATION

Unfortunately, there are plenty more of these tricks:

- *Feigned intimacy.* Early on in the relationship, the narcissist reveals intimate details (which will probably turn out to be fabricated) about themselves, which inspires you to share things about yourself—and these admissions will eventually be weaponized and turned against you.
- *Guilt-tripping.* The narcissist finds ways of blaming everything that isn't frictionless in your relationship on you.
- *Indirect insults.* These are more or less subtle disses, concealed beneath a layer of feigned benevolence: "I like it when you wear that dress—it makes you look so slim!"

- *Insinuations.* This is the use of statements so ambiguous it's hard to determine what's being said. For example: "You know, you could make so much money doing white-collar crime!"

- *Vacuous statements.* Narcissists put no weight on anything they say. They might say anything that seems appropriate to them in the moment. For example: "I love you." It might give you a moment's relief, but it won't really mean anything—narcissists aren't capable of love!

- *Minimization.* The narcissist convinces you that what they did wasn't really so bad: "What? Doesn't everyone do that? It's not like anything happened! You're getting caught up with the minutiae again."

- *Lies.* How do you detect a lie in the midst of all this non-sense? If you observe the other behaviors here, you can safely assume the narcissist is lying to you, too. About everything. Constantly. Are their lips moving? Start the recording.

- *Condescension.* This is a classic gambit, which involves down-playing every opinion, emotion, or experience you give voice to. For example: "You really shouldn't be feeling that way. You're kidding, right? Surely that was no big deal."

- *Charm.* Narcissists will often seek to win you over with charm first. They don't often start out insulting you—that approach hasn't worked too well for them in the past. You'll be told things nobody has ever said to you before. And honestly, who wouldn't enjoy being swept off their feet by a load of lovely compliments?

- *Deliberate forgetfulness.* Narcissists "forget" to go shopping before dinner, even though they promised they would. Or they forget your anniversary. Or they forget to call you from their hotel room . . .

- *Rage.* Shouting and screaming to get you to back down if you object somehow to the narcissist's bizarre behavior.

- *The victim card.* This is one of the major strategies. Narcissists are capable of some degree of self-pity. And they can play victim with the best of them: "I knew nobody would want me on their team. Of course—why would a bore like myself expect anything else? I'll go alone then, I suppose."

- *Rationalization.* This is a common defense mechanism, only applied deliberately in this context. It involves giving logical reasons for illogical actions. For example: "I'm sorry I hit you—I just got so mad when you provoked me." Or: "I know I shouldn't drive when I've been drinking, but I wanted so badly to get back home to you quickly."

- *Flattery.* Does this one need an explanation? We all know how having somebody express appreciation for our looks, intelligence, or taste can make us feel. It's not lost on narcissists, either.

12

Who Is in Danger of Falling Victim to a Narcissist?

Out of your vulnerabilities will come your strength.

—SIGMUND FREUD

People who complain about the state of the world, or how they are the victims of tragic circumstances that have kept them from getting the exact job they want, or their long commute to work, or the fact that the local coffee shop didn't have their favorite brand of oat milk have one thing in common: They've probably never been victimized by a narcissist, a psychopath, or a sociopath. They simply don't know what they're talking about.

Narcissists are able to fix their sights on anybody who possesses a particular human ability: empathy. It doesn't matter if you're beautiful, rich, competent, successful, well liked, popular, funny, or mentally strong—a narcissist could still deceive you completely. They use the same methods as psychopaths to ensnare people. Love bombing is just one of them, and it even works on coworkers, although, of course, the application will differ.

People like this use manipulation techniques you could never come up with in a hundred years.

Countless mental coaches, psychiatrists, psychologists, and therapists who don't specialize in this particular field are duped by narcissists and psychopaths every week. People with a strong sense of empathy are some of their favorite targets, because these people are always prepared to open their arms to anybody who looks like they could use a little help. Narcissists are skilled at playing the victim, even when they are actually the aggressors. It's a bit like a wolf calling for help after spotting a sheep.

I've combed the available literature for any correlation with the intelligence levels of the victims. There are no obvious connections; intelligence appears to offer no protection against manipulation. Instinctively, my theory would have to be that being smarter actually makes you more vulnerable. It's not a very comforting thought. Why would that be the case, though?

The greater your intelligence, the more you are able to think rationally. Psychology studies have shown this. It's not that you can disassociate yourself from your emotions, but rather that you rely more on logic when observing other people's behavior. You look at what they do, and think that there must—*must*—be a logical explanation for their strange behavior. You base your interpretations on yourself. I think we all do this. It's not a very useful strategy for dealing with narcissists, though.

Whether you're susceptible to the manipulations of narcissists or not depends rather on your degree of vulnerability, which has nothing at all to do with your intelligence. This could be caused by past traumas you've suffered—and may even have forgotten about!

Unfortunately, there are lots of stereotypes about victims. A common misconception, for example, is that female victims of domestic violence are somehow the same. It's often assumed that they have poor self-esteem and possibly lack employment. However, this simply isn't true. In fact, women with good self-esteem who are employed are *more* likely to be victimized by a domestic abuser. They could be as smart, successful, and talented as you like. None of that protects them from jerks. Or narcissists. On the contrary, it could actually trigger violent responses in narcissists who can't tolerate being questioned. There can only be one winner in a relationship like this—and it will always be the narcissist.

The most dangerous thought you can have is this: *Nobody could ever manipulate me. Nobody could entangle me in a web of lies and strange behavior. I'd see it coming a mile away.*

No, no, no. Forget all that stuff. I used to think like that, and I turned out to be painfully wrong. You have no idea what it ended up costing me.

Narcissists don't seek us out because we're like them; they seek us out because we are their opposites. We are empathic, and we want the best for others. Our hearts, if you will, are too big. We feel compassion for the weak, we possess emotional intelligence, and we have genuine confidence, which the narcissists can't emulate.

One of my favorite examples is that of world-renowned psychologist and psychopathy expert David Hare, who managed to have the wool pulled over his eyes in prison, by a psychopath he had diagnosed personally. What the guy said sounded so good, though . . . Another researcher lent his Mercedes to a narcissist who had just been released from prison—and never saw his car again.

How is this possible? you might wonder.

Well . . . This is just what narcissists do.

CAN YOUR BEHAVIORAL PROFILE TELL YOU IF YOU COULD BECOME A VICTIM?

Things would be a lot simpler if all we needed to concern ourselves with was the mischief that narcissists get up to. However, the problem is a lot more complicated than that, as you know. A narcissist is able to manipulate and deceive a great variety of people, and there is no particular type that is always safe. Especially not in a relationship context. When emotions, which are in many ways opposed to logic, enter the picture, things can go sideways in no time.

Even though nobody is immune to manipulation, we probably all have slightly different weaknesses to address. Let's take a look at the kinds of thing a narcissist might consider when selecting a victim.

YOUR WEAKNESSES

Just like psychopaths, narcissists are on the lookout for your weaknesses. They are essentially cowards, and so they tend to prefer victims who are weaker than average. Now, strength is not a watertight protection, here—there are plenty of highly motivated psychopaths who have torn the strongest people you could imagine to shreds. But in any case, you're far more likely to run afoul of somebody who wants to manipulate you if you're somewhat the worse for wear emotionally.

There is a difference between narcissists and psychopaths that's hard to define precisely. Although both of them are habitual manipulators, psychopaths are without a doubt more dangerous. They see life as a game, and themselves as masters of it. They could cause a world of trouble for others just to stave off a moment's boredom. All other humans are perishable assets in the deliberations of a psychopath.

Narcissists are more likely to be aware that what they are doing is probably wrong, but as they feel entitled to the best of everything, they do it anyway. I wouldn't go so far as to say a narcissist is particularly troubled by pangs of conscience, but they are at least more human in outlook than psychopaths.

Psychopaths are a lot more cunning, too. They are always looking for an angle to get the upper hand on somebody. The world is just a buffet to them, and they feel entitled to help themselves to anything they want. In comparison, narcissists seem more like overgrown toddlers, flailing at the floor when they don't get their way, while psychopaths are always learning, in every situation, always refining their techniques. Psychopaths also seem—although this is hard to prove—to be a lot more ruthless. They can set their mind on avenging some slight or another and proceed to do anything in their power to destroy another person utterly.

What others might think matters less to a psychopath, while narcissists will be constantly considering the image other people have of them. It's all a bit complicated, and as I've pointed out in the past, there's no sharp boundary between these two disorders. Since narcissism can be highly preoccupied with an individual's emotions, it might be interesting to take a brief look at how the different colors might respond to different situations here.

The stereotype is that Yellows wear their emotions on their sleeves and can't hide anything they feel, while Greens are the exact opposite: They actively seek to conceal their emotions, at all times. Blues are assumed to have hardly any emotions at all and mostly present as stone-faced, and Reds tend to experience just a single emotion: rage.

Apart from being rich in generalization, these observations also have a nugget of truth to them. The charts on the following page provide some examples of how this can manifest.

HOW LIKELY ARE REDS TO FALL VICTIM TO A NARCISSIST?

Reds are strong, and forceful, and don't take crap from anyone. They believe in instant payback. Tough, gnarly, competitive types, who enjoy a good tussle. How could anybody ever get to them?

Anger

D

The higher the D factor, the more the individual will tend to be impatient and short-tempered.

This means they will be prone to frequent rages.

The anger itself can often be controlled, but the people around them will pick up on their impatience and irritability.

The lower the D factor, the more patient the individual will be.

Patience

Optimism

I

The higher the I factor, the more the person will tend to look on the bright side of things.

That means the person will largely trust other people.

Nothing is impossible to them, and they energize the people around them.

The lower the I factor, the more pessimistic the individual will tend to be, and thus, the less trust they will have in others.

Pessimism

Doesn't Show Emotion

S

The higher the S factor, the less likely the individual will be to express their emotions.

To keep from burdening the people around them with their problems, they repress most of their emotions.

This person will often claim that all is well even when it isn't.

The lower the S factor, the more you will see and hear the individual's emotions.

Shows Emotion

Fearfulness

The higher the C factor, the more likely the individual will be to follow rules out of fear of being found out, punished, or having to confront authority figures.

The more C factor somebody has, the more they will stick to the rules.

Others won't always pick up on the underlying fear.

The lower the C factor, the less fear they will feel. Rules will become mere recommendations, there to be broken.

Fearlessness

Now, Reds aren't constantly arguing with everyone around them, but if you need to get a Red to do something they don't want to, you'll have a conflict on your hands. How does the narcissist react? By caring less than most people do. They see the angry face, they hear the angry words, and the aggressive insults aren't lost on them. However, their main concern will still be whatever it is they want. There are countless examples of narcissists successfully redirecting a Red's anger in ways that benefited them personally.

The Troublesome Weaknesses of Reds

Boorish, arrogant, aggressive, steamrollers, bad listeners, rushed, commanding, controlling, intolerant, and egotistical.

The narcissist's best approach here is to dare to do the unexpected. People often keep their heads down a little around Reds. So what do you think might happen if they came across somebody who didn't?

Only somebody who is prepared to take on some serious risk would do that. Psychopaths are the masters of this, but narcissists are also able to do it. For example, it might seem suicidal to head into the office of a boss who is known to detest bootlickers and immediately proceed to praise them to the skies.

However, this is all just a game to a narcissist. That's the part that Reds have a hard time understanding. They can be taken in completely by somebody who fails to register the danger. Narcissists radiate confidence. Reds are good at detecting confidence and tend to respect it. Sometimes they will even feel a certain admiration for it.

What works on Reds is praising them—subtly, though, don't forget that—for something they are more often criticized for. For example, many Reds are constantly being told how insensitive they are. While some Reds might be amused that people are scared of them, they're just like everyone else, really—they want very badly to be liked and respected just as they are. The difference is just in the way they show it. So, when somebody dares to show appreciation for *these particular characteristics,* it hits home.

Conclusions

The thing with Reds is you can't do anything too openly. That's why skilled manipulators prefer a more indirect approach. The narcissist's method for winning the trust of a Red is simply to show nerve. As I mentioned earlier, narcissists aren't as troubled by situations like having to lie through their teeth to their boss's boss as you or I would be.

Reds also tend to avoid asking for help. They try to solve the problem on their own first. This is great news for ambitious manipulators, as this means they will be able to feed their victims more and more of their medicine, over a prolonged period of time, until the Red finally goes to someone else for help.

HOW LIKELY ARE YELLOWS TO FALL VICTIM TO A NARCISSIST?

The weakness of Yellows, to a great extent, is their aversion to talking about weaknesses. It's a big downer, and people get way too negative about this stuff. Yellows are typical relationship-oriented people. They want to be surrounded by people whenever possible.

The downside of this is the dependence on others it entails. Without other people, Yellows grow bored or run out of ideas. They can't speak to, joke with, or laugh with others, and they can't refer to the people around them.

This is the key to a Yellow's vulnerability. Social isolation—perhaps the worst fate known to man. Any driven narcissist who is looking to manipulate a Yellow will begin their efforts by ensuring the Yellow is isolated from the outside world. The narcissist makes a point of cutting the Yellow off from their friends, family, and work-related social events. After-hours workplace get-togethers are out of the question. Bit by bit, the victim's contacts are eliminated, and the victim is thus brought closer to the narcissist, step by step.

If the victim has nobody to talk to, the narcissist will be quick to be the only person who listens to them. Somebody who actually appreciates the Yellow, despite all their obvious flaws and weaknesses. The narcissist will put themself forward as the only person who even cares. As a result, they will become so much more important to the victim.

But how does the narcissist pull it off? It's devastating in its simplicity. They exploit the Yellow's weaknesses and turn them against them. So, let's take a look at these weaknesses of Yellows.

The Sad Shortcomings of Yellows

Selfish, superficial, egocentric, excessively confident, all talk and no action, lacking in focus, messy, forgetful, irritable, sensitive, disorganized and chaotic, giggly and lighthearted, talks too much and for too long, terrible listener. It doesn't matter how much pain it causes a Yellow to be reminded of these things. The narcissist wants to get their way.

For example, a deceptive, manipulative narcissist might tell the victim in confidence that somebody they care about a great deal said something very unpleasant about them. Maybe their best friend, even. A stab in the back!

Yellows are particularly sensitive about relationships breaking down. This brings them stress and disrupts their balance. Keeping them out of balance after this involves planting tiny, tiny seeds of doubt in themselves and in their abilities. Or, perhaps, their popularity.

Comments like "Why do you talk about yourself all the time?" are simply met with confusion. If anybody is talking about themselves, it's the narcissist, of course. Sure, a certain degree of self-centeredness is part of the Yellow package. However, a narcissist will make a point of guilt-tripping you over it. They will keep pointing out how egotistical the Yellow is. Quite soon, the Yellow will stop daydreaming and being creative and be well on their way to disaster instead.

There are other ways to break a Yellow, too. Constantly mentioning how they really ought to take things more seriously, not laugh so much, and not joke around all the time. Just be serious, for once. The narcissist can feign personal insult over practically every joke a Yellow cracks. Any joke will become inappropriate, even insensitive. "How could you?" Their sense of humor, which is essential to Yellows, breaks down and fades away. People will stop recognizing them and will increasingly seek to distance themselves from them. They've become so introverted and weird.

Conclusions

Isolation. "Give up the childish nonsense. Don't play around so much. Give me more attention—much more! If you don't, I'll leave you." This catches the Yellow in a trap.

There are plenty of individuals who make more or less subtle attempts at separating their significant other from their old friends. Jealousy is often a factor here, of course. This is not okay. If somebody tries to control you, you should take a step back and ask yourself why they are behaving as they are. This kind of influence needs to be questioned immediately. And of course, not everybody who uses this method is a narcissist.

HOW LIKELY ARE GREENS TO FALL VICTIM TO A NARCISSIST?

The main weakness of Greens is their tendency to shy away from conflict. Conflict is uncomfortable at best. Only troublemakers get involved in that kind of thing, and uncomfortable truths are troublesome to a Green.

Greens are change-averse, particularly when it comes to changes that are rushed. Being the center of attention is dreadful, as is public censure. They don't even really want public praise. They're introverted and something of an observer type. It can be hard to get a straight answer out of them, even to the most direct of questions. Hearing a Green say yes when they mean no is a common occurrence.

Which of these weaknesses are Greens aware of? All of them, I'd say. Greens tend to be quite self-critical.

Greens and Their Weaknesses

Conflict-averse, impractical, change-averse, stubborn, grumpy, buttoned-up, cowardly, passive, evasive, irresponsible, dishonest, talking about people instead of talking to them, overly sensitive of criticism, and indecisive.

If a narcissist is trying to sink their claws into a Green person, they will tend to target the Green's sensitivity to criticism and aversion to conflict. An insensitive comment can get a great deal of work done here.

Let's take a look at a personal relationship. A Green person will not uncommonly know that they are somewhat slow to act and lack initiative. In a relationship with an equally Green partner, they would tend to stay at home, leaving their dreams to be just that.

Paradoxically enough, this leads us on to Red behavior: a strong personality who acts with clarity and intention in every situation. A Red who is in a good mood can achieve an incredible amount in a very brief time. Building a fence or painting a garage takes them hardly any time at all.

Of course, this example is quite simplified, but I'm sure you understand the principle. The way to get to a Green can be to exhibit Red behavior. Since Greens like to get out of having to make difficult decisions, they will be happy to delegate all their decisions to others.

Once a narcissist has won the trust of a Green and managed to get close to them, they'll be ready to get to work manipulating their victim.

Turning People's Strengths Against Them

Greens don't exactly have inflated egos. They're more likely to put themselves down and keep pointing out how badly they suck to themselves and anybody else prepared to listen. All a narcissist needs to do here is reinforce that.

Let's say a Green woman complains to the mirror about the weight she has put on. Any man knows that this question is a veritable deathtrap—but if you're actually interested in keeping your significant other down, just agree with them: "Yes, I think you might have put a little weight on." The victim's self-esteem, already fragile, takes another knock.

Cooking, then: Was this sauce really as good as it could have been? Couldn't it have been spicier, less thick, or warmer, or colder? It doesn't take much to keep a Green guessing. If they object at any point, all the narcissist needs to do is raise their voice a smidge. One loud argument every week should be enough to keep your Green compliant indefinitely.

HOW LIKELY ARE BLUES TO FALL VICTIM TO A NARCISSIST?

During my past research into psychopathy, I concluded that Blues might be the hardest people of all to manipulate. Blues recall what you've said in the past, and they have a good sense for details. They take notes, save emails and text messages, and know how stuff works.

At this point, you know that narcissists often lie just for the sake of it and they always have new lies ready in case they get caught out and need to muddy the issue. Naturally, narcissists won't be able to resist trying to dupe a Blue. Things will soon get challenging, however. Blue coworkers or bosses or friends or partners are always the quickest to see through a lie. This is because they remember exactly what they were told last time around.

If a narcissist wants to manipulate a Blue to gain some advantage or another, it's going to take some work. Loudly announcing that *it's actually like this* isn't going to get the narcissist far. Blues look stuff up. Rational and naturally inquisitive as they are, they will simply march back to the office narcissist and point out the error. How does the narcissist get out of this?

In a relationship, you can't simply say, "I paid for the couch," or, "Your share is eight hundred dollars." A Blue partner or friend will ask for the receipt. This isn't necessarily because of some suspicion they're harboring—they just want to see the receipt.

You can't treat a Blue any old way and expect to get away with it. Many people study up on certain subjects, at least enough to be able to seem like they know what they're talking about and make people listen. Blues, however, go all in on everything. One of their most noteworthy traits is their inability to let things lie; they have to dig into things and find out how everything works. Sometimes this can be annoying to others, but in this specific context it's definitely to their advantage. Note that Blues won't necessarily make too much of the narcissist's antics. They have no need to tell the world how they feel. Deep down, however, their minds are made up. There's no trusting that person at the end of the hall, and that's something that will be factored into every decision going forward.

So, does this mean Blues are immune to manipulation?

Unfortunately, it's not quite that simple.

The Frustrating Flaws of Blues

Evasive, sullen and glum, suspicious, picky, whiney, impossible to satisfy, sticklers for procedure, indecisive, buttoned-up, dispassionate, socially inept, sluggish, et cetera.

Blues have weaknesses, too. Usually, narcissists try to identify these weaknesses in order to exploit them. It's going to take time. The manipulator understands that it's imperative to tread lightly. One way of making people distrust a Blue is to eliminate the Blue's credibility. This is achievable, too, by convincing everybody else that the Blue has become careless.

Narcissists know better, though. They will set their charm to work, gathering a group of allies to do the narcissist's bidding. These allies will be comprehensively manipulated, and will consistently maintain that the narcissist is the most amazing person in the world. Each time the narcissist is criticized, these unwitting pawns will come to their aid, making the source of the criticism—the Blue, in this case—seem grouchy and difficult.

If you remove every opportunity to point out any mistakes you've made, you might be able to get them to doubt themselves in the end. The fact that their colleagues are declaring their allegiance like this won't alarm the Blue as such—but if they are denied the opportunity to do quality work, the Blues will suffer a blow to their confidence.

Conclusions

It's probably much easier for an attractive female narcissist to deceive a Blue who has weaker relationship skills. This is a pretty basic example, and I know how outdated it can sound in 2022. But I think you know what I'm getting at. Imagine a man who has yet to meet the one. Suddenly, a beautiful woman is pledging her love to him. She is giving him every kind of attention, and emphasizing all his strengths. He's never experienced anything like this before, so he's incredibly vulnerable to her advances. But this can go both ways—a charming narcissistic partner is hard for anyone to resist.

Blues may be less dependent on personal relationships than most, but they still tend to form very close private bonds to the people they do engage with.

13

How Are Narcissists Made?

An abnormal reaction to
an abnormal situation would be
normal behavior.
—VIKTOR FRANKL

A reasonable question to ask at this point is how somebody actually becomes a narcissist. Is it innate, or learned behavior? It's an interesting question, particularly when viewed in the light of psychopathy.

Psychopathy is a personality disorder that more or less encompasses everything that's part of narcissism and combines it with an additional set of even less appealing characteristics. The question of how an individual becomes a psychopath appears to have been resolved by science at this point. I say *appears* because consensus, as is so commonly the case in the field of psychology, has yet to be reached on the issue of psychopathy. There are still some psychologists who claim that psychopathy ought to be treatable, but we'll have to think of this as more of a theoretical assumption. Nobody has so far managed to explain how it could be done.

However, not all people who behave like psychopaths actually are psychopaths. Some of them are sociopaths.

Sociopaths are more or less the same as psychopaths in terms of actual behavior. They are also manipulative, unempathic liars, who wouldn't think twice about doing anything to get what they want. As I've established by now, they are not pleasant to be around.

However, psychopaths were born with their disorder, as MRI scans of their brains have revealed. The amygdala—that is, the emotional center of the brain—is less developed than in normal individuals.

Sociopaths, on the other hand, have been shaped by their environment. Hence the term, "sociopath," which explicitly refers to the society around the individual. By making people endure long, difficult childhoods, often rife with abuse at the hand of their caregivers, you can produce people with stunted empathy and emotions. For example, this is how child soldiers are trained. By nature, children know nothing about killing people, but with guidance and a gradual increase of the pressure, their natural compassion can be removed. This is a dreadful procedure, but that doesn't prevent it from happening in several parts of the world. Those places are practically sociopathy plants. Children who grow up in bad enough conditions can turn into emotionally numb automatons. The process of restoring them to the people they could have been is a difficult process that succeeds far too rarely.

In the world of science, there is pretty much a consensus on this: About 50 percent of an individual's attributes depend on their genes, their nature. This has been tested for more than a century, through experiments involving pairs of twins, which as far as I can tell have covered every imaginable human trait. Statistically, this suggests that narcissism is half dependent on genes. The rest is a result of the treatment one receives growing up, and there are thousands of different contributing factors to take into consideration. This is a massive area of inquiry, but I'd like to spend some time now focusing on the nurture part of the equation.

My question for this chapter is this: Can a narcissist be created, like a sociopath can? I suspect this to be the case.

Fortunately, it is rare for parents to set out to deliberately turn a child who has previously displayed few, if any, narcissistic tendencies into a full-on narcissist. But their treatment of the child is bound to have consequences.

There are several competing theories regarding how narcissism arises within an individual. In general terms, it comes down to either nature or nurture, or a combination of the two. However, we lack any precise knowledge of how the phenomenon is produced.

There are some clues. Many researchers in the field of antisocial personality disorders agree that there are some specific risk factors that will contribute to a child's development of NPD. Some studies suggest that children who grow up to become narcissists are often the children of narcissists. Other studies have failed to find any strong correlations.

However, the children of highly successful children are also at greater risk, particularly if they lack the talents that made their parents so successful.

And, of course: pampered children from well-to-do families. Oops.

I realize that this whole thing can seem a bit sinister, but if you do observe tendencies along these lines, you'd do well to pay attention to them. It's undeniable that parents influence their children; the question is simply how much and in what ways. Of course, having a child go through a variety of trauma, such as contentious divorces or parents using the child to get back at each other, which is quite common, can cause its share of problems. Different kinds of childhood trauma could cause a child to "shut down" their empathic abilities. Their aim in doing this is self-defense, and they probably don't do it consciously. Psychologists refer to this as a narcissistic injury.

Perhaps it's not that surprising that children can be traumatized by bad living conditions. But this is still only half the equation.

The second, more complicated and—I presume—less digestible part is related to the most recent theories about what might happen to children who are overvalued and excessively cherished by their parents. Parents who, with the best of intentions, allow their children to stay children until they're well past an appropriate age. These parents might be of the opinion that their particular child is God's gift to creation, even if there is no evidence at all that their child possesses any remarkable abilities in comparison to others. Systematic *overvaluation,* as opposed to *derogation,* might very well cause a spoiled child to develop an excessive sense of entitlement to all the good things in life, and will rarely help them learn to be considerate of the emotions of others. Basically, they are taught to think they are better than their peers.

Several studies reveal that parents who keep telling their children that they are special, more so than other children, are actually producing narcissistic children. In one report, it is stated explicitly: "Narcissism was predicted by parental overvaluation, not by lack of parental warmth. Thus, children seem to acquire narcissism, in part, by internalizing parents' inflated views of them (e.g., 'I am superior to others' and 'I am entitled to privileges')."

This produces the grandiose variety of narcissists. In schools, these children are known as "pompous children." In China, they are called Golden Children. Children who can't walk through the door without expecting the whole world to conform to their needs. I hardly need to point out what happens when they're expected to cooperate with others. These other people might even think of themselves as number one. If so, things are likely to get quite interesting.

While working on this book, I've had several conversations with teachers, and I've found it fascinating to hear what teachers who work in relatively affluent neighborhoods have to say. Naturally, many children and young adults from fortunate circumstances present as polite and well adjusted. They are often good at showing consideration and respect for others. However, a significant number of them seem to have remarkably inflated self-images. They genuinely believe themselves to be part of some particularly privileged group. And apparently, they sometimes behave accordingly.

TRAUMA AND ITS EFFECTS

Several studies have also revealed that this same sense of being entitled to more than others is common in children of parents who were permissive of bad behavior and who allowed their children to run roughshod over others without even apologizing afterwards. The parents who taught their children to think of themselves as inherently amazing and wonderful creatures seemed quite apathetic about the world around them. They spoiled their children rotten, even when they behaved terribly. Nothing the child did ever had any consequences. The parents simply cheered for their children's efforts, no matter what kind of disaster they might have caused.

However, parents who set boundaries for acceptable behavior raised children whose attitudes to rules and regulations were much healthier. Transgressing boundaries is a highly typical characteristic of narcissists.

Another phenomenon that seems to trigger narcissistic tendencies is when parents treat their children like trophies. This downgrades their kids to mere objects to be shown off, like a handbag or car. It also teaches the child to view other people as objects, rather than as individuals made of flesh and blood.

Convincing the child that they are perfect as they are—better than everybody else, even—while simultaneously treating the child like an object and offering no valuable feedback to help the child explore their true identity has proven to create a complex psychological cocktail. This combination of overvaluation and neglect can produce children who exhibit narcissistic behaviors.

Constantly being told how perfect and adorable you are, no matter what you get up to, but never being given any genuine feedback about your actual behavior can cause issues. You won't have the frame of reference when you need to judge what is actually okay and what isn't. The outcome will be a child who feels entitled to everything they want, regardless of whether they actually deserve it or not. Any connection to one's own performance has been lost. These children frequently come to focus excessively on a specific thing or another. It could be appearance, material obsessions, or what other people think about them.

It's clear that very few, if any, parents would deliberately set out to create these little fiends by purposefully neglecting their need for balanced feedback. And, as I mentioned earlier, parenting and specific genetic variations are commonly both contributing factors. When children have no genetic predisposition to narcissism, parenting might not be as significant a factor, and so you might be able to get away with inflating their egos. The problem, though, is that there is no way to tell how children are going to respond ahead of time.

This lack of certainty regarding the effects has caused some psychologists to urge caution. If things go too far, we won't be able to undo them.

The damage to the amygdala that the victims of narcissistic abusers present can potentially trap them in a permanent state of fear and anxiety, and cause them to respond poorly to any environment that reminds them of their suffering at the hands of the narcissist. In other words, victims of narcissistic abusers are in a state of constant alertness to a danger that is no longer present in their lives.

This hypervigilant mind-set will also cause the children of narcissists to suffer panic attacks, phobias, and other mood disorders that can significantly restrict their ability to live full, productive lives.

SHOULD WE PITY NARCISSISTS?

All we know for certain is that somebody who lives with a narcissist will suffer some kind of mental harm as a consequence of this relationship. Their partner's lack of empathy and morals can cause havoc for everybody they come across. Everything they do is done at the expense of others. In fact, one could even ask oneself, *Does the reason for my partner's narcissism matter?*

After writing about psychopaths, I've received comments to the effect that it isn't the psychopath's fault that they are a psychopath. Seeing as they can't help themselves, they're actually completely innocent. Some even claim that the psychopath—or, in this case, the narcissist—is the real victim. Why am I having a go at narcissists? It's not as though they asked to be that way.

I guess. But if your baby is about to be torn to pieces by a hyena, what would be your main concern: the baby's well-being or the hyena's?

Having a personality disorder does not absolve you of all responsibility for your actions. Rather, it's a reason for an individual to seek help with regulating their behavior before they end up completely isolated.

Things tend to play out in fairly predictable ways for narcissists. In many cases, people gradually cut them off, until they have nobody left to admire them. In the end, everybody sees through the façade. That's the problem for narcissists, you see:

Nobody likes them. Not really.

14

The Challenges of Narcissism

I imagine one of the reasons people cling
to their hates so stubbornly is
because they sense, once hate is gone,
they will be forced to deal with pain.

—JAMES BALDWIN

For the narcissists themselves, it would probably be better if their situation was curable. There is an unfortunate trap here that people seldom think of.

The idea that a little narcissism might actually be a good thing is actually quite common. It might be phrased in different ways, but they all share the same general outline. In our competitive world, it's advantageous to be tough, hard-nosed, and ambitious. A strong desire to reach the top will definitely increase your chances of success. Having to step on others to get where you're going is simply an unfortunate, but unavoidable, side effect.

Promoting yourself has become both more common and more necessary than anybody is really comfortable with. And yeah, you can make a whole career out of it if you want. Our TV screens are bursting with people who don't really do anything besides talk about themselves, show off their homes and cars, and, if we're being honest, exhibit a revealing degree of self-centeredness.

Is it entertaining? I guess, but nobody could have gotten away with something like that a number of decades ago. Being famous for being famous wasn't a thing back then. You had to do something people cared about first. These days, you can make your name doing nothing in particular. This change has been a gradual one, and it's been underway for some time. Now some people will do literally anything to get to be on TV. Social media provides an abundance of examples of this. My own improvised, intuitive explorations of the issue have revealed that a new influencer is born every twelve seconds or so.

THE MOST INFAMOUS NARCISSIST IN THE WORLD

Instead of giving you a long list of examples of this kind of personality, I thought I'd use a single one, whom nobody will have been fortunate enough to be ignorant of: Donald Trump.

He is a real estate tycoon, a businessman, a reality TV celebrity/star, and a general celebrity, with a long history of picking fights with people all over the place—like talk show hosts, for example. He put his name on everything he got his hands on. Trump Tower is just one of countless examples. Did you know his name has also been used for wine, water, golf clubs, airplanes, a university, restaurants, apparel, watches, vodka, perfume(!), and more? Although this list isn't endless, it's still impressively long.

He topped his whole career off with a four-year term as president of the United States of America. Despite all the controversy surrounding his person, he ended up being elected. Does this mean we can assume narcissism actually can help you reach the top? There are certainly many experts who have argued that his behavior gives him away as a narcissist. It's worth noting that he has a huge number of supporters.

You have to invest in yourself, emphasize your strengths, and take what's yours! You might even have to trample a few other people on your way to the top. "Eat or be eaten" has been the rule for ages in some circles, after all.

On the other hand, it could be that there are at least as many, if not far more, individuals who are more successful than he is but whom we've never ended up hearing about. They just keep their nose down and don't worry about showing off on TV or in social media. It was hard to overlook Donald Trump even before he became the US president. Despite this, he is very obviously not the best at anything at all—apart from attracting hostility from practically every quarter. As far as I can tell, he is a world-class talent in that regard.

WHEN DO I GET MY FIFTEEN MINUTES?

It's not too difficult to see the appeal in seeing your own reflection and thinking to yourself that you're actually pretty great. Or pretty, hot, cool, or badass—whatever you prefer. I suppose that's why so many people post photos to Instagram—to get to read those same things about themselves. Who wouldn't like to have somebody tell them that they are *totally the hottest*? I don't know of anyone who's fully immune. Self-deception is a treacherous yet blissful activity.

So is being the follower of somebody successful, perhaps at the expense of having to push a few people out of the way, and getting to feel how the limelight rubs off on you.

All of these things can make some people feel less like failures and more successful, even if this means closing their eyes and ears to criticism and past failures. Just like an alcoholic or a thrill-seeking serial adulterer, they enjoy not having to take personal responsibility for things.

Initially, the effects are all beneficial. Life's a thrill, and everything feels great.

Little by little, though, the trap is closing in around them. Excessive self-centeredness and egotism are a strain on everybody else, and many find they just can't take any more. They distance themselves from anybody who exhibits too much narcissistic behavior for too long.

Eventually, you'll have to face the facts: You're not really that special. You're actually much the same as everybody else. You're no Dwayne "The Rock" Johnson, nor are you Kim Kardashian. Sorry.

Now don't get me wrong. There is nothing wrong with who you are. I'm actually convinced that you're a genuinely amazing person. However, you might still be headed for a rude awakening—unless, of course, you pick yourself up and start moving in the right direction. That's something else entirely. If your dream is to be successful, physically fit, or famous for something important, get to work on that instead of wandering through life trying to convince yourself that you've already arrived.

The people you admire and might want to emulate didn't become who they are by chance. They worked for it. I'm not trying to suggest that they all started out with nothing. Some of them received help from all kinds of quarters, including well-meaning parents who may have had the financial means to invest in their children. However, nobody can even hold on to an existing fortune without making some kind of effort. It takes genuine commitment to make something out of even the best of circumstances.

However, the majority of successful people started out almost at the very bottom. To take a somewhat strange, yet nonetheless interesting, example, a significant majority of all the billionaires in the world earned their fortunes themselves. They didn't inherit a penny of it. There's no easy way to tell you this, but you're going to have to work for what you want, too. Nothing is free in life. Scrolling through endless social media feeds of photos of expensive sports cars, luxurious mansions, or elegant handbags is not going to make you successful. It could make you envious, but that's about it.

Ultimately, because we can only ignore reality to a certain extent, some narcissists end up struggling with depression. Perhaps, by this point, they will already have alienated most of the people they know. They could very well be isolated from everybody they used to know, as their old friends saw through them in the end.

These friends grew tired of all the trouble that the narcissist's inflated ego and mischief were causing and found themselves unwilling to go on suffering the consequences that came with their previous role as an accessory to the narcissist. Now they won't even pick up the phone.

IS THERE A CURE?

Assuming you don't want the people around you to think poorly of you, is there something you can do about all this? Some psychologists still think that narcissists are misunderstood, stigmatized, and in need of treatment. They suggest that there might be some "cure" for people who have been diagnosed with NPD. Unfortunately, there is insufficient evidence that therapy, for example, actually has any kind of significant effect on narcissists.

Treating NPD can be quite the challenge. A great deal will also depend on the individual's readiness to engage in and continue therapeutic treatments. Several varieties of therapy have use in the treatment of NPD. Let's take a look at some of the ones people tend to suggest.

THERAPEUTIC APPROACHES FOR NARCISSISTIC PERSONALITY DISORDER (NPD)

The person giving the treatment, an experienced psychotherapist with specialized training, begins the procedure with an assessment of the subject's psychological function. In this stage, different diagnoses will be considered, along with coexisting conditions, before a treatment plan is suggested.

NPD therapy is intended to do the following:

- help the narcissist overcome their resistance to therapy
- identify narcissistic behaviors that cause problems in their life
- explore past experiences and assumptions that may have led to narcissistic behavior
- help the narcissist admit that these behaviors impact others
- replace grandiose thoughts with more realistic ones
- explore new behavior patterns and help the narcissist practice them
- help the narcissist see the advantages of these newly learned behaviors

PSYCHOTHERAPY

In one-on-one sessions, the causes of the narcissist's emotions and behaviors are explored. Understanding your past will help you focus on relevant emotions and behaviors, which will in turn make your thoughts and emotions easier for you to manage.

COGNITIVE BEHAVIORAL THERAPY (CBT)

Here, unhealthy thought and behavior patterns are identified and subsequently replaced with healthy ones. The narcissist will practice new skills. They will also be assigned homework to do so that they can refine these skills between sessions.

SCHEMA THERAPY

Schema therapy combines elements of psychotherapy with elements of CBT. The idea is to identify negative patterns and mechanisms that stem from early childhood experiences. Once the narcissist has discovered these harmful schemas, they can learn to change them.

GESTALT THERAPY

This is another variant of psychotherapy. In this case, there is more emphasis on the present than on the past or the future. Past life experiences are viewed through the lens of the effect they have on the narcissist's life today. The narcissist is encouraged to reflect on what is going on in their life at the moment. They will work on improving their self-awareness and self-responsibility.

The drawback to all these methods is that no matter how well-intentioned they may be, and no matter how well they have been designed to treat and even cure narcissists of their problematic behavior, there is simply no conclusive evidence that they have any tangible, real effects at all. If a single study had been able to verify that a particular treatment was actually effective, it would have been a huge deal. Perhaps such a study will arrive one day.

It's also worth noting that there are no drugs that are used specifically to treat NPD. But the true challenge to treating a narcissist is that treatment, of any kind, hinges on the voluntary participation of the person to be treated.

THE REAL PROBLEM

The true source of the problems is obvious: What reason could a narcissist possibly have for wanting to be *cured*? *Cured from* what? one wonders. From their ability to use other people or get their partners or parents to help them out with anything they might need? From their promiscuity? From their inability to feel regret, guilt, and shame? Why on earth should a narcissist want to be free of those things? What reason could they possibly have for wanting to lose the feeling that they are at the top of the food chain?

They simply have no motivation to change. Narcissists maintain their lifestyles at the expense of other people, and they have no intention at all of stopping. Psychotherapeutic treatments are not their first option by a long shot.

I often think of cats in this context—they might be the most narcissistic animals in existence. Try telling a cat what to do. Good luck trying to perform tests on them—it's almost impossible to get them to play along for more than a brief moment.

However, there is one context where you actually could help a narcissist. This applies to narcissists who lack the grandiose behavior that most narcissists display. The more introverted ones, who have weaker self-esteem, function differently. These are the ones we refer to as *vulnerable narcissists*. They are more aware of how skewed their notions of superiority are, and they also don't harbor any illusions as to their actual superiority—however badly they happen to desire to be superior. These individuals can develop depression—and that is definitely treatable.

With the right treatment, these narcissists could very well get back on their feet and return to their true selves. Standing strong, tall, and proud. But they will still be narcissists. Again, this begs the question: Good for whom?

What I'm trying to determine here is if it would actually be a net positive for society. A narcissist in great form will do psychological harm to many potential victims before they are done. Do we really want to encourage that?

Is this a simple issue? Far from it. I have no idea what the right answer is here.

Regardless of this particular case, it seems that people with narcissistic traits struggle more and more as the years go by as it becomes harder and harder to maintain a grandiose self-image in the face of the psychological and physical realities of aging. Psychopaths are similar in this regard: Aging causes them to lose some steam, but they don't ever stop being psychopaths. Or narcissists.

PART III

How to Handle Narcissists

. . . .

15

The Challenges of Being Close to a Narcissist

> To be yourself in a world that is
> constantly trying to make you something
> else is the greatest accomplishment.
> —RALPH WALDO EMERSON

What's it like to live with a narcissist? Given all the typical narcissistic traits I've discussed so far, it will also depend somewhat on who you are. Some of us are more tolerant of poor behavior than others. Since narcissists can often seem charming at first, it's not always easy to know who you're dealing with.

My simplest, most basic advice is this: Be on the lookout for a certain set of behavioral patterns whenever you enter into a new relationship, whether it be romantic, platonic, or professional. This chapter will be of use to you if you suspect you may actually be involved with a true narcissist, but it should also be helpful if the person you're interacting with is merely exhibiting some narcissistic behavior. It's not always easy to tell the difference, so you need to be on your toes.

Now, I'm not in any way suggesting you should live your life in fear of meeting new people. All I'm saying is that it can be good to maintain a healthy, alert, and natural attitude when you're around people you don't know anything about. Think of it as being in traffic. If you think about it, traffic is incredibly dangerous. All those lunatics riding bicycles and driving cars. Still, the danger doesn't stop you from getting around. All you need to do is keep a lookout and pay attention and you'll be fine. On the vast majority of occasions, nothing bad happens.

The most important pattern for you to be looking for is whether what the person says, perhaps even repeatedly, really matches up with what they do.

Naturally, all narcissists don't behave exactly the same and do all the same things all the time, but there are patterns.

SO, HOW DOES A NARCISSIST BEHAVE IN A RELATIONSHIP?

You'll notice a constant state of disappointment. Their partners disappoint them in every way: They don't make enough money, they aren't educated enough, they aren't attractive enough, they're far too ignorant, they don't take very good care of the family, or their background is all wrong. Whatever they do, it'll never be quite good enough. There's always cause for criticism and dissatisfaction. Life was supposed to be a lot easier. It's enough to make you wonder why anybody would want to move in with a loser like that.

Comments along the line of "my ex was a lot better at XYZ than you" are common. It could be that the narcissist in this relationship is keeping tabs on all their exes (there is most likely a small legion of them) to see if any of them look like they're about to have some kind of financial windfall. The narcissist might stand to gain somehow— ideally by getting back together with their now wealthy ex, but failing that, they can at least ram the news down their partner's throat.

ALWAYS CHOOSING THE WRONG SIDE

Another warning sign is when one person in the relationship never sides with their own partner but tends rather to side with anything or anybody *against* them, whether it be a matter of taking a stand, voicing an opinion, or planning to do something. There is both a stated and an implied mistrust of the person they live with. Other people's opinions are used as evidence that their significant other is clueless.

A practical example of this could be when you're redecorating the house, like fixing up a kitchen or bathroom. Whatever the other person does, however they do the work, it won't be good enough. When people come to visit, the narcissist brings up every single mishap along the way, and they might even hire a professional contractor to clean up the mess. This is an effective way of humiliating somebody. It's important to realize here that there isn't necessarily anything wrong with the work they did. The whole point, rather, is to make them feel useless and incompetent. This is a way for the narcissist to keep the upper hand.

Narcissists want the best, after all, and they feel entitled to demand it, too. Often, they are imaginative enough to paint a vivid image in their mind of what their life should have been like, as opposed to the misery they are currently suffering. These fantasies might be about money—making more of it, or their partner making more of it, wealth and riches that the narcissist really should have received ages ago.

MOVING ON FROM MATERIAL CONCERNS

This isn't limited to material possessions, however. Fantasies and daydreams could be about achieving career success, fame, and all the things that might have been. If only they hadn't taken up with that loser. Things would probably have been a lot better if they'd been with somebody else. Perhaps their ex was a lot better at arranging for the narcissist to achieve an appropriate degree of success. Perhaps they should have listened more to their parents, who warned them that this wasn't the kind of person they should spend their life with. However, if their partner were to do things that satisfy the narcissist's needs, like taking a new job that pays better, the narcissist will be in favor of this solution even if it means they will hardly get to see each other. It will improve their situation in material terms. More money coming in is always welcome news, seeing as everything they make is spent almost immediately.

The partners of narcissists also end up suffering for the sins of others. They end up paying for what other people did or didn't do. It could be imagined past offenses, which the narcissists still bear grudges over. As soon as the opportunity arises, they will vent all their frustration onto their partners. Imagine a punching bag in the basement. Whenever something annoys or angers the narcissist, they can go down there and pummel that punching bag. It didn't do anything to cause offense. It just hangs there. But it has to pay for all the narcissist's baggage. This could happen in any relationship, of course, but it is highly typical of relationships involving a narcissist.

WHAT ABOUT EMOTIONS?

Emotions are a complicated part of all this. Narcissists can be quite cold, and they aren't really that emotional. They like to keep their partners at a slight distance, to leave some room for doubt about their feelings for the other person. This seems to work, too, judging by the hordes of people who seem to be prepared to put up with almost anything to win their acceptance. The emotional terrain can get pretty bumpy here. Just like psychopaths, narcissists occasionally shower their partner with terms of endearment, only to be completely dismissive a moment later. None of this happens by chance. It's all part of a manipulation technique.

One version of this is making your partner feel guilty for wanting to be intimate with you. You shame them for having the nerve to suggest anything like that. Again, the objective here is to make the other person feel isolated and alone.

ISOLATION FOR ISOLATION'S SAKE

Another pattern that many victims of narcissists have reported is being prevented from making new friends. When their partner makes a new acquaintance, the narcissist makes a big deal of what an inappropriate person this seems to be. Their complaints can be rather fanciful. Any kind of support needs to be cut off, because they want the partner to be isolated from other people. If the narcissist's partner were to complain about the narcissist's friends, they would simply be called a control freak.

Nobody's perfect. Nobody, that is, except a narcissist. They never need to change anything about themselves. As they feel they are perfect just the way they are, there's no real need for them to take any kind of criticism seriously. Not from anybody, least of all the person they live with. However, there is an obvious double standard here: The narcissist, of course, reserves the right to criticize anybody as they see fit. Often, the narcissist will lash out at anybody who dares criticize them, and their assault can be quite ferocious.

EMPTY THREATS AHEAD

Along with these methods, there is of course the conventional approach of threatening to leave the relationship. Although this threat might be frightening enough, there is often more to come. Narcissists also often threaten to sue or press charges against their former partners. Their complaints vary from arguments about money to who gets to keep the house, or even taking a child custody battle to court.

Grandiose narcissists are aggressive by nature, and they don't mind starting a fight. Conflict doesn't bother them as much as it bothers other people. Even though they are less emotionally detached than psychopaths, they don't mind causing mischief in other people's lives; to them, maintaining a relevant threat level is an exciting challenge.

If the narcissist's partner says they can take the kids, the threats might become financial instead. If there's plenty of money in their estate, you can always tell the other party to go ahead and take what they want. And since narcissists want to cause real harm, they can always threaten to spread vicious rumors about their partner. Or use social media to assassinate the character of somebody who was their soul mate for six months.

There are other signs that might suggest that the person you're living with is on the narcissistic spectrum. But I think I've covered enough of them here. As I said before, you need to be on the lookout for patterns. Remember, not all narcissists do all these things all the time. On the other hand, being regularly subjected to just one or two of these abuses might be more than enough.

Realize this: If it doesn't *feel good*, it *isn't* good. You owe it to yourself to do something about it. But what?

Well, that brings us to the next important question: How do you liberate yourself from a narcissist once and for all?

16

Breaking Free from a Narcissist

The cave you fear to enter
holds the treasure you seek.
—JOSEPH CAMPBELL

This is where things get really complicated: addressing issues in existing relationships, whether they be with romantic partners, relatives, coworkers, or friends. When something feels off and you don't quite know what to do about it, here are some ideas for how you could approach it. If there's anything I've learned from supporting psychopaths' victims these last few years, it's that you have to listen to your emotions in these situations.

If things feel wrong, they are.

WHAT YOU MUST NEVER DO—PART 1

This next part is perhaps too obvious to need explaining, but I'll go over it anyway. The reason why I want to belabor this point is that it would be very easy for me to be all smug and suggest that this stuff isn't challenging. But it is. It's difficult. It can even feel completely impossible, and if you know that feeling, I promise, *I feel you*.

Anyway, here it is:

You must under no circumstances accept any kind of abuse from a narcissist (or anybody else, for that matter). Physical abuses leave visible marks, and I've explained that no immediate connections between narcissism and violence have been found so far. It's actually much more complicated than that. But I'm in full agreement with the advice women are given about men who are physically abusive:

Walk away at the first sign of abuse.

Any man who's enough of a spineless coward to raise his hand against a woman deserves to waste away in solitary confinement forever. This behavior provokes me on a level I can barely express with words.

Don't stay. I'd also like to tell any men who are reading this that if your partner strikes you, you should also walk away immediately. This is not the right person for you.

We should also address psychological abuse. I want to be very clear about this: I'm talking about *abuse*. This isn't about insults or disagreements about what to watch on TV while you eat dinner on a Saturday night. After the publication of *Surrounded by Psychopaths*, a woman asked me about her ex-husband, who was refusing to return her books to her. Well, some of her books, anyway. Might he be a psychopath?

No, no, no!

Disagreements are a natural part of any separation. There are reasons why people grow apart. The fact that they are causing trouble for each other is no indication of psychopathy or narcissism.

Being insulted is one thing; suffering psychological abuse is something else entirely. If you're regularly being put down, called names, made a fool of in front of other people, threatened, or publicly humiliated, there's no reason to accept it. None of that is okay. But remember, we're not talking about comments along the lines of

"Are you wearing that shirt to the dinner party?" However rude and snobbish that might be, it isn't what I'm talking about right now.

Besides, people often say things they end up regretting in the heat of the moment. Normal people calm down and apologize for their behavior. They move on.

But if you're subject to regular psychological abuses, you need to draw the line. Do *not* accept it.

Know that narcissists often plan ahead—way ahead. They might well perform their role as Prince or Princess Charming for months before they show their true colors. They will charm everybody you know on a number of different occasions, firmly establishing their image as the perfect partner. Then, once your entire family is crazy about this person you've met . . . they spring their trap.

LOOK FOR PATTERNS

It might start with something small. Something simple, that doesn't really matter too much. You might think to yourself that it was a bit of a mess, but you leave it be, because you like the narcissist. You've just been put through the first test. If you don't react and question their behavior, there will be more to come. Much more.

If you've been living with a narcissist for the last twenty years, you might want to consider this: Would you have moved in with them in the first place if they treated you the way they do now? Consider the last month of your relationship: Would you have moved in with them if you knew this was what you had to look forward to?

If it feels wrong, it is wrong.

A relationship needs a whole number of things in order to function, and some of the nonnegotiable ones are trust and confidence. If you can't trust your partner, it's not going to work out. If you don't have any confidence in the person you live with—whether in all areas or just specific ones—it's not going to work out. Trust between two adults is the determining factor that gives people the courage to let their guard down and be themselves. The courage to show weakness. The courage to lose their temper. The courage to bring up difficult issues. The courage to ask for help. The courage to cry on somebody's shoulder. The courage to expose their flaws to somebody else.

However, trust has a limited shelf life. You can't trust your wife or husband based on how they acted two years ago. It's how they acted last week that's relevant. Maybe even how they acted last night. Or even this morning. It's the person they've become that you need to focus on.

Trust has to be earned anew, every day. That goes for you, too. Perhaps you're somebody who knows that you're in danger of being seen as a narcissist by the people in your life. If so, you need to realize this: It's your most recent behavior that reveals who you are. That's how you prove yourself worthy of trust. Not by referring to something you did months ago.

Trust has a limited shelf life.

Once it expires, the relationship is over.

End of story.

WHAT YOU MUST NEVER DO—PART 2

There's another warning I'd like to give you here. It might seem tempting to be more proactive about solving your problems. Depending on your own personality and mental state, you may end up deciding to tell the world what an insufferable jerk your narcissist is. You decide to smoke them out, basically.

Think long and hard before doing this, though. You're a good person, after all—you don't lie to, cheat, or manipulate people. The other person might not be like you. You might not be on a level play-ing field. They lack empathy but know that you don't. You're an open target for emotional attacks that could do further harm to you. And for all you know, the narcissist might have been preparing for this breakup for years. When you call the people you think of as your allies to tell them the truth, you might well find that you're a little late to the party. I'm sure you can imagine the kinds of things the narcissist will have told all the people you care about.

Although narcissists can cause a great deal of obvious harm to many people, many will still refuse to see them for what they are. That's how manipulation works. You might be thinking that this seems hor-ribly unfair and just wrong. You'd be right. But they might also have been subjected to years of manipulative behavior. If you really want what's best for them, you should probably abandon your propaganda efforts.

Letting the world know that the narcissist is less of a catch than everybody thinks might seem like a good idea, but the backlash could come swift and hard. Narcissists have a highly vindictive streak. If you burst their bubble, they will simply regroup and come after you. Perhaps they will even muster the troops and turn everybody they can convince against you. It's happened before, and the victims of this tactic don't always recover fully.

Smoking the narcissist out might prove too costly, then. Don't do it unless you're on incredibly firm ground, with allies you have abso-lute confidence in not to waver from your side.

WHAT YOU CAN TRY

You need to decide whether to take any action at all. In cases where the person you're dealing with is an acquaintance, a family member, or a coworker, it's less clear-cut. If the person in question isn't in your immediate orbit and nobody appears to be in any immediate danger, you could decide to leave things be.

If, for a variety of reasons that I hope at least you can understand, you decide to keep a narcissist in your life, make sure to put as much distance between yourself and them as you can. Stay out of their immediate vicinity, basically. The air gets more toxic the closer you get.

Increasing the distance a little will make it easier for you to gain the narcissist's acceptance, as you won't be reacting as strongly to their antics. This can be a good way of flying under the radar.

One example that comes to mind is a distant relative of mine, who has a classic mean aunt in her family on her husband's side. She's a truly awful, grouchy woman, who complains about everything and is always arguing with somebody. Attacking others is her way of life. She can say extremely negative things about people she's never even met. She thinks she's all-knowing, which is ironic considering she somehow believes the whole family loves her. What she doesn't know is that practically everyone has had enough of her and her hostilities. Even her own kids despise her, although they don't have the nerve to say it out loud.

This aunt makes herself the subject of every conversation, mainly by constantly repeating how unfair life has been to her. There's no end to her imaginative narratives in which she is always the victim of some vast conspiracy to hold her back in life. It remains highly unclear who is supposedly the mastermind behind this plot.

Her husband is visually impaired, but she won't let him listen to audiobooks on his CD player because she doesn't like having cords littering the floor. Yep, you didn't misread anything. Her needs trump his, even though this means he can't enjoy reading anymore, which used to be one of his greatest pleasures in life.

This aunt passes her venom around to everyone and everything, and my relative avoids her whenever possible. Sure, he gets the odd angry phone call, but he simply listens and hangs up. He doesn't point out to her that she's a blatant narcissist—all he does is limit their contact as much as he can.

If we replace the relative with a friend, the situation will be less sticky. Just don't respond to text messages or phone calls as quickly as you used to. Don't get in touch, in any way. Don't comment on anything this individual posts to social media. Ignore them. Tell them you're sick the next time you're supposed to meet.

All this will have a single important effect: It will make you a less appealing option to latch onto and seek to manipulate. The narcissist will look for new hunting grounds. If you meet in the future, at some social event or another, you can always be polite—just as long as you're not inviting! Don't ask any questions. Don't be dismissive, but don't encourage anything, either. When the narcissist complains that you're boring, you'll know you're on the right track.

The same goes for the workplace. If it's your coworker who is a narcissist, avoid all contact whenever possible. If it's your boss, find a new job. I mean it—you have no mandate over this person, and there's no way you can win. Walk away.

It will work. Think about whether this might be a suitable approach for you. In the end, it might still be wisest to sever the ties completely, rather than just ceasing to care. It's certainly the safest option.

WHAT YOU'LL PROBABLY END UP HAVING TO DO

If you have to face up to reality and accept that the person you allowed to get so close is actually bad for you, you'll need to resort to more drastic measures. Let's suppose the person in question is your partner. This isn't a challenge I'd wish on anyone, but many will come to some hasty conclusions after merely scanning the narcissism checklist.

Let's further suppose, then, that the person you're living with is *not* a narcissist. If that's the case, you can simply bring up your complaint and ask for some improvement. If they're a reasonable person, this will work as long as you make sure they know you're serious about it. Address the conflict. It's definitely worth it. If they're a jerk, things might not work out anyway and the solution will, once again, be to move on. Why give yourself a jerk to deal with?

Don't use the words "narcissist," "psychopath," "freak," or other similar terms. That would only provoke them. Nobody is ever going to say, "You know what, I never thought of it before, but I think you're right—I think I'm a narcissist!" Not going to happen. Forget about it.

Limit yourself to commenting on behaviors. Simply come out and say it: "What you're doing to me is unacceptable, and I want you to stop immediately."

Be specific. Avoid bringing up emotions, as this will only give the narcissist more ways to get back at you.

Don't say, "You're always so rude to me! It hurts me quite badly."

Instead, say, "Yesterday, you told me in front of my family that you think I'm starting to look a little old and worn. That's not okay."

Don't say, "You treat me like a walking ATM, and I find it humiliating."

Instead, say, "You borrowed another fifty dollars from me last month, and you told me you'd pay me back within three days! Pay me back the money you owe me immediately."

Under *no circumstances* say, "When you stay out all night, I don't know what you're getting up to and it makes me feel insignificant and unloved."

Instead, say, "I'm not okay with you being out partying all night. That's not a good foundation for a functional relationship."

Another thing you should avoid is making (empty) threats, because this might trigger aggressive behavior on the part of the narcissist.

Therefore, don't say, "I'm going to break up with you if you don't stop texting your exes."

Instead, say, "Any real man would pay attention to his current woman, rather than his past ones. So what'll it be?"

My advice is that you simply take out a pen and paper and write down what the problem is and how you might bring it up in the clearest, most neutral way possible. When you've figured out exactly what you're not happy with, add what you'd like to see instead.

No emotional outbursts, no threats about doing this or that.

Just put it out there. "I'm not okay with you doing X. I wish you would do Y instead."

Your partner might never have thought of this. If that's the case, you might have a fruitful discussion, and things could end up better than ever between you.

If your partner is of the more common, stubborn variety, you might be told that they get where you're coming from, but they still don't intend to change. In that case, at least you're free to leave.

A narcissist might try to unbalance you by changing the subject and hurling accusations at you. "Like *you're* so perfect?" Remember, in this sense, narcissists are pretty much overgrown children.

Your partner might even say you're right and promise to improve. All you need to do then is keep an eye on what they do next. Stop paying attention to what they say, promise, or explain to you. Simply observe their behavior. That's all that matters.

One of my most important mantras in life is this: Compare what people say they will do with what they actually do. That's when everything comes into view.

Does the change fail to materialize? Does the other person soon return to their old, bullying ways? Pack your bags! There's no way to sugarcoat this: You need to get out of there.

Make sure you have your allies nearby. If the narcissist has taken all your mutual friends, figure out who is still on your side. There are plenty of interest groups that shelter women who need help, but far fewer groups will take care of men in similar situations. In any case, you need to make sure you have a whole team on your side, however small. You might be too vulnerable on your own.

You owe yourself this much. Your future self will thank you for it. Your future children will thank you for it. Your friends and family will gradually recognize the old you, and they will thank you for returning to them.

17

A Complete System for Breaking Free Once and for All

*The answer to the problem of humanity
is the integrity of the individual.*
—JORDAN B. PETERSON

Do you need a more detailed plan? No problem. Here are my suggestions for the various steps you might need to take if you genuinely think you might be dealing with a true narcissist, or at least a highly skilled manipulator. This method will work on anybody: family, life partners, or people you have unfortunate encounters with at work.

BREAK THE PATTERN

The most common response to being manipulated is to take immediate action. This isn't always a great idea, because you might still be off-balance if you're too quick to respond.

It's better to wait awhile and put some time between the event and your subsequent reaction. The problem with hasty reactions is that they will amplify your adjustments to the manipulator—you'll be doing the exact thing they hoped you would. This person might even understand you better than you do yourself. Think about it. Go over the events that took place. Don't follow your gut reaction.

The phone is a perfect tool for slowing the pace of a conversation that might otherwise be too fast for your own good. It could be a case where somebody is trying to pressure you to agree to something you haven't had time to consider properly. Basically, they are trying to trap you into agreeing to something that could end up costing you hundreds of hours of unpaid work.

Your immediate response should be one of the following:

- "Hey, I need to ask you to wait for a minute. I'm sorry."
- "Someone's coming; I have to go. Call me back in five minutes!"
- "I'm almost out of battery! I need to find my charger—I'll call you back later."

Note that there is no asking for permission going on here. There's nothing rude about your behavior. You're just letting them know you'll have to get back to them later. Seems entirely reasonable. It might easily have been true, too. While you're collecting your thoughts, you'll have plenty of time to think over what was actually said, and how you should respond to it.

If you received a text message, there's nothing to it: Just don't answer. Or wait for a couple of hours first. Or a week. Rushing your decisions can be costly.

If you're together in the same room, things can get trickier, of course. However, there's always coffee to fetch, bathrooms to visit, or people to greet. Pick up your phone and pretend to see an email that needs an immediate response. Hold your finger to the air and smile apologetically. The effect will be the same either way: You get some breathing room and time to think.

Use it. *Think*.

Maybe all of this seems almost ridiculously simple to you. You'll see how simple it is once you've given it a try. You know that there can be consequences if you don't play along with the narcissist's antics. It's awkward. But if you can't even find the courage to try, this only goes to show how badly you need to do it. There's something that doesn't quite add up here.

If you can't think clearly even after you've had a moment to calm down, you can always carry on refusing to respond:

"I need some time to consider what you said, so I'm going to get back to you when I'm done with that."

"That question requires a great deal of thought, so I need some more time to deliberate. I'll get back to you as soon as I can. Thanks for being so understanding."

"I'm afraid I am still unable to respond. I'll definitely be considering your proposal, and I will get back to you as soon as I'm able to do so."

"This sounds like an important question to me, and I'm going to need some time to give it the thought it deserves. When I have, I'll be in touch."

If you're a Red, you might already have moved on to the next chapter, but either way, you'll be painfully aware of how often you get things wrong in haste. Sometimes you just move too fast for your own good.

If you're a Yellow, the challenge will be keeping your mouth shut and not letting a load of unfiltered opinions out. Stop. Think.

If you're a Green, stick with what you do best: Don't respond at all. Ignore your aversion to conflict for a moment, and bring out the main weapon in your Green arsenal: passive-aggressive behavior. Shake your head and tell them you'll sleep on it. Don't say yes when you mean no. Now repeat that to yourself eleven times.

Finally, if you're a Blue, you might already see how reasonable my suggestion is. You won't have any problem staring at the manipulator while you think it all over. Silence doesn't bother you, and now you have a neat, practical solution—empirically proven, at that—to apply whenever somebody tries to get you to give an immediate response to something or other.

Now, your manipulator might certainly question your behavior at this point. The partner who wants to "borrow" money to hold them over until payday will shout at you that they always pay their debts—even if this is a blatant lie—your mother who will burst into tears and complain that you've grown so heartless and that you've forgotten how she used to do "everything" for you. Your boss might try to tempt you with some vague promise of a promotion before giving up and handing the suicide mission over to somebody else.

These are manipulators we're talking about. They manipulate. They can't be trusted. Don't expect to stay calm and balanced throughout the ordeal. You might actually need to use the bathroom, for real. The respite you get might not last very long. Hostilities might ensue. Remember this, though: Your newfound resistance is a result of your feeling unhappy with the relationship you're in. It's dysfunctional, and you want to see a change.

BE A BROKEN RECORD

I want you to repeat your message over and over and over and over and over . . .

Your manipulator knows exactly how to apply pressure to you. But you must resist. There's no need to apologize or ask to leave. Simply repeat that you'll be getting back to them about X. No excuses or long explanations are necessary.

Don't get engaged in some debate over why you're not responding to the original question now. You also don't need to tell them when they can expect their answer. Setting yourself a deadline might mean giving up control.

Be consistent. Stay on message. Behave consistently. Don't change. People who do exactly what they say they will enjoy a great deal of respect from other people. If you can demonstrate that you won't be caving into pressure in the form of tears, screams, threats, promises, or whatever might work on somebody like yourself, you'll have reclaimed control of the situation. The power of consistency is *astounding*.

Here's the sound of a broken record:

Narcissist (N): Since you're so good at organizing things, I've decided that you will be in charge of a huge project that's coming up.

You: The other line is ringing. I need to take the call. Excuse me. [Breathe, and decide if you want to take this suicide mission or not.]

Let some time go by. Try thirty seconds.

You: Thank you for waiting. I need some time to think about your proposal. I'll get back to you as soon as I can.

N: What is there to think about? Are you saying you won't take the project on? There are a lot of people involved in this . . .

You: I understand if this comes as a surprise to you [validating the narcissist's actual emotions], but I need to think about it, so I'll have to get back to you.

N: Well, I have to say, I won't be able to wait for too long. This is a very important project, you know. Everything depends on this right now. I need your answer right away.

You: I understand your concerns, but I need time to consider this. I'll get back to you as soon as I can.

N: [Getting annoyed over the unexpected resistance they've encountered] You're not listening! You're putting us in a tight spot, here. We need your help! There's really nothing for you to consider.

You: [Deep breath.] I understand your frustration, but I'm going to have to get back to you on this one. Goodbye.

Yep. You hang up, just like that.

Naturally, you could just tell the narcissist to stick it from the start. The problem with doing that is that your relationship might turn sour and you don't know for certain if they're even aware of their own manipulative behavior.

The power of consistency. There's nothing like it.

DEPROGRAMMING FEAR, ANXIETY, AND GUILT

Fear of something can be a difficult thing to carry around: Rejection, making a mistake, not being accepted, being criticized, making people angry, being ostracized, those are just a few of the things most of us fear at one time or another.

Anxiety tends to be more abstract. It may even revolve around things that never actually happen.

Look back on your life to date, and consider some of the things that have caused you anxiety over the years. You'll notice that only a very small portion of your anxiety was actually merited. I'm told Mark Twain once said, "I've had a lot of worries in my life, most of which never happened."

In the end, guilt is the feeling of being responsible for other people's feelings—that it would be your fault if the narcissist was to get sad or feel mistreated.

A manipulator will want you to be off-balance, and will be prepared to scream at you, threaten you, sob, cry, or play the victim and the martyr all at once, just to get you to feel either afraid, anxious, or guilty. Until now, it's worked, too. But no more.

RED FEARS

If you're a Red, just think of all the things that are out of your control. What on earth are you doing? I know you don't intend to show it, but don't deny that you feel it sometimes: You're not that cold. Reds are, generally, terrified of losing control of all the important things in their lives.

YELLOW FEARS

If you're a Yellow, you'll live in constant fear of rejection. If all your friends were to shun you, where would that leave you? Social isolation is one of the worst things a Yellow can endure. Not being able to spend time with people and socialize all the time can be a great strain on them.

GREEN FEARS

If you're a Green, you'll be very aware of your fear of conflict. If somebody raises their voice ever so slightly, it makes you weak at the knees—in the bad way! You're also afraid of rapid change. You'll back down if somebody threatens to shake your existence up too much.

BLUE FEARS

Blues fear one thing above all else: public humiliation. It could be in the workplace, in a relationship, in some situation where they might appear ignorant—they'll go to great lengths to prevent this from actually happening. Making an absolute and total fool of themselves would cause them so much shame that they might never recover.

WHAT COULD POSSIBLY GO WRONG?

When you've decided to break your manipulator's hold on you, you'll experience several of the following emotions: You'll worry about what might happen; you'll fear some very specific outcomes. Worst of all, you'll even feel a degree of guilt for thinking you can change.

I realize that you're less than perfect, but that doesn't mean you deserve to be manipulated and deceived. While you're liberating yourself from a narcissist, you'd do well to consider your own well-being. In time, you'll have plenty of opportunities to work on your weaknesses and cultivate your personality. However, there's no need to do all that right now.

One thing you will have to address immediately is your own aversion to these unpleasant emotions. Carrying fear, anxiety, and guilt around can be very cumbersome. Believe me, I've given all three a solid try. For a time in my life, I was a virtuoso of anxiety. However, that was back before I realized that most of the things I would worry about never ended up happening.

How do you do it? It's simple: You tackle your own discomfort head-on. In much the same way as we treat claustrophobia, you need to expose yourself to your fears in small doses.

Are you afraid of riding the elevator? Look at a photo of an elevator first. That's all. Then walk inside a building with an elevator, and look at it from a distance for a while. Next, look inside the elevator for a few minutes. You don't need to step inside. Eventually, though, you'll be inside it, while somebody else holds the doors for you. You stand there for a bit, before exiting the elevator again. Next time, perhaps you'll allow the doors to close while someone else is in there to keep you company. Maybe you'll ride it for a floor or two, and so on.

That's how claustrophobia is treated. You face the fear, one baby step at a time. You could do it, too.

PUT EVENTS INTO WORDS

As long as the implied contract between you and your manipulator is in effect, the manipulation will be in effect, too. Therefore, it is imperative that you break the contract and voice your concerns. I keep using the word "manipulator," because I want to emphasize that not all manipulators are narcissists. Sometimes manipulation can even be a subconscious behavior—I discuss this elsewhere in this book. If you're not sure what you're dealing with exactly, I would recommend the following approach:

Nobody can read your mind. So, instead of waiting for that to happen, you confront the manipulator with your experiences. Do this just between the two of you. There's no need for a fancy dinner or any other great effort on your part, but make sure you can speak without disturbances for a while.

Put what you need to express into words. To avoid misunderstanding, each of the following phases needs to be included.

Here's what you say:

1. "When you . . . [describe the behavior that you want the manipulator to cease] . . ."
2. ". . . I feel . . . [describe in detail the negative emotions that this produces in you]."
3. "If you could stop [the troublesome behavior] and . . . [describe the behavior you would prefer to see in this situation instead] . . ."
4. ". . . I would feel . . . [explain exactly how you'd like to feel when you're with your partner/boss/coworker/mom, or whoever the manipulator happens to be]."

In that precise order. Your message will get through, and there is a good chance that the other person will actually listen to you. If this is somebody who is essentially decent but has got themselves caught up in inappropriate behavior, you'll see changes with this method.

Here's an example from when I was coaching an individual a few years ago:

1. "When you complain about everything I do all the time . . ."
2. ". . . I feel insufficient and useless."
3. "If you could give me some positive feedback, too, and even some praise . . ."
4. ". . . I would feel that you valued me more and I would be a lot more at ease."

Or, perhaps, this way:

"When you call to complain to me about feeling so lonely, it makes me feel misunderstood and underappreciated. If, instead of going on about how lonely and miserable you are, you could just get in the car and come over instead, it would be easier for me to take you seriously."

At work, you might use something along the following lines:

"When you complain about my work performance in front of the whole firm, it makes me feel completely hopeless, and I just want to hand in my notice then and there. If you could acknowledge my efforts now and then, I'd be encouraged to develop my skills and try to do an even better job."

If you're feeling particularly strong that day, you might even try something a little less restrained:

"When you keep complaining about your health and implying that I'm somehow to blame, it gives me stomach cramps. If instead of staying in bed to nurse your imagined afflictions you could just get up, put some clothes on, and give me a hand in the kitchen from time to time, I might be prepared to stay in this relationship."

Boom. How's that for a broken pattern?

Each individual statement conforms to the formula of 1, 2, 3, and 4. Get pen and paper out, and give it a try. What's the first situation that comes to mind? How does their behavior make you feel? What do you need to see more of from now on? How do you want to be feeling instead? Write down your entire script, and read it out loud to yourself a few times. Refine it, and think about the responses you might get. If you can predict some of the more common reactions, you may even be able to prepare answers to them from the beginning. This is called preventing objections, and it works like a charm.

Practice it a few times and you'll find it much easier.

Besides, you can always put a stop to everything by saying this:

"It's up to you if you're going to continue shouting/crying/blaming it all on me, but at least you know now how unhappy/afraid/worthless/insecure/pissed off it makes me feel."

Now you've repeated something the manipulator was never expecting to hear from you. On the one hand, you've labeled their behavior a conscious choice. On the other hand, you've agreed that your emotions are your responsibility. If you had told them that their behavior is the cause of your emotions, that might have invited a discussion, which might have resulted in you being coerced into admitting that you're imagining things, that you're wrong, and so on.

DESTROY THE MANIPULATION UTTERLY—MAKE SURE THERE IS NO NORMAL TO RETURN TO

You're on the verge of regaining control of yourself, your emotions—your whole life, even. And it's all going to be worth it. You'll feel a lot better if you can make your way through this step, too.

The narcissist—whoever it happens to be—is not going to like this one bit. Don't expect them to tell you, "Ah! I had no idea! I'm terribly sorry—I'll stop doing it right away!"

No, making the shift from bad to good behavior can take months, and that's why I'd like to bring up the power of consistency again.

No take-backs.

If you've said you won't accept a certain kind of behavior, you have to stick to your guns. A truly daring manipulator might decide to call your bluff, after all. You've just robbed them of a great deal of comfort. It only makes sense to be prepared for more of the kinds of attacks you've seen before.

The power of consistency.

When the narcissist subjects you to stifling silence, shouting, cursing, door slamming, table punching, angry looks, mocking laughter, tears, sobs, being ignored, threats, or whatever worked for them in the past, you simply respond, "That's not going to work on me anymore. You can stop trying now."

It might all sound something like this:

"I know that you want me to pick up your slack, but your threats won't work on me anymore.

"I understand that you'd like me to solve your problem for you, but trying to get me all worked up and imbalanced isn't going to do anything for you.

"I realize that you want me to do this, but your raging and cursing have no effect on me anymore. Cut it out."

Going forward, the narcissist will have to treat you with respect.

DICTATE YOUR TERMS FOR CONTINUING THE RELATIONSHIP

If you have a manipulative boss, you have a decision to make. The wrong boss can really hold you back in life. Your career can hit a standstill. You might not have any kind of mandate to make decisions.

All you can do is appeal to your manager's common sense. If your boss is genuinely refusing to listen, perhaps you should pursue other options instead.

This is really a case where personal matters might actually be easier to deal with. You can always tell your partner, mother, siblings, rude aunt, or uncle by marriage that you'll be removing them from your life completely if they won't show you some respect.

It's easier said than done—I know. But if you've determined that your partner is a narcissist and the relationship is making you uncomfortable, at least you'll have figured out why.

If you want to avoid any unnecessary breakups, you would do well to communicate your terms for continuing the relationship. Note: The idea here is not for you to get back at them for past injustices. You'll have to let that kind of thing go. But you do need to explain a thing or two before you can move on from the issue. Establish a framework for the relationship.

Here's what I'd suggest:

1. Explain that you'll be making your own decisions about what you want or don't want to do from now on. You're going to put more emphasis on your own needs, but not to the point of neglecting your partner.
2. Explain how you expect to be treated going forward: considerately, sincerely, with more friendliness. Explain that it is high time the narcissist acted as though they valued you as a partner, daughter, lover, or whatever it may be. Explain, in direct terms, that you're not going to agree to be hurt anymore. End of story.
3. Set clear boundaries. Explain that you're not going to put up with any more of the narcissist's antics (feel free to exemplify based on your observations). Don't make threats—it

will only make things worse. Explain that you don't intend
to get into any discussions that involve the behaviors you've
singled out.

4. Ask them to recognize that your needs, principles, opinions,
    and values are not necessarily wrong, even if they happen
    to contradict theirs. Explain that just because they think
    they're right, that doesn't make you wrong.

5. Explain that you're expecting more from your relationship
    from now on, now that you've set clear boundaries for your-
    self.

6. Finally: Ask the narcissist (a friendly smile and big eyes
    might help here) to confirm that they have heard what you're
    saying. And ask them to commit to making an effort going
    forward.

That's it!

Again, you shouldn't expect an individual who has been manipulating you for years to just go, "Sure, no problem. Let's do it your
way from now on." However, if you've already implemented the five
preceding steps of your plan for reclaiming your dignity, the sixth
isn't going to come as a total shock to them.

Again: I can't overemphasize the power of consistency. If you
choose it as your weapon, you'll be able to resolve this issue once
and for all.

A WORD OF WARNING

There is a specific criterion that can cause this whole approach to fail
miserably: whether or not the person in question is actually a clinical narcissist who would be diagnosed with NPD. If they are, these

measures will only work for a limited time. A narcissist of that kind is simply incapable of change, just like a psychopath. Which brings us back to the message from the preceding chapter:

Walk away, and don't look back.

18

Is Missing Your Abuser a Thing?

*I think it's important to realize you can
miss something but not want it back.*

—UNKNOWN

Let's say you manage to break free of the person who's been causing you anguish for all those years. It could be a romantic partner, a close relative, a parent, or—why not?—your boss. Naturally, we must all determine for ourselves how much we are prepared to accept in the way of mental or physical abuse. Personally, I believe in the zero-tolerance policy. If you let little things slide, they might grow bigger. In any case, you've stuck with your plan, you've been consistent and clear, and you've genuinely done everything in your power to get the bad treatment to stop. Let's say that in your particular case, the narcissist backed down. Or perhaps you broke up. Separated, or got divorced. Relationships can turn pretty toxic. It's sad, but it's also inevitable sometimes.

WHAT NEXT? IS EVERYTHING PEACHY NOW?

Many survivors of relationships with narcissists have noticed that this phase can get quite challenging. Despite suffering years of mental abuse at the hands of a narcissistic partner, a person who manages to break free might actually still miss, or feel that they are still in love with, the person they left just six months ago. Somehow, a void has opened up in their life. This is in no way logical—it probably sounds completely irrational. However, our emotions control us more than anything else.

To begin with, it might be wise to let some time go by before drawing any conclusions. What you mistook for love might turn out to be nothing but a habitual pattern embedded in your mind. These kinds of patterns tend to fade with the passage of time.

I know—this is a strange, confusing thought.

Be that as it may, some people still experience their newfound freedom as a loss. So, let's take a brief look at why exactly this is. If you've ever missed somebody who you knew was actually bad for you, then perhaps you'll be able to find an explanation.

First, it's simply reflective of how human beings work. We don't enter into relationships thinking we'll give it a go and see if it lasts. When we marry, for example, it's supposedly for life. We've had happy endings stuffed down our throats since before we even learned to spell "Hollywood." That's why we're prepared to invest so much of ourselves in another human being. It's not meant to end. Thinking that a relationship isn't going to last makes us feel sad. Also, and this may sound a little odd, you can still love somebody, even if you don't like them very much.

HOW YOUR OWN MEMORY DECEIVES YOU

Now, we should also consider that our memory can be devious. Our brains organize things by association, not chronologically. If you experience a situation that reminds you of something, it basically doesn't matter how far back in time the memory is: You'll recall it as clearly as if it were yesterday.

One technique that narcissists use to give the appearance that they are the ideal partner is to engage in a very intense courtship. This could involve anything from giving their partner flowers every other day, or taking them out to nice dinners, and showering them with little gifts and declarations of love early on in the relationship. This is intended to do one thing: create a false sense that you are appreciated. It works, too. You're bound to remember it, because it's very possible you've never experienced anything like it before. Even if it was all fake.

For example, seeing a bunch of flowers right after a separation can bring back memories of all the flowers you received during the love-bombing phase. Your early days with the narcissist made a strong impression on you, and you're still feeling it. Flowers, text messages, stolen kisses, and passionate nights. It's all there, inside your mind. However well you may have internalized your rational realization that you were being manipulated, the *feelings* remain.

Bad things can make you feel wanted and loved, too. For example, in the context of a romantic relationship, jealousy is an emotion that involves worrying about competition for your lover's attention. Psychologists have claimed that these emotions might stem from childhood memories, like being completely or partially neglected in favor of a sibling, for example. A skilled manipulator might offer any of these things as an explanation for their jealousy. Poor self-esteem can play a major role here, but as we know, it can be feigned. It can also cause you to feel sorry for your narcissist.

JEALOUSY

When you sense that the narcissist is exhibiting jealous, possessive behavior—which is obviously a negative—you might very well mistake this for true love, or a genuine fear of losing you, and this might be very attractive to you. It makes you feel special, and suddenly you find yourself believing the narcissist's fantasies about how special your future life together is going to be. The sense of grandiosity the other person is carrying around can even rub off on you. If the narcissist criticizes you, you might take it as evidence that they truly care and genuinely see you. At least you weren't invisible then. Not like now. Now you're not triggering the slightest bit of jealousy in anybody. Who are you even anymore?

And—here's a troubling thought—you might experience some pangs of jealousy yourself, which are directed at whoever your old abuser is presently wooing with endless declarations of love. Resist this! Remind yourself of all the pain you've suffered at their hands.

WE ALL HAVE SOME REDEEMING QUALITIES

There are other reasons why you might miss your former abuser, however. Of course, it's entirely possible that the narcissist possessed some other characteristics, which weren't altogether bad. They might have had a wonderful sense of humor, for instance. Some of them might be good listeners, or good at making you think they're good listeners. We shouldn't underestimate the significance of physical attraction here, either. It's a strong reason why people stay together, even though everybody pretends to only care about inner qualities.

Imagine if this person was the most beautiful, or even sexy, individual you had ever seen. Narcissists are often believed—by themselves, at the very least—to be more attractive than the average person, but this mainly comes down to the effort they take to look good. There is no evidence at all to suggest they have better-than-average looks. However, confidence is an attractive quality. I'd have to say I consider this to be well documented, particularly among males—alpha male behavior seems to be quite attractive to prospective partners. On an intellectual level, we might question this, of course, but our nature is sometimes difficult to resist. No longer being the object of this kind of person's attention can sometimes cause a sense of abandonment.

As narcissists aren't the only people who follow patterns, there's another thing to consider here: You might also find yourself constantly attracted to the same kind of people. We can't rule out the possibility that the narcissist you just left reminds you of some other narcissist from your past. It could be a parent, an older relative, a past boy- or girlfriend, or anybody at all who has mattered in your life. Maybe they behaved similarly to the person you just broke up with.

Or maybe it has to do with how invested you are in the individual in question. Here, I'm thinking of all the time you've spent thinking about them each day, daydreaming about what's going to happen, planning how to express yourself so as to be understood, and satisfying them in whatever ways they require this week. Perhaps you used to spend a lot of time tidying your house, in order to please your narcissist.

However, you should also factor in time spent hoping things will improve, worrying about what mood they will be in when they get home—angry, happy, or anything else, it's all out of your control. Basically, narcissists can be pretty hard work. The worse they are, the more time you'll end up wasting on them. Once they're finally out of your life, it can leave you feeling quite empty.

Strong feelings tend to live on in people. Negative experiences are easy to recall. Neuroscientists have recently figured out why we are more easily controlled by our negative emotions than by our positive ones. It turns out that it's all a matter of survival. Fear has a greater role to play in your survival than happiness does. If you don't know fear, you'll get eaten, because you won't respect danger. However, if you're unhappy, that won't pose any immediate threat to your existence. Everything gets even more complicated when you consider all the negative experiences you've shared with your narcissist. In some bizarre way, you're connected through the pain your relationship has caused you.

The dreams your narcissist tricked you into believing. All the things you thought were in your future. All the promises you were given of freedom, travel, fine things, children, love, and growing old together. If you're something of a romantic, it will hurt a lot when you realize that you're still waiting. You've been living on the hope that things would change soon . . . but soon never came. Sometimes you might just want to get to enjoy sharing these dreams again.

But, more than anything, I think this longing, or even love, for somebody who spent such a long time being a genuine threat to you is caused by an addiction you've developed. You've given up the narcissist for the same reason people give up drinking: You've realized that the short-term pleasures don't make up for the long-term costs.

THE CURSE OF AA

You're much like a member of Alcoholics Anonymous. Even now—after one, five, ten, or even twenty years of sobriety—you can still feel that itch. That's why AA members never touch a bottle again once they've broken free. They know they would only relapse. There's no such thing as *just one drink*.

You don't need to mourn this, you don't need to feel miserable, but if you do, that's okay, too! If any of this resonates with you, all that tells us is that you're human. There's nothing wrong with you. You are just as you should be. Maybe getting divorced is a bit like dying, after all. Then let it be!

It's okay to grieve. Allow yourself to.

ONE THING LEFT TO DO

If you'll allow me the liberty, I'd like to tell you what to do once you've managed to break free of a narcissist: Increase your distance from the person in question as much as you possibly can. Physically, geographically, emotionally. That's the only way you'll manage to hold on to your new freedoms.

Walk away, and never go back.

Never.

Never.

19

Linda Revisited—An Analysis of Her Behavior

Courage is what it takes to stand up and speak.
Courage is also what it takes to sit down and listen.

—WINSTON CHURCHILL

Do you remember Linda, whom I discussed earlier in this book? Feel free to go back to that example and see if it reads any differently to you this time. Let's indulge in some speculation on the future of our fictional Linda. Behaving as she does isn't exactly endearing, but that doesn't make it a crime. The consequences can be dire, however.

For a start, she's probably not going to start working until her parents decide to cut her off. When she hits twenty-five or so, her mother may finally have managed to convince Linda's father to close his wallet. Maybe they have other children—they can't give all their time and resources to the squeakiest wheel all the time.

So, Linda applies for a job, fully convinced that she will be offered it. It might work. Many employers value confidence. Let's say she gets the job, then. Does this mean her personality will suddenly magically transform from the immature, sullen teenager she has been and she will become the wiser, more responsible adult she really ought to be already? That's quite a question.

Here's what I would expect to happen next:

Linda gets to work. However, she's still in the sabbatical mind-set. And it's not like she ever had to make any effort before. So, she carries on as usual. Late mornings, early evenings.

However, the difference between a workplace and a university is pretty significant. At school, your job is to learn. In a way, you're investing in yourself. Nobody else really cares how you do. In a workplace, on the other hand, your job is to invest your time in the business. You might be expected to put in at least eight hours each day, five days a week, forty effective weeks a year, or something like that. If you've never had to do this before and have grown accustomed to getting by on the charity of others, this can be quite a change.

Many young people have experienced this challenge before. The majority of them have accepted their situation, picked themselves up, and risen to the challenge of their adult responsibilities. In other words, these things tend to work out okay, more or less.

Linda may be able to get away with her late mornings and early evenings for a while, until her colleagues let her boss know what's going on. Or perhaps the boss will notice it herself and ask Linda to join her in her office for a chat. "What's the problem?" Naturally, Linda promises to do better, but not without managing to squeeze in some reasonably acceptable excuses for her behavior. She's used to faking things to get her way; why should this situation be any different? However, a week later, her boss is back in her hair. She's diligent when it comes to following up. She went to the management class. "Didn't you say you'd be trying harder?"

Linda sees it differently, though. She's used to having to fight for what she thinks of as rightfully hers. She goes home and cries about it to Daddy. Her boss is such a meanie! Her demands are so unreasonable. Next, Linda asks if maybe her dad could have a word with her difficult boss? Just a little phone call, like he's done countless times before for her. He loves his favorite daughter, doesn't he?

Her father, who lives in reality, explains that this is out of the question. Work isn't school. She's in the private sector now; you either perform or you go home. After all, this is the profession she went to school for four years to learn, and this is what all those tuition fees were for. However, he wants her to explain how she ended up in this situation.

Linda goes into her usual spiel. She insists that she really has done her best. No matter how hard she works, all she gets is criticism. She doesn't get it. However, her father knows his daughter. He knows, in his heart of hearts, that she hasn't done her best at all. He tells her the only thing a responsible parent could say in this situation: "You'll have to get your head straight. Grow up."

At this point, Linda throws a violent tantrum and threatens to kill herself if he won't help her—he's lost track of the number of times she's tried this before. Dad stands firm. She's an adult now. She'll have to fix this situation herself.

Linda storms out of her family home and spends her whole trip home wallpapering her social media with the news of how badly life has treated her. She deserves better than this. But no support is forthcoming. Her real-life friends, who have all grown up by now, have already turned their backs on her. They've seen through her and know she is a fraud.

Her boss doesn't relent, either. She insists on receiving the services she's paying Linda to provide. If Linda can't do that, she'll have to leave her job. "Get your act together."

Here's a question to reflect on:

How did Linda end up in this situation? She was a smart young woman, with nice, generous parents, who was raised in an average middle-class home, without any special challenges. She had the peaceful, secure upbringing many can only wish for. What went wrong?

Which narcissistic behaviors can you identify here? What do

you think constitutes true narcissism, and what is simply ordinary spoiled-brat stuff? How did she become the person we see before us?

Is it possible that Linda herself is not to blame for the way she behaves? What if there are other explanations that we haven't even considered yet? Was she born that way, or did something make her that way? If it's the latter, what's the cause?

PART IV

A Narcissistic Culture

. . . .

20

When the Problem Affects More than Just a Few Individuals

The world suffers a lot. Not because of the violence of the bad people.
But because of the silence of the good people.

—NAPOLEON BONAPARTE

Up to this point, I've been discussing narcissism as the object of more or less scientific study. My examples of narcissistic behavior, whether they be individual or collective, as in the last chapter, are clear in that context. Naturally, we all recognize many of these patterns, too.

We've seen them, we've experienced them, and we've probably even engaged in our own share of narcissistic behavior in the past. I know I have, and the more I learn about the unflattering reality of narcissism, the harder I try to avoid it. Of course, talking about yourself is fine—but it's a good idea to know that you can very easily overdeliver in that regard. The trick, as you might have guessed, is to figure out where exactly to draw the line.

It's no easy feat.

In the last few years, the issue of the spread of narcissism has been much discussed. It all began with a book, *The Narcissism Epidemic* by Jean M. Twenge, PhD, and W. Keith Campbell, PhD, which was first published in 2009. The thesis here was that narcissism has reached beyond the domain of the ordinary clinical diagnosis. Even people who aren't narcissists in any way have suddenly begun to exhibit behaviors that seem suspiciously narcissistic. Basically, the pathology seems to have been introduced into our culture. Wanting to be seen, to claim more space, to promote oneself in more or less obvious ways.

I tend to think they had a point. But before we get into this subject, I want to point out that some people believe that this couldn't possibly be explained as a cultural phenomenon. As usual with matters of human psychology, consensus has proven to be an elusive goal here. Some claim that the time we live in simply gives people no choice but to fudge the details of their résumé—it's the only way to compete with all the other frauds out there!

This faction tends to conclude that no fault lies with the individual. People are basically forced into this kind of behavior. It's what everybody expects of you these days. This idea has spread like a plague, particularly among younger people. However, I do agree that it seems wrong to be calling people narcissists just because they've adapted to changing rules.

I can buy that. But on the other hand, if it isn't the *individual's* fault and it's really all just a matter of people choosing to adapt to new circumstances . . . if, in other words, it's the *culture* that has grown increasingly narcissistic . . . then what's going on, exactly? Can we simply refer to the whole phenomenon as a narcissistic culture? And might it not then be true that narcissism is on the rise, as Twenge and Campbell claimed back in 2009?

I'll readily admit to finding this a difficult question. However, it seems too important for me to ignore, so I'll pursue it: Is there really a chance that narcissism is on the rise in our society? Consider my arguments and make up your own mind.

Next, we'll be looking at what happens when the concept of narcissism is applied on a social level and what this might give rise to.

As you read the following discussion, try to consider it in the light of this question:

HOW MUCH NARCISSISM CAN THE SYSTEM HANDLE BEFORE IT BREAKS DOWN?

That's the obvious challenge here. We can't compare narcissism to schizophrenia, for example, as the ill effects of that disease mostly impact the person suffering from it. Narcissism is not a mental illness. It's a personality disorder. This means that narcissism isn't some isolated phenomenon that only impacts a small percentage of the population. Some researchers claim that between 15 and 20 percent of us are narcissists.

How would that even be possible?

If we know anything about narcissists, it's that they have a peculiar self-image. As I demonstrated in various ways in part 1, they are highly infatuated with themselves and they genuinely feel superior to the rest of us.

The question is whether you can act inappropriately from time to time without being a full-on narcissist. What would it mean if somebody who was essentially like you or me began to focus on themselves to an unhealthy degree? How far could things really go before they unraveled? How powerful are the defense mechanisms we rely on as individuals?

Believing in yourself is a nice feeling. If you genuinely believe in yourself, you'll try something more than once before giving up. You'll keep going, over and over, because you actually believe that you'll make it.

As many could report, liking yourself is a lot better than disliking yourself. But is there a point where it might have gone too far? Is it possible to like yourself a little too much, even for those of us who aren't narcissists?

To answer that, we'll need to take a look at the big picture. After having studied individual narcissists and expressed our outrage over their amoral behavior, we need to allow for the possibility that this problem may reach beyond different individuals, and that the scope of our investigations might need to be expanded. There are two kinds of narcissism: On the one hand, there is the kind of narcissist who would fit the defined diagnosis of NPD based on the specific criteria it involves. On the other hand, we have all the people who exhibit narcissistic behavior from time to time—or all the time—without necessarily fulfilling the diagnostic criteria. That's precisely what I and many others call a narcissistic culture. Behaviors that are undoubtedly narcissistic but have become so common and accepted that they have been integrated into our culture. Part of our zeitgeist, if you will.

IS NARCISSISM ON THE RISE, OR ARE WE IMAGINING THINGS?

A US study was carried out involving thirty-seven thousand college students, and the results showed clearly that since the 1980s narcissistic behavior had been increasing just as rapidly as obesity. One in four college students agreed that most of the criteria on a standard checklist for narcissistic traits applied to them.

These behaviors haven't really been associated with any specific clinical diagnosis—and having so many individuals suddenly develop full NPD seems highly unlikely, of course. So, there must be some other cause. On top of this, the increase seems to be accelerating, and occurring at a greater rate in this decade than ever before.

Researchers believe that there is a narcissistic culture of some kind, hiding just beneath the surface. It could actually influence both people who do exhibit narcissistic behavior and less self-centered individuals who don't.

As this problem is by no means limited to the United States, I thought I'd introduce you to an idea you may never have even considered.

A NARCISSISTIC CULTURE

Jean M. Twenge and W. Keith Campbell argue that narcissism, just like any ordinary illness, is caused by certain factors, spreads through certain channels, presents a variety of symptoms, and might be alleviated somewhat by prophylactic therapies and cures. They suggest that narcissism is a psychological plague, rather than a physical disease, but that the analogy works surprisingly well.

Just like the obesity epidemic, this supposed affliction has different effects on different individuals. More people are overweight than ever before, just like more people are narcissists than ever before. However, that doesn't change the fact that plenty of people get a healthy amount of exercise and maintain a good diet, or that plenty of people are able to behave considerately and maintain a humble outlook.

Less self-obsessed individuals have seen narcissistic behavior on TV, online, in real-life situations with people they know, and even within their families. Even the ones who don't get carried away after seeing it will have come across it, and will thus be influenced by it to some degree.

It has become more common for people to use the word "narcissist" as an invective, just as the word "psychopath" is sometimes used as a general term of abuse. However, it's rather difficult to find any scientific evidence of narcissism outside the world of academia. There are plenty of books on the subject of narcissism, but there is still a dearth of precise evidence in favor of one particular theory or another. Often, you end up having to draw your own conclusions based on your observations, and that's what I've done in this book. It will probably be decades before we can confidently say we fully understand psychopathy and narcissism. If we ever will.

"Narcissism" is an attention-seeking term, and I don't use it lightly. This book is full of examples of different narcissistic behaviors, and I refer to various studies. Now that I'm moving on to discussing narcissistic culture, things are going to get even more complicated.

Cultural narcissism is potentially even more dangerous, because it appears to be becoming more common. At least that's my own opinion, which I've arrived at after spending the last two years learning about the problem. Naturally, many of the things I am discussing here occur in most individuals who would be given the regular NPD diagnosis.

Narcissism isn't merely a case of excessive confidence, or a healthy sense of self-worth. As we've seen, narcissists go beyond being confident: They literally have an irrational faith in their own abilities. They are also much less interested in having close, emotional relationships, a trait that distinguishes them from people who have regular confidence and self-esteem.

21

Expressions of a Narcissistic Culture

*Attack the evil that is within yourself
rather than attacking the evil that is in others.*

—CONFUCIUS

Let's take a closer look at what a narcissistic culture might be like, and see if you agree with my conclusions. As I mentioned in the previous chapter, I'm not discussing people who would receive the full NPD diagnosis, but rather a set of phenomena that should be regarded as narcissistic based on the checklists and criteria that have been used to diagnose narcissism.

HERE'S AN EXAMPLE: THE LESS-THAN-PERFECT ROLE MODELS

In Sweden, we have certain people who have made careers out of basically being good at one thing: making negative statements about other people. However, this can be done more or less gracefully. Poorly spelled posts on social media are one extreme, while established writers will be able to express themselves more forcefully. The purpose is the same, though. If you have a way with words and time on your hands, you can do a lot more harm. Especially if you've somehow acquired a large platform.

Sweden has a bunch of popular bloggers and podcasters who've spent years messing with whomever they set their sights on. To protect any sensitive egos out there, we can refer to them all collectively as Bruno the Blogger. It's hard to do justice to the mischief Bruno has caused collectively over the years. He's tried to rob so many people of their respect and prestige. This also happens to be a bit of a trap, as it only attracts more attention to the phenomenon. He's targeted Swedes of every class: the royal family, professional football players, business leaders, single mothers, his neighbors, and his own former spouses. You get the picture. Anybody could find themselves the target of a Bruno the Blogger hit piece, because that's all he writes. Or all she writes. Female bloggers can be mean, too.

BRUNO THE BLOGGER

Bruno the Blogger is occasionally quite a celebrity who writes for major newspapers. He's often part of the trendier crowds. From time to time, one of his TV appearances is canceled because of something he's said or done, and this makes him angrier than anything else. But this is simply another pattern we recognize from the clinical narcissists. Bruno gives himself the right to mock, ridicule, humiliate, or mess with anybody he likes, for the ostensible purpose of trying to get a laugh. Bruno seems to feel people need to grow thicker skin. In some ways, I have to agree. I don't think this is a good time to be overly sensitive. But if anybody pays him back in kind, his demeanor shifts completely. Whenever somebody has a go at him in the media, he immediately launches a ruthless counterattack.

Sometimes Bruno has a run-in with one of his peers. This is like

Christmas for the mass media. The headlines write themselves. Remember, Bruno has a huge audience.

Why aren't more people expressing their horror at how all these Brunos are behaving? Is it because they are paid to be mean, or is it because they do it for no real reason? And why, why, *why* do people take such enjoyment from being cruel to one another? What does that say about our current culture?

A Bruno will soon realize: *The more vicious, cold, and heartless my statements get, the more my readers enjoy them. I find myself despising my own followers more and more.* There we go; that's as good an example of narcissism you could get: "The audience, the 'fools,' don't know any better." On the other hand, Bruno's fans are his lifeblood—he wouldn't exist if it weren't for them.

This is a good time to go back to our checklist of narcissistic traits. Callousness and lack of empathy is one of them. We should remember, too, that a narcissist feels entitled to behave any way they like, because they feel superior to the rest of us.

WHAT IS THE DANGER HERE?

If you have this disposition, every time you get away with something you'll feel the urge to try something else. And what might seem entirely innocent at first glance could soon lead to other things.

A professional soccer player's fans are young girls and boys who want to play soccer and become pros one day, too. This keeps the soccer academies busy in the summertime.

An actor attracts admirers who would also love to be on the silver screen. Many people would love to work in theater, film, or TV.

A celebrated musical performer attracts people who would like to write and perform music. The Idol series of reality shows is successful for a reason.

A bestselling author attracts large numbers of people who dream of being writers. Author is the number one dream profession among Swedes, for some reason. Creative writing classes are popular, and our annual book fair is one of our largest trade fairs.

Successful entrepreneurs attract people who want to start businesses. Start-ups are common, and many entrepreneurs end up making the leap after hearing various success stories.

What do vicious bloggers and narcissistic podcasters attract? I wonder. And what kinds of behavior are they encouraging in others?

You get my point.

SOCIAL MEDIA AND CULTURAL NARCISSISM—ARE THEY CONNECTED?

Let's assume, hypothetically, that we all have some kind of drive that makes us susceptible to deceiving ourselves into thinking we're somehow special and a cut above everyone else. What dangers would exist around us, and what would we need to treat with caution? Much of what goes on in social media actually defies all rational explanation. Until, that is, one considers the mechanisms of narcissism. That clears up some things a great deal.

Many people go around dispensing facts about themselves that nobody ever really asked to hear. I'm not the first person to joke about what things would be like if people walked around town loudly declaring what they had for lunch, or what they think about some celebrity's new sneakers. The comparison isn't entirely fair, I suppose; an accurate metaphor would actually involve calling all the people you've met at least once in life and whose phone number you happened to have to deliver the same message. It's at least selective to that extent, if we're being honest.

IS A SOCIAL MEDIA PRESENCE MANDATORY?

Well, that's the million-dollar question, isn't it? If narcissism has become an integral part of our culture . . . how could you not be present? Would you even exist if you weren't on social media? In defense of social media, I might mention that nobody forces anybody to watch, read, or comment on someone else's posts on Facebook, Instagram, TikTok, or Twitter. So, if I'm one of those boring types who takes offense at seeing others act out like that, what am I doing on social media in the first place? It's just like when you're watching a TV show you don't enjoy: You can always change the channel; nobody's forcing you to write an angry letter to the producer. You could even just turn the TV off. That's actually a pretty good idea. I do it myself quite often, and I haven't suffered any adverse effects so far.

But sure, I use LinkedIn, Facebook, and Instagram. I don't do it because I find it enjoyable—I actually tend to feel a little down after spending just a few minutes using them. However, as a writer and lecturer, I keep getting told that I simply have to have an online presence. Like I said, if you're not on social media, you may not even exist. Until you have a sufficient number of followers, you're simply deluding yourself into believing you exist.

Personally, I'm quite bad at it, unfortunately. I don't feel genuinely passionate about posting advice and tips on these platforms, and I suspect that my small band of brave followers have actually caught on to that fact. I'm also not too comfortable talking about myself and my personal life. Showing people pictures of myself in various situations just makes me feel silly, which doesn't help anything. I'm in no way claiming that my way is the right way. All of this is just a matter of personal preference.

There are obviously some really great things people use social media for. Spreading information and important ideas is one of them.

Engaging in interesting discussions with people you disagree with is another. Trying your ideas out on your network. It's not always easy to solve the logistics of getting people together for a talk. And you can discuss something with ten people at once in a single thread. Even just staying in touch is valuable. If you don't want to call your friends, you can always send them a text. The possibilities are endless.

So what's the appeal of social media? What's in it for us?

Lots of studies have set out to investigate this. Most of them have made rather obvious findings along the line of "humans are social animals, and we enjoy communicating and interacting with one another."

On the other hand, it's not like that began with social media. And the pictures we share of ourselves online (on your own favorite platform, for example) are not always . . . how do I put this . . . accurate representations of objective reality. Adding a filter to your photos is a great way to appear younger and better looking. The art of photo editing is an interesting one. However, we've known for a long time that we do it for other reasons. We want to look more tanned, or less acne ridden, or slimmer, or whatever it is. Of course, the technology works just as well for making people less attractive, but based on my own research into the subject, there aren't many examples of people doing that.

The same people who spent decades tut-tutting the touched-up pictures of models in glossy magazines are now routinely adding a bit of pizzazz to their snapshots from dinner with their (happy) families before displaying them to the world. Although why anybody would want to post their pics to the Internet is beyond me—once you post them, they're not going away. Ever. They will be eternally stored on a server somewhere, even if you change your mind and delete your post.

Maybe I'm just being old-fashioned. Maybe I just don't get how exciting it is to see everybody's homes and dinner plates at the end of the day. That's probably it. I probably just fail to appreciate all this stuff.

That's kind of my point, though. These days, this narcissistic inclination has become so common that nobody ever questions it anymore. It's become a part of our culture, basically.

Social media took off when people started taking photos of their lunches. This has been the subject of quite a few jokes over the years, and I can see why that would be the case.

Here's an amusing anecdote from lunch, I think it was two years ago. There are two girls sitting at the table next to me. They look about sixteen or seventeen. When their lunch arrived, they styled it, adjusted the plating, then proceeded to photograph their plates from every possible angle, worrying loudly that the pics weren't coming out right. They worked on their pics for a good fifteen minutes, and then posted them on some platform or another, complete with chirpy posts and catchy hashtags. One of the girls was very anxious to see what people would say about her pasta. The other one soon commented that her pasta was cold.

She summoned the waitress over to complain. The waitress calmly explained that if they had started eating when the food was served, it wouldn't have gone cold.

THE SELFIE BUG

This stuff is all very amusing. I've seen people elbow their way into violent demonstrations just to get a selfie among the chaos; I've seen a guy standing on the bed of a truck that was going 70 miles an hour just to get a selfie, hanging upside-down off the side of a bridge, standing in front of a car that ran off the road, and standing on a pedestrian crosswalk with a barbell loaded with weights.

Perhaps the idea is to show the world what a fascinating person you are? I'm not claiming to know what the deal is in each individual case, but there has to be some explanation for this behavior.

THE ICE BUCKET CHALLENGE

Back in 2016–17, there was a fundraising drive in support of research into Lou Gehrig's disease, or ALS. The idea was that people would raise awareness and help gather donations and either show proof of their donation or be doused with a bucket of icy water. Naturally, people felt compelled to film it all and post it online. As these things go, it was really quite innocent and fun, and the cause was a good one.

But I doubt it would ever have worked without a healthy dose of narcissism in the mix. If nobody had been prepared to either show off their donation or be seen with a bucket on their head, this whole goofy trend would have been dead on arrival.

Countless people make occasional donations to different charities from time to time. But apparently, some people will only give change to a homeless person if they get to film themselves doing it. The psychology at work here is fascinating. Where does someone get the idea they need to announce how virtuous they are to the world? Why is it not enough to just be . . . a good person?

WHOM DO WE MEASURE OURSELVES AGAINST?

Even the names of the different social media platforms can be revealing. Myspace, one of the early ones, really said it all. Facebook is perfectly named: It's all about being seen as your very most presentable self. Early on, YouTube's slogan was "Broadcast yourself." Sure. Why not? Maybe I should do it from my i[ndividual]Phone?

Different generations are on different platforms. It would be quite pointless for me to get into what age groups frequent what platform, because whatever I write is bound to be outdated by the time the book heads for the printers.

It's obviously become part of our culture for people to promote themselves and keep presenting the best possible versions of themselves. There's no longer anything unusual about reporting every move you make (or don't!)—why wouldn't all 567 of my followers be interested in seeing my new sneakers from eleven different angles? With a bit of luck, somebody will get envious, and then I'll know that I'm better off than at least a few people.

The problem is that the narcissist will have to resort to increasingly extreme measures to assert themselves. A century ago, all they needed to do was look across the road and compare their fields to their neighbor's. If the neighbor looked like they were doing better, that could be upsetting, of course, but at least you could walk over and ask how they did so well with their harvest.

Often, that would be the end of it. You had a single rival to outdo if that's what you were into.

It's different now. I hold in my hand a tool that gives me access to all of creation. No exceptions. Everybody reveals everything. Only an improved, touched-up version. Hardly anybody writes a Facebook post about their disappointing Friday night or the Sunday roast they burned to a crisp. The heart-wrenching arguments with your mother-in-law during Christmas dinner get edited out of the official narrative. Kids with runny noses or dogs with upset stomachs are nonstarters. Who wants to see that stuff? Nope, online, we're all beautiful, in great shape, successful, popular, inspiring, dynamic, and—most of all—tremendously happy. Just like the narcissists always did, we now all find ourselves trying to present a perfect picture of ourselves.

And what do you do when the whole world is your point of reference? For example, as I write this (in December 2020), Facebook has

2.7 billion users worldwide. That's more than every third person on the planet.

As I see it, we have three options here:

1. We could break down and get depressed over how everybody else is so much better, more attractive, and more successful than we are.
2. We could just ignore the whole thing. Watch the show without participating. Or we could just log out completely. Pretend it's 2005 again.
3. We could decide to join this race and look to get a competitive edge by any means necessary.

The final choice will be a lot easier if you have a healthy dose of narcissism in your system.

This makes sense. These platforms are ideal for self-lovers. Who can take the hottest selfies? Who has the most friends? Who has the best house, the most attractive partner, the most amazing vacation, and the most illustrious career? Who's taking the time to keep putting this information out there, too?

This has been studied in depth. There is no doubt that people who score high for narcissism are masters of self-promotion, making superficial acquaintances, and emphasizing their best qualities, including a few fictional ones. Many of us also see through our friends' more, shall we say, "solipsistic" tendencies.

Others fail to, though.

I wasn't fully immune myself. Why did I have so few Facebook friends compared to everyone else? Only 136 friends? Others had 5,000! How embarrassing was this? I must be so repulsive.

It took some time before I realized that those "friends" people were showing off were just long lists of names of people who couldn't possibly be genuinely acquainted with the person at the center of the whole thing. Perhaps it would be better if we referred to them as "contacts." If you think about it, it's probably quite unusual to have more than five close friends in real life. I've never really had huge groups of friends in real life, either. I was always better at maintaining a smaller number of deeper relationships.

But that whole friend-collecting thing was something that happened during the infancy of social media. These days, we've moved on to comparing our numbers of followers instead—and a follower could be anybody who pays any attention at all to what I'm doing. The most sociable person on Instagram right now is the football player named Cristiano Ronaldo. Just under a quarter of a billion people follow his everyday adventures through their smartphones. People can't get enough of watching him drive his Bugatti, it seems. Second place goes to singer Ariana Grande, who has close to 210 million followers. Third is actor and entrepreneur Dwayne "The Rock" Johnson, with just over 200 million. The Rock was named the nicest person in the world during the holiday season of 2020. I like him, too, but I couldn't possibly tell if he's the nicest person in the world or not. I've never even met him.

Facebook belongs to Ronaldo, again, where he has more than 122 million followers. Second on Facebook is singer Shakira, with about 105 million followers, and third is actor Vin Diesel with just over 103 million.

On TikTok, it is Zach King, with about 67 million followers. I must confess that I'm not familiar with his work, but I'm sure he's a fine young man.

Twitter is dominated by former president of the United States Barack Obama, who has more than 130 million followers.

You and I have our work cut out for us, then. And as I said, you'll need to pull something special out of the hat if you want to be competitive. Basically, social media causes some kind of endless social inflation. If humanity were to be judged based entirely on what goes on in social media, we would definitely seem significantly more narcissistic than we actually are.

A few years ago, an American university carried out an extensive study of which strategies perform well online. Frequent posters are rewarded. Ideally, you should post several times a day. Just don't offer anybody any real help or ask any questions—either will be punished immediately. The study concluded that what people wanted to see more of online was superficial exchanges rather than any in-depth discussions.

There are certainly exceptions, and I would guess this is at least in part a generational phenomenon. Whatever the truth may be about that, we can no longer deny that there is a great deal of demand for superficial fluff.

22

A Literal Look in the Rearview Mirror

Every action has its pleasures and its price.

—SOCRATES

I'd like to give you one more example, if that's okay. This one is kind of fun, and it relates to a theory I have. You might find this farfetched, so bear with me. I can't prove the first thing about this, but I still find it amusing. Let's go!

Let's talk about car design. I don't know too much about cars, but I have eyes, and I can see. For one thing, contemporary cars have grown huge. I suppose this is because of all the equipment and safety devices that even small cars need these days. Some are significantly larger than others, however; some of them are so big they could probably count as trucks—except all they're hauling 95 percent of the time is the driver.

Have you noticed how the design of the fronts of cars has changed over the last thirty years? The "face" of the cars?

WHAT AUDI AND TOYOTA HAVE IN COMMON

Let's compare some cars from the past with current models. I've chosen an Audi, which is one of the more popular high-end brands, and a Toyota—because this development is not limited to Audi. The left image is of a 1990 Audi. The right is of a 1990 Toyota Corolla, the best-selling car model of all time.

Whether these cars are beautiful or nothing special is all in the eye of the beholder, of course. Personally, I'm not too impressed, but I don't think I would have felt the same way thirty years ago. However, these pictures are unlikely to frighten anybody.

Here are the Audi and Toyota Corolla from the year 2000. Ten years later.

What's happened? Not too different, eh? Still neat and tidy, without any excessive details. The look is a little more modern, but there's nothing here that would cause you to raise an eyebrow.

But now look at these fronts from 2010. Still an Audi and a Toyota Corolla.

Something has changed this time. But what? Apart from being bigger, the front looks a little . . . aggressive. It looks far from timid, anyway. The headlights are beginning to resemble eyes. Suddenly, you kind of get the feeling the car is looking at you. Go back to the year 2000 and note the difference. If this really is a trend, it may have started at some point between 2000 and 2010.

But what comes next? Now let's look at a Toyota Corolla and an Audi from 2015.

It's starting to show, right? These maws are pretty large, and the headlights are like a pair of irritable or even combative eyes. Narrowed, and wary. There is a distinctly predatory expression to them. These cars will be noticed, and not exclusively in a good way. Their design is intended to communicate two things to the world: (a) you have a new car, and (b) you're something of a big shot. This is quite the nod to individualism. Look out!

So, how do they look in 2020, as I write this? Let's google "Audi+grille+2020." Of course, we'll look at a Toyota Corolla, too. On the following page is what I found:

Whoa! The kid gloves are off, it seems. These cars look like they want to eat you. Their grilles are like angry mouths, threatening to devour everything in their path. You must admit that these car hoods are far more aggressive looking than their ancestors from 1990. These cars look mad, to put it bluntly.

I can definitely see why people would get out of the way when a predator like this appears in their rearview mirror. It also provides an excellent way for the driver to make the *first impression they want*.

If you love your Audi or Toyota: I'm sure these are great cars. You might even reckon they represent the pinnacle of car design.

This applies to many other car manufacturers, too. But that's not what this is about. I also don't think it's about being trendy, either. Cars just look aggressive nowadays. They look ticked off. Testosterone is simmering all over our parking lots. (Men *are* more aggressive than women. There is evidence of this in prisons all over the world.) Vehicles are completely inhuman now.

If you saw a bunch of new cars driving down the street, you could be forgiven for believing that alien robots had invaded our planet. Some models these days are so over the top that they almost make you want to challenge whoever is behind the wheel to find out how tough they really are. What's more badass: you or your car?

This gives us some clues. People wouldn't be buying cars that look like this if they didn't somehow appeal to them. Something about getting into a car like this, rather than one that looks friendly, gives them a feeling they enjoy.

In the early 2000s, I had a car my daughter's friends from day care called the happy car. It looked to them like it was smiling. I liked that. I haven't seen any cars like that in a while, though.

My own theory—I'm mainly interested in the effects here; a car designer and a psychologist might do better at explaining the underlying causes—is that a lot of people basically feel better when they look a little dangerous. It makes them feel a bit tougher than the average person. This could definitely be indicative of a kind of aggression. Probably passive aggression, in the form of a cocky car, but aggression nonetheless. We also know that narcissists tend to be more aggressive than other people.

So, what came first? That's an interesting question. I'm sure you would agree the mood in traffic has grown a little testier where you live. It's worth reminding ourselves that there's less elbow room in traffic these days, that people are driving faster, that the risks have become greater, and that traffic violations (such as bicyclists going the wrong way on a one-way street or people using parking spots reserved for the handicapped) are committed more often in our urban neighborhoods than they used to be. They seem to risk their lives habitually, in ways that seem inconceivable to me. Cyclists wear hardly any protective gear, but this doesn't stop them from running red lights to hurl themselves into intersections, seemingly unconcerned about whether they will survive the day. Or do they simply take their safety for granted?

Where does all of this lead?

This isn't an ironclad conclusion, of course, but it does seem to me that society is getting colder. What else can we expect, if even our cars look pissed off? This makes me wonder: Might phenomena like these be generating more aggression?

23

Aggression and Collective Narcissism

*Any person capable of angering you
becomes your master.*

—EPICTETUS

There is a widespread idea that aggression is the same thing as losing your temper frequently. It's not that simple, however. Getting really mad is an emotional state, while aggression is actually a behavior. Punching or insulting somebody who made you angry is a behavior. When you lose your cool, you'll often feel like doing all sorts of things, but thanks to your good upbringing, you're unlikely to do more than spit and curse over it. Ideally, you might even address the issue that caused it.

AGGRESSION: MORE OR LESS?

Not all narcissists will resort to aggressive behavior, but a fair number will, and this group tends to cause much more trouble than the rest.

What would you respond to this question if you were only allowed the answers "More" or "Less"?:

"Are we seeing more or less aggression in our society than thirty years ago?"

If you answer sincerely, your answer will be "More." But why is that, exactly? Perhaps your neighbor bought an angry-looking car. A pretty simple explanation would be that more people were angry than before. That is, they are performing more actions that can be interpreted as aggressive.

Amusingly, a fair number of people aren't even bothering to be subtle about it. It's actually a bit of a paradox: Why would a narcissist, whose main objective is to be admired by others, be interested in attacking anybody, whether verbally or physically? Wouldn't that imply that we need to rethink our ideas about narcissism?

There is a fairly common idea that suggests that people who like themselves have an easier time liking others. Some psychologists I interviewed for this book even claim that you can't love somebody else if you don't love yourself first. If you like other people, you're not going to be aggressive.

However, narcissists can actually become aggressive *for this very reason*. Usually, they feel that their own needs ought to trump everyone else's, and people who get in their way could well become targets for their aggression. Their inability to empathize when others are suffering, along with their sense that people aren't giving them the respect they deserve, make them capable of lashing out at anybody. In any way. But it won't be happening constantly, and maybe not every time. When unprovoked, they behave much like the rest of us.

ARE NARCISSISM AND AGGRESSION ONE AND THE SAME?

In an American study a few years back, the objective was to find out whether self-esteem, narcissism, and aggression were connected to one another. A series of rather exciting experiments was performed on college students who were asked to write papers and then receive feedback on their work. The people giving the feedback were other students who had been asked to go after their peers and tear their work to shreds. They were told to say things like "this is the worst writing I've ever read! So awful! Is this the best you can do? Worthless. Poor quality."

Eighty percent of students with narcissistic traits became more aggressive than non-narcissists did when they were insulted the same way. Some of the narcissists' reactions went way beyond what seems reasonable for some feedback on an essay. Threats of physical violence unless the feedback was changed were made.

The teachers—whom one would take to be natural authority figures in this context—weren't spared, either. One would think that college and university students, who are adults, would have learned to behave decently to one another. But even so, college professors are assaulted each week by dissatisfied students. Some students have even ended up in jail because of their reactions to things like being given a failing grade for a class they felt certain they would pass. They simply can't accept anything less than the top grade, because that's what they feel they deserve in their own minds.

ABC News filmed part of the experiments I just mentioned. One student—let's call him Nick the Narcissist—won the whole thing by a landslide. He managed to score a whopping 98 out of 100. The TV team asked him if he really wanted to be featured in their segment. "Absolutely!" Nick responded. "I'd love to!"

A member of the research team took him aside and pointed out to him that he was in danger of seeming like an aggressive narcissist. Perhaps that wasn't the kind of reputation he wanted? Nick the Narcissist, however, felt that he looked so good that he was bound to come across well on TV. He was asked if perhaps they might blur his face out, at least? "No, no, I want people to see me," Nick explained.

"I'd like to have my name mentioned, too. It's a shame," he added, "that you can't reveal my phone number during the broadcast, too."

As outrageous as this example is, it still reveals some things to us about the inner workings of narcissists. He didn't mind seeming like a total jerk as long as he got to be seen on TV.

SELF-ESTEEM AND AGGRESSION?

The same research team investigated the connection between self-esteem and aggressive behavior with the objective of discovering whether narcissism might contribute to acts of aggression. This was tested in a variety of ways, but the conclusion was the same each time: People who exhibit strong self-esteem *and* narcissistic behavior tended to be more aggressive than others. More, that is, than people with *poor* self-esteem and *high* degrees of narcissism, or *strong* self-esteem but *low* degrees of narcissism, or people with *both* poor self-esteem and low degrees of narcissism.

When studying kids aged eleven to thirteen who displayed strong self-esteem and physically aggressive behavior, the team found that these individuals would simply rationalize their behavior if challenged. They convinced themselves that the kid they beat up was a real jerk, who had somehow actually deserved the beating they received. These bullies' behavior simply made them feel better—superior to their victims.

I realize this might not be fun to read. It's a little depressing. Discussing sensitive issues is tricky these days.

What am I saying, here? More or less *any* topic can cause controversy today. You see, there are people out there who actively seek out things to be outraged over. They can be pretty organized at times, too. Are you sitting down?

Say hello to the collective narcissists.

COLLECTIVE NARCISSISM

Just think of political slogans like "Make America Great Again," which Donald Trump used in 2016, or "Take back control," which was used by the Brexit campaign in Great Britain that same year. These messages were intended to suggest that national sovereignty was somehow impaired in the United States and Great Britain, and that it must be restored as a matter of urgency. What needed to be protected was the nation itself.

Because of how complicated politics can get, and because anybody could end up in trouble at any time for practically nothing, I'd like to emphasize that I am not commenting on the politics as such. Left, right, or anywhere in between, it's nowhere near my area of expertise. However, taking an interest in human behavior, I find myself fascinated with how political messages are communicated. And I'd like to be clear about one thing: Although I just mentioned Trump and Brexit, which generally belong to the right on the political spectrum, I don't think the people on the other side are really any better. Neither the left nor the right has a monopoly on collective narcissism.

Who are collective narcissists, then? They are individuals who demand that their group be accepted by others, without any questions. They possess a heightened sensitivity to any indication that this might not be the case.

The core aspect of narcissism is dependence on other people's admiration and recognition. When the same recognition is sought on behalf of a group, the narcissism takes on a collective dimension. Note: These two varieties of narcissism aren't always directly related. Individual narcissists, whether diagnosed or not, are not automatically collective narcissists. Some of them might even be so far gone to narcissism that they're unable to cooperate at all.

The group in question could be formed around anything. A

political ideology. A specific attitude to taxation. A particular view of feminism. The faith one adheres to. A sports team, climate change, or anything else that can trigger an emotional response.

It could also just be a family. "If you go after my family . . ."

EXPLAINING A PHENOMENON THAT'S MAKING HEADLINES

What are the prevailing attitudes in groups that are characterized by collective narcissism? Here are some common examples:

- *I wish other groups would be much quicker to recognize my own group.*
- *My group deserves special treatment.*
- *I won't be satisfied until my group gets the recognition it deserves.*
- *I demand that my group be given the respect it is due.*
- *It makes me really angry when others criticize my group.*
- *If my group had significant influence over the world, it would be a better place.*
- *It upsets me to see other people overlook the achievements of my group.*
- *Far too few people properly appreciate how important my group is.*
- *The true value of my group is often misunderstood.*

Assuming you've kept up with public discourse at all over the last few years, I'd be surprised if you hadn't come across some of the preceding statements being expressed by one side or the other in regard to some issue. When collective narcissists take control, anybody who *isn't* part of their group had better watch out. This kind of group is always going to be prejudiced, regardless of the members' ages, genders, educational levels, or political ideologies. No group is immune from this. Through some bizarre logic, everybody else suddenly becomes the enemy.

Collective narcissists carry around a set of carefully selected prejudices. They attack anybody who poses the slightest threat to the group's grandiose self-image. It's hard for them to accept that people can be oblivious to their self-avowed greatness.

Collective narcissists are keen to exact their vengeance on anybody who fails to award the group public recognition as clearly and promptly as they expect.

This pattern has actually been tested in a scientific context. In a study, collective narcissists from the United States were asked to read a fabricated interview with a foreign exchange student, who made some disparaging remarks about their experiences of studying in the US. This entirely fictional exchange student had some opinions about US culture and was troubled by some things he had seen and experienced during his time there. After reading these negative comments about their country, the collective had particularly harsh words for the exchange student's countrymen. They slated an entire nation based on the opinions of a single (fictional) individual.

Here's the plot twist: Even after the team running the study informed the participants that there was really no exchange student, and that the whole thing had been made up for this test, many of the subjects remained agitated anyway.

One of them made this comment: "I don't care if it's true or not. It sucks either way."

Collective narcissists also tend to perceive slights where nobody else can. Often, you can't even make a joke without offending some group or another. Nothing slips under the radar these days.

A well-known British actor stated a few years ago that he was troubled to find out that some of his British colleagues who came from minority backgrounds felt that it could be easier to get work in the United States than in Britain. If you listen to what he said, it's impossible to misinterpret his intentions: He is undoubtedly siding with his Black colleagues. However, he also commits a mistake so unforgivable that it will only ever be noticed by people who are prepared to go to great lengths to take offense.

In the interview, he uses the term "colored people," the accepted expression at the time. But just before the interview was given, the acceptable term in the United States had become "people of color." The actor, who is from England, was not aware of this difference, which is barely noticeable in purely linguistic terms.

But that was all it took.

Some quarters reacted with such violent rage that he might as well have used the N-word. All hell broke loose, and the actor was suddenly being made out to be some kind of white supremacy activist. How could this happen? He sought absolution; he made a heartfelt apology.

Much ado about nothing? Perhaps. But he wasn't prepared to put his career in acting at risk.

This is what happens when you accidentally knock over a hornet's nest like this. There are plenty of these examples, too: countless individuals whose careers, relationships, and lives have been ruined by these kinds of efforts.

Are these signs of an increasingly narcissistic culture? What would you say? Things were pretty different just a few decades ago, anyway. While people may have been suspicious of opinions that differed from their own, deplatforming, cancel culture, and groups that silence those they disagree with, are definitely fairly new phenomena.

HAVE THE COLLECTIVE NARCISSISTS
TAKEN OVER?

There seems to be no end to collective narcissists' capacity for taking offense on behalf of their groups.

Success for another group, or increasing influence for a minority, can both threaten the position of the majority. Collective narcissists seek to protect the privileges of their own group by undermining the motives of other groups. It's also worth remembering that anybody who seeks recognition for their group is likely to feel that overlooking said group is a serious transgression. According to the logic of collective narcissism, a crime like that must be avenged. I'm using the word "avenged" quite deliberately, here.

The whole phenomenon is alarmingly fertile ground for conflict, and even violence, as groups of this kind feel maltreated in the course of some political process or another. Collective narcissists are more likely than others to propose retribution for any act that puts their grandiosity into question.

Collective narcissists deliberately provoke hostilities between different groups. There doesn't even have to be a legitimate threat in the first place. Since they insist on getting to set the agenda, they are free to invent any threat that might help them demonstrate their power to the world. They feel entitled to be deceptive, as it's for a good purpose.

We haven't quite figured out how to address this problem in a constructive way yet. Studies have shown that individual self-esteem in groups of collective narcissists is actually quite low, and that they tend to experience negative emotions. This doesn't match up with individual narcissists, who, as I've covered elsewhere in this book, will tend to have strong self-esteem and think very highly of themselves. The problem, then, is highly complicated. Collective narcissists will no doubt remain a force to be reckoned with as long as they're able to weaponize social media for their cause.

Engaging with an exaggerated collective self-image seems to be a way for human beings to fulfill their universal need for social belonging. We all want to belong to *some* group, after all.

To have any chance of deterring further escalation of hostilities between different groups, we're going to need a better understanding of collective narcissists, as they clearly aren't going anywhere anytime soon.

CHARACTERISTICS OF COLLECTIVE NARCISSISM

Within the collective, it's more common for members to be strongly against something than strongly in favor of something. There is often an explicitly negative aspect to what one does and says. The question is this: How can you tell if you've ended up in a group that suffers from collective narcissism? Fortunately, there are signs to look for.

Commonly, the group will have singled out a specific issue or problem as their concern. Nothing takes priority over this issue, and everything else is negotiable. They express themselves in incredibly categorical ways. Their views on things are extremely binary, and their arguments lack nuance. You're either with them or against them.

Having gathered as a collective, they rarely encourage free thought. The group's leaders will demand that everybody use the right expressions and have the same ideas. Nobody in the group is allowed to question anything. There's no more thinking to be done. "We already have all the answers."

Individualism is banned. Groupthink dominates everything. You can hear it in the arguments they use: "They're such-and-such a group of people." "Those people are like this, or like that." The number one objective is for the members to unite behind a single idea rather than unite in harmony. This single idea, whatever it may be, is kept under strict control.

Compare it to an orchestra. They all have different instruments, which make different sounds. Not all members of the orchestra play all the time—the strings will occasionally pause to wait for the percussionist, and so on. But the orchestra is still able to cooperate, as they're all working from the same sheet music. That's not the case with collective narcissism. Here, it is mandated that all the musicians must play the trumpet.

This coercive mode of thought is very powerful. You must; you have to; it's a requirement; everybody has to do the same thing. Think the same thought. Independent thought is an unnecessary evil, because the agenda has already been written. The most telling warning sign is when you hear somebody say, "We don't need to listen to them. We already have all the answers."

That's all an illusion, of course; nobody has all the answers. But the point is to avoid dialogue, as it has the potential to cause the group to implode.

Anybody who deviates from this will suffer brutal punishment. If you try to sneak off, you'll be seen as a quitter and be mistrusted and disgraced. The group will do anything to prevent its members from breaking with its established norms. If you don't embrace the group's agenda, that makes you evil in their eyes—it's as simple as that. And group members who do this will be punished far more severely than any outsider guilty of the same crime. Does this make logical sense? I'm not sure.

The pressure to exhibit loyalty to the group demands open displays of solidarity. "Go out and tell the world what *we* think." Open displays of adherence to the group's ideas are mandatory, whether they actually make sense to you or not. Passivity is a surefire way to attract censure.

Within the group, people are expected to adhere to an idealized, whitewashed view of the group itself. They genuinely believe they are the only people to see the world for what it really is, and that their opinion is the only reasonable one. Any objectivity is out the window when it comes to collective narcissism. *"We're better than them."* Any legitimate positive will be amplified and exaggerated. Any negative will be suppressed and downplayed.

Collective narcissists display some of the same traits as individual narcissists and so aggression breeds like bacteria in warm weather.

Raging fury is just one ill-formed thought away. The group is extremely testy and irritable and keeps getting into conflicts. The following is useful to keep in mind for anyone who likes to question and discuss political dogma: If you pick on one of them, the whole group will turn on you. It's like walking up to a beehive and punching one of tens of thousands of bees. You might not survive being attacked by their 9,999 friends.

CONSEQUENCES

There's no way you could force your way into a group like this, even if you wanted to. It's too tightly knit. Nobody will care about your contribution as a unique individual. You have to be part of the group to count.

This phenomenon appears here and there in contemporary society. With just about any issue worth discussing—along with a great number that don't merit any kind of attention—we're seeing a pattern emerge in which a certain group acts so deliberately aggressively that it becomes clear that the last thing they really want is debate. What they want is to destroy their imagined enemies.

The enemy could be another group that holds another opinion, or it could be a group that has no opinion at all about the issue in question but has for some reason been singled out as the enemy by the narcissistic collective. The enemy could also be individuals who may or may not actually have taken some controversial stand or who haven't actually opened their mouths at all but are unfortunate enough to belong to the wrong group. If they get picked up by the swarm's radar, they could be done for.

CAN YOU DO ANYTHING ABOUT THIS?

Let's assume you know yourself well. You know how to stay strong enough in yourself to never resort to behavioral narcissism, and you don't go around making enemies. Does that mean you're safe?

No, because you're still living in the same world as the rest of us. It's hard to resist this cultural development if you don't pay close attention.

I warned you earlier not to challenge a true narcissist. The same advice applies here. Create distance and then maintain it. Don't take unnecessary risks. If you'd like to go over that advice again, you'll find it in chapter 16, "Breaking Free from a Narcissist."

However, you should also be on the lookout for collective patterns that can sometimes arise spontaneously within the population.

In medieval Europe, many women were tortured and put to death simply because they had been accused of being witches. Today, we marvel over how this could happen and shake our heads at the sheer madness of it. But the fact remains that some people managed to convince the public that some women could use witchcraft to ruin harvests or cause ships to sink at sea.

Somebody accused a specific woman and the notorious witch trial was performed: She was thrown into a lake with her hands tied behind her back. The reasoning was that if she really was a witch, the lake would refuse to take her and she would float back up to the surface. If she wasn't a witch, the lake would accept her with open arms. Regardless of the outcome, the woman would die. Whoever came up with that solution was a real class act. More than 150,000 women were murdered before people realized that this wasn't okay.

How can crazy ideas like this take root at all? And why would anybody listen to this kind of madness?

The answer is simply that collective narcissism existed in the past, too. People would unite over some idea, whether logical, fabricated, or simply evil and malicious. They would decide to make this idea their truth. Then they would start eliminating anybody who disagreed.

Disturbed lies are taken as truth, in order to execute power. And nobody dares speak up. The collective has grown so strong at this point that simply asking questions can be dangerous.

These patterns also exist within some of our contemporary political movements. Social media is fertile ground for this kind of behavior.

I'd advise you to be cautious when it comes to groups like this. It can be a good idea to study their claims more extensively before you decide that they sound reasonable. Also, you should pay attention to how any movement treats nonmembers.

Remember, people have always disagreed about various issues. That's not the remarkable part. Basically, the point where things get weird is when a group wants to destroy anybody who disagrees with them. It's unhealthy, it's dangerous, and you want nothing to do with a movement like that. Think what you want, believe what you like, and promote any values that are important to you. What matters here are not the specifics of your chosen way of life. But you should remember that it's unhealthy for a group to begin to view its opponents as subhuman and feel entitled to do anything in its power to destroy them.

That kind of thing can cause wars, bloody revolutions, and tyrannical dictatorships. In Nazi Germany, the Soviet Union, and Maoist China, it led to the mass murder of tens of millions of human beings.

When you start silencing people and making them submit to your demands regarding the words they use, you're already heading for a disaster.

24

How Did We End Up Here?

There are always four sides to a story:
your side, their side, the truth
and what really happened.
—JEAN-JACQUES ROUSSEAU

So far, it definitely seems like the concept of cultural narcissism reflects something real. Let's assume that it is a trend in society. Where did it come from? Did it appear out of nowhere? What's the hen here, and what's the egg?

At some point, this all began when somebody decided that the rules others have to live by didn't apply to them. But when was that, exactly? There are competing theories for how we ended up where we are right now. When it comes to a starting point, I agree with those researchers who have looked for causes all the way back in the 1970s. I can't give you a specific year, as this theory isn't too precise. However, during the 1970s many of the inhibiting and restrictive ideals of the early 1950s were abandoned. Fashion changed as the seventies progressed. Tapered suits gave way to extremely flared trousers and huge spectacles. Loud colors. It's no coincidence that cars were often lime green, bright orange, or deep blue back in the seventies. But regardless of how loud the colors were, they didn't have the aggressive demeanors of the cars we know today.

THE GLAMOROUS SEVENTIES

Somehow, finally, the freedom to be whoever you wanted had arrived.

In my part of the world, the "Old" World if you will, we have in many respects taken after the United States. Much of this began in the fifties and sixties. Women entered the workplace in force, and the service economy underwent explosive growth. Santa Claus began to get more media coverage than Jesus Christ. The economy was booming, and most people were better off than before.

It spread to my part of the world, too. In war-weary old Europe, hope was burning more brightly than ever. Personally, I have mixed feelings about the seventies. I grew up during the Cold War, and I felt a numbing fear of nuclear war as a child. I read of the horrors of Nazi Germany and the Second World War throughout my school years. The successors to this abysmal legacy, communist China and the Soviet Union, were another nightmare altogether.

On the other hand, perhaps it wasn't too strange that people saw better times ahead after the time the world had just spent at rock bottom. Somewhere around this point, people from various groups began to stand up and demand their rights. Black people fought to end discrimination; women started their epic struggle to be judged on equal terms with men. There are many examples of movements that have done a lot of good and set a tone for the future that followed. They made the world a better place.

Of course, this is an extremely, almost unforgivably, abbreviated account of history, but society slowly began to shift from an ethos of conformism to one of nonconformism. Drug culture and hippies in the 1960s. The student revolts of 1968. All highly nonconformist, I'd say.

INTROVERSION FALLS OUT OF FASHION—BRING ON THE EXTROVERTS!

I started school in 1972. At some point during my years of elementary and middle school, our collective focus shifted from introversion to extroversion. I would always talk too much, and my parents kept getting told that although I did well enough in terms of academic performance, I was too talkative. "Could you ask him to stop doing that?" Although it's worth pointing out that it was the teacher who asked the parents to solve the problem (the opposite seems more common today), this pattern changed when we were a little older.

At first, the more extroverted kids would be told to sit still and listen, but as time went by, introverted kids were gradually encouraged to step up and claim more of the space: *"Own the room!"*

I'm afraid I can't say when this happened, but this is the problem, anyway: Extroverts didn't like sitting down and being quiet, and introverts wanted nothing more than to do precisely that. If you ask me, both these views are incorrect. Both approaches discriminated against about half of the kids. The interesting thing, though, is that this shift occurred at all. After teachers previously preached humility, the opposite became the ideal: Everybody was supposed to be engaging in self-promotion.

Is this a consequence of encouraging everybody to invest in themselves? Where I grew up, we saw a shift from a norm of introversion to a norm of extroversion. Now everybody has to do some self-promotion.

THE HUMAN POTENTIAL MOVEMENT

Initially, people fought for specific groups who they felt had suffered from discrimination.

Then the focus shifted to the Human Potential Movement. The purpose of this movement wasn't really to promote any kind of self-admiration; the goal was to promote the utility of introspection.

In California, members of the movement began to hold seminars based on psychologist Abraham Maslow's hierarchy of needs:

1. Physiological needs: food, water, air, shelter
2. Safety needs: security, stability
3. Social belonging needs: family, friends, love
4. Esteem needs: self-esteem, power, recognition
5. Self-actualization needs: becoming anything you want

Maslow suggested early on that nobody could skip any steps along this hierarchy. This issue has been much discussed, but there is reasonable consensus at this point that this is the most promising idea. It's hard to get things done when you don't have food and water. Being afraid won't help you form a social bond. Improving your self-esteem is hard to do without having people around.

In his day, Maslow claimed to have met very few people who were genuinely located at the top level: self-actualization. This makes perfect sense if you consider that self-actualization is a particularly complicated concept, derived from a series of equally complicated points of view.

However, Maslow positioned self-esteem just beneath self-actualization.

Self-actualization is difficult.

Self-esteem is simple in comparison.

As more and more individuals took an increasing interest in their own growth, they replaced the almost hopeless goal of self-actualization with the far more accessible concept of self-esteem. And why shouldn't they? Going over the available literature on this subject, I find endless information and ideas about self-esteem in books, magazines, documentary films, and even children's shows, but precious little about self-actualization.

Maybe Maslow was right, after all. Self-actualization is hard to achieve.

THE EMERGENCE OF THE SELF-HELP INDUSTRY

In the end, the goals for collective growth of the 1960s were abandoned in favor of a more alluring emphasis on the self. The stage was set for self-investment to become the zeitgeist. It was time to make more room for *me* in the world. This is really quite a logical development considering that individualism had never been practiced in any seriously organized form before. We had to try it out sooner or later. In this context, reference is often made to writer Tom Wolfe, who pointed out that "rather than spending our newly won financial gains on improving the world, we spent our money on self-help instead."

One of the big winners here was est (yep, it's a lowercase acronym!), or Erhard Seminars Training. Hundreds of thousands of people spent their hard-earned money on classes promising to teach them how to put themselves first, how to explain to others that we are all ultimately responsible for our own fates and how nobody should ever accept victimhood, as you can always shape your future.

Note: This is *not* narcissism. I'm firmly committed to these ideas myself. I have no doubt whatsoever that we can form our futures as we see fit, as long as we make it our main priority. I'm also fully on board with the notion that the responsibility for my own well-being lies mainly with myself. There are plenty of examples of people who have come to this realization, stopped waiting for the world to come and rescue them, and set to work improving themselves, their families, their occupations, and their lives. So far, this is all uncontroversial stuff.

Self-help is so ingrained in society today that it's hard to say where it begins and ends. School kids are learning yoga. Inmates are taking mindfulness classes. People hire coaches for all kinds of things. To sum the message up in basic terms: You can do it.

The seeds of this can actually be found in one of the bestselling nonfiction books of all time: *Think and Grow Rich* by Napoleon Hill. It was published back in 1937, and some sources claim it has sold an incredible 170 million copies worldwide. In brief, the book claims that a strong mental focus is all you need to achieve anything you want, including curing serious diseases, getting as rich as you could ever want to be, and being universally loved and praised. The sky's the limit, really.

Another huge international literary hit was *The Secret* by Australian author Rhonda Byrne. Since its publication in 2006, it has sold a staggering 30 million copies globally. The message of this book is that you can have anything you want as long as you want it enough. Think about something hard enough, and it will come to pass.

However, on further consideration, one soon realizes that this message is actually a lot older than that. Didn't Jesus say something about *faith moving mountains in the Bible*? Who knows how old it is, really?

In any case, the methods used to achieve maximum happiness and success and become the best version of yourself are constantly changing, and this has nothing to do with the self-help industry. However, there is a trail for us to pick up here, which will take us straight to something that nobody could have predicted.

Because what happens when you want a happy, carefree life but *don't* quite feel like rolling up your sleeves and doing the actual work? When keeping a log of everything you do, eat, and think seems like too much trouble? When you can't quite motivate yourself to organize your messy thoughts, and would just like to have that luxurious, fabulous lifestyle immediately, thank you very much. What then? This is where the vague concept of narcissistic culture starts to become more distinct.

WANTING TO HAVE EVERYTHING FOR NOTHING

The simplest way, I guess, is to just pretend you're already there. It suits narcissists very well to conjure up these visions of success and then try to convince themselves that they have already achieved them. And live as though this were true.

I'm not suggesting that accepting your fate and going on living in misery is somehow a better option. If you manage to identify a problem in your life and decide to solve it, I will be the first to cheer you on.

But reading a book about self-actualization and then putting it down and thinking to yourself that you already knew all that stuff won't do anything for you. You won't see any results unless you start trying out the methods suggested in the book. There will be no improvement, and the problem will remain—assuming it doesn't get worse.

The potential narcissist we all carry a version of inside ourselves is all about the destination, and wouldn't mind skipping the journey.

It's a bit like having easier access to a source of money than is actually good for you. I can borrow money, buy myself a fancy lifestyle, and pretend I earned it all, rather than *actually working* for what I want.

At some point, even somebody with narcissistic tendencies will have to face the fact that there are no free lunches. Whenever you get what you want, you'll always be paying for it in some form or another.

25

Self-Esteem: More Trouble Than You're Worth

Whoever fights monsters should see to it
that in the process he does not become a monster.

—FRIEDRICH NIETZSCHE

I dedicated a significant portion of the earlier chapters of this book to the subject of self-esteem. Let's take a quick look and see if that discussion has any tie-ins with our current circumstances. Essentially, of course, self-esteem being on the rise in the world is good news. People who are content with themselves are healthier, suffer from physical and mental illness less often, live longer, are more productive, and cause fewer problems for other people.

Meanwhile, there is a group who is experiencing increasing unhappiness, a fact that is blamed on social media. The abundance of opportunities social media offers for comparisons with the very best, most attractive, richest, and most popular people on the planet is not necessarily a positive.

In his book *12 Rules for Life: An Antidote to Chaos,* Canadian psychologist Jordan B. Peterson writes that we shouldn't compare ourselves with one another so much as with our own past selves.

Naturally, we can learn many lessons from those who have already achieved success at something.

But this is only true as long as it motivates you and feeds you the energy you need to keep working towards your own goals. There is a real danger that you might demotivate yourself if you keep comparing yourself with those incredibly successful people. It could stifle your future performance, rather than inspire you to improve it. It's easy to imagine that you'll never be as great or successful as them, and if that's the case, you'd be better off competing with your own past self. That way, with a bit of luck, you'll see some change for the better.

The line between these two attitudes is incredibly fine, so keep your wits about you.

And remember to think!

Before the Internet, you might have compared yourself to your brother, neighbor, buddy, or that guy in the next town over who made a fortune doing something or other. Nowadays, we can access information about the absolute elite in any discipline, anywhere in the world. At the simple press of a button, we can find out what the number one practitioner of some craft or another is up to, how much money they've earned, their current lifestyle, exactly how happy their kids are, and so on. It's all available for public viewing. It's like comparing a ten-year-old girl who dreams of being a singer with Beyoncé. Is that comparison inspiring or deflating? If we adopt the wrong attitude at the outset and spend too much time worrying about what others are getting up to, we'll run the risk of suffering full-on burnout. This can, doubtlessly, cause your self-esteem to crumble.

Especially if you keep looking at people who've actually earned their success. That's the main threat to some people's contentment, after all—it would be easier to accept that somebody won a fortune in the lottery.

How can that be easier to accept? Well, basically, because we believe that *we* could win the lottery, too. But that person who spent twenty years working like a maniac, making endless sacrifices along the way, never going to parties, never buying a BMW, but constantly investing everything into the vision they formed and remained true to and then actually going on to be successful, and maybe even famous, making the big money—that person is a serious threat. My own achievements won't look very impressive next to theirs.

STRONG SELF-ESTEEM = SUCCESS IN LIFE?

For the longest time, I believed that this was the case. Now we could certainly define success in a variety of ways. Whether a person thinks of themself as successful is a highly personal matter. I go over the topic of how you might define success for yourself in some detail in my last book, *Surrounded by Setbacks,* so this time around I'll settle for stating that the definition of success will vary depending on whom you ask.

However, there will be interesting insights to consider. Different psychological tools associate an individual's core values with a variety of personal characteristics, and self-esteem is often one of them. A decade or so ago, an extensive study was carried out on subjects from a variety of professions, and my own self-analysis put me somewhere in the middle of the pack. My self-esteem is neither remarkably high nor alarmingly poor. It's fine. Just between you and me, I kind of expected—and hoped—to score higher.

I asked my contact which professional group usually scored the highest for self-esteem. When I was prompted to guess, I suggested that maybe it was elite-level athletes. Or perhaps corporate management at some of the larger or more well-known organizations. Professors holding prestigious positions at esteemed universities. You see, I associated strong self-esteem with actual achievement.

My contact shook her head. The answer was something else entirely: pig farmers. They were, for all practical purposes, extremely content with themselves and felt that they had nothing to prove to anybody. They weren't at all interested in, say, what others might think of their chosen careers. According to this model, high achievers in most areas tend to be individuals with poor self-esteem, who feel that they have a lot to prove. They're never satisfied with anything, so they keep working hard. Is this a good or a bad thing? It's hard to say.

There is some correlation between self-esteem and quality of performance, but studies have shown that we may have gotten the wrong idea about how they are related. It seems that better performances lead to better self-esteem, rather than the other way around. I have to confess that my own assumptions about this were wrong all along. Now, success and achievement certainly aren't everything in life. People can be satisfied with far less, of course. Managing to avoid getting all worked up over nothing can also be taken as a measure of success. And if your self-esteem is strong, you'll probably find it easier to appreciate and be grateful for the things you already have.

Besides, there are other factors at work here that are skewing these results. Young members of the upper classes, for example, tend to have better self-esteem and higher grade point averages than working-class kids. Some individuals who struggle with their self-esteem are poor achievers, but this appears to be caused by childhood issues, such as living with parents who are addicts. Basically, it's difficult to identify any *automatic* connection between strong self-esteem and success.

If a knack for self-admiration alone were a foolproof recipe for success and first-rate performance, young Americans, for example, would be world-class at just about everything they do. Young Swedes would be pretty amazing, too. The numbers don't differ that much.

One study showed that 39 percent of American eighth graders

felt strongly confident that they would pass their math classes, as opposed to just 6 percent of their South Korean peers. However, a comparison between the two populations' actual results reveals that the South Korean kids wiped the floor with their unfortunate American counterparts.

The South Korean kids dominated Swedish kids, too. Student achievement is in decline in the West; meanwhile our kids keep growing increasingly confident each year. I'm happy for them and I wish everybody could feel that way about themselves, but at the same time I worry about their long-term prospects in life. It's hard to forge a career out of walking around feeling content with yourself. Life is probably going to place greater demands on them than that. Perhaps I'm being a bit too critical about this, but either way, this issue is undeniably a complex one.

LET'S BOOST EVERYONE'S SELF-ESTEEM NO MATTER WHAT! WHAT'S THE WORST THING THAT COULD HAPPEN?

The scientific method is our best approach for figuring out causal relations. It allows you to experiment with different kinds of treatment and see what happens. This is where things get really exciting. Because, of course, studies have been carried out on these things, too.

Students whose achievements were average or below average were divided into two groups. Both groups were sent one email each week, which included a homework assignment for them to carry out. Group A received nothing but the assignment. No comments or explanations, just an admonition to "get it done!"

The second group, B, received another email as well, which included messages that were intended to boost their self-esteem. For example, they were informed that people who perform poorly in some context often experience negative thoughts and hopelessness and feel inferior to their fellow students. A reference was made here to a (fictional) study, which suggested that students who had strong self-esteem didn't just get better grades but also managed to maintain a high level of confidence. So, these students were encouraged to hold their heads up high and maintain high levels of self-esteem. Later, they retook the test.

Sometimes it can be good for us to challenge our own preconceived notions. The results, you see, flew in the face of the researchers' expectations.

Group A, who were given nothing but their assignments, achieved more or less the same results as before. No better, and no worse.

Group B, who had received the assignments alongside the weekly confidence-boosting messages, achieved significantly *worse* results. Their scores dropped from 57 points (out of 100) to 37.

Now, some of you may be thinking that group B might have had lower self-esteem *despite* their weekly confidence boost. Perhaps it wasn't very effective? Or maybe they simply didn't buy into what those emails were telling them?

The research team wanted to find out, too.

So, they decided to measure both groups' levels of self-esteem. Strangely enough, the students in group B proved to be feeling very good about themselves. Their self-esteem had improved. Most significantly, they felt better than the first group, A, despite producing a far inferior performance. How can we explain this?

After all, this can't exactly be welcome news to a culture that's so keen to inspire confidence and self-esteem in people.

For the record: I wasn't very impressed when I first read this. You see, I've always been of the opinion that self-esteem is essential for good performance. Feeling good beats feeling bad every day of the week; there's no debating that. And still, I can't help thinking about this.

The aspect that troubles me has to do with how this connects to narcissism.

WHAT CONCLUSIONS SHOULD WE DRAW FROM ALL THIS?

Strong self-esteem, it seems, is something of a double-edged sword. It works very well up to a certain point, after which it can go off the rails.

I can't stress this enough: I am not in any way claiming that we should be wandering around feeling insecure, disliking ourselves, and tearing our own confidence to shreds. All I'm saying is that paying a less excessive amount of attention to yourself and your thoughts isn't necessarily a bad thing. Being able to focus on the well-being of the group and invest time and effort into supporting others isn't necessarily evidence of deep self-loathing.

It should be possible to succeed without having to overcome your own ego every time. After all, that's the whole point of the self-esteem movement. Cultivating your self-esteem has been fashionable for some time now, and I think it's essentially a good thing to accept and like yourself and think of yourself as deserving of a good life. But, as we've seen, there are dangers, some of which can't be overstated.

While working on this book, I discussed the subject of self-esteem with a whole load of people. Occasionally, I would end up in some rather heated debates. Some people seemed to respond with particular rancor: "Oh, we're supposed to go around hating ourselves now, are we? Is that what you're saying?"

No, that's not what I'm saying.

The opposite of obesity isn't anorexia.

There is a whole range of attitudes that lie somewhere between self-hatred and narcissism. Some people do walk around actively disliking themselves, and we need to help them. In any case, you can appreciate yourself without having to indulge in pathological, harmful self-infatuation. As I mentioned earlier, you'll know that you've gone too far when your self-centered focus starts to impact others. That will mean that you're straying dangerously close—or have already crossed the line—to narcissistic behavior patterns. You just might not know it yet.

However, the case can also be made that you've actually gone too far the moment your behavior has consequences for someone else you may care a little about: yourself.

Or, to put a generous spin on it, in case you're recognizing your own behavior in this, perhaps it's not all your own fault that you're in the particular mental state you are in today. There is a narcissistic culture that's gaining ground out there, and many researchers and psychologists are starting to raise the alarm. It's not entirely a matter of individual responsibility.

Who knows? Perhaps you've been encouraged to believe that life will be easy and that you actually do deserve the best of everything, without having to work for it? That no effort at all will ever be required from you, and that the world is terribly unfair for not giving you what you deserve.

Sound familiar?

If it does, you know what we're going to have to do next: take a look at your parents.

26

Normalizing Narcissism

Sometimes people don't want to hear the truth
because they don't want
their illusions destroyed.

—FRIEDRICH NIETZSCHE

At this point, I'd like to remind you what we're doing right now:
We're trying to identify the causes behind what might be a prolifer-
ation of an increasingly narcissistic culture.

A current trend in our part of the world is that first-time parents
tend to be older now than they were a few generations ago. Many
people stay in school longer, take sabbaticals to travel, work for a
few years, or pursue self-fulfillment. Once all that is over and done,
they're ready to move on to starting families. These days, it's not un-
common for first-time parents to be close to the age of forty—an unthinkable state of affairs as recently as the 1950s.

Does any of this really matter, though? If you can keep up in purely
physical terms and if your financial situation is stable, couldn't it
actually prove to be a good thing? It does seem like a much better
option than becoming a parent at seventeen, after all.

And while we must remain open to the truth that there are many
competing views on this, a pattern nonetheless reveals itself: Anyone

who has a child at the age of forty will, naturally, have arranged their life in a specific way. They will have established their routines and a long list of habits, good and bad, that grow increasingly difficult to break as they grow older. A habit you've kept up for twenty years will be far more firmly entrenched than one you picked up six months ago. And, to top it off, a twenty-five-year-old will, on average, have more energy than a forty-year-old. Biologically, we should really be having children by the time we're seventeen or eighteen. Relax! I'm not actually advocating that; I'm simply pointing out that this is what evolution seems to have designed us for.

On the other hand, a forty-year-old is bound to have more life experience. Much more. They'll feel more self-secure and are also more likely to enjoy the financial stability needed to raise a child. They've learned to control their impulses. Hopefully, they've also learned to stay calm even when things get out of control. Small children have a way of making things do that.

What makes an ideal parent? I have no idea.

But I do know that the older you are when you have your first child, the fewer you'll be able to have. When I was a kid, Swedish families had an average of 2.1 children. This number dropped to 1.5 children per family, before rising again, to just over 1.8 children per family. Only children have always been a thing, and they are growing more common. I have one sibling. My parents have three each. Their parents, on average, had six siblings each.

What happened? Historically, a greater number of children was necessary to secure the family's livelihood, but as societies come to enjoy increasing wealth, the number of children born by each woman decreases. You can't argue with the data in this case. Nobody is trying to deny it: Increased wealth equals fewer children.

In addition, almost every child survives childhood nowadays. In the poverty-stricken Sweden of the early twentieth century, it was common for just five out of ten siblings to make it to the age of five.

Child mortality dropped as our society's wealth increased. In Africa, child mortality recently reached the same levels that Europe saw in the 1950s. It's not something we often talk about, but genuine progress has been made in this regard.

Now, you may be wondering what all this has to do with narcissistic culture. One theory might be that parents who have just the one child, rather than five, are more likely to attach a great deal of significance to the well-being of that child—I'm talking about 100 percent of their offspring, after all.

What do people do when they only have one most cherished thing in life?

Naturally, they try to take care of it in the best way possible. They protect it with everything they've got. They have zero tolerance for failure—this might be their only shot at this! So, they listen to their only child, look after them to the best of their ability, and try to satisfy all of the child's needs in a way that would have been unthinkable for parents just a century ago. There simply wouldn't be time for that in a family with ten or more kids.

Consider, then, that many who have been raised by parents who were older than average and tended to their children's every need have grown accustomed to receiving a great deal of attention. Ever since they saw the light of day, they've been surrounded by proof that they are the center of the universe, and there's no doubting how much they matter to their parents. Now they are adults, ready to make their way in the world and pursue happiness on their own terms.

So, what does all this actually have to do with narcissism?

THE DANGERS OF FLYING

During a long flight, my wife and I were in our seats, reading our books. Behind us was a woman, in the middle seat, who was traveling with a child who kept kicking the back of my seat. Anybody who has experienced this particular phenomenon knows that in the end, all you can think about will be those kicks to your seat. My wife turned around and asked the child to stop kicking the seat right this moment.

The kicking ceased immediately.

But the part that interested me was the mother's reaction: I heard her mumbling, "There's no need to be rude about it!" Apparently, asking not to have to endure several hours of being kicked in the back is rude now. I'd like to add that my wife was not at all abrasive about it. She was as calm as ever, although admittedly, her eyes may have been a little . . . intent.

Why didn't the mother react? After all, she probably wouldn't have liked to have someone kick her seat like that. We never interviewed her about this. As we were disembarking the aircraft, however, I noticed her giving us some rather hostile looks. You would have thought we had slapped her child or something.

HOW NARCISSISTIC TENDENCIES ARE NORMALIZED

I have a memory from much earlier, when my daughter came home from day care one day and announced that she was a princess. Stunned, I responded instinctively, "No, sweetheart, you're not."

You might think that there's no harm in indulging your kids and playing along with their ideas that they are princesses, talented soccer stars, influencers, future reality TV stars, YouTube phenoms, or just the most fabulous creatures alive. Why not let them dream of playing for their favorite team, with their favorite star? Or marrying a prince and receiving half the kingdom? What harm could it do?

I agree that it might seem a bit excessive to get worked up over something like that. Until you think about it a little more, that is. Small children soon grow into bigger children. Before you know it, they're teenagers. During the late teens, a rather awkward phase that's rife with narcissistic behaviors begins, and the last thing any parent should want to do is let this get out of hand.

Your objective is for the kids to grow up to be the best versions of themselves they can be. Of course you want them to be strong and independent. But you also don't want to give them the wrong idea and make them think that the world is their oyster. The real paradox is this: How do you give your children everything they need without robbing them of everything in the process?

But let's start at the beginning first.

HOW A SIMPLE T-SHIRT CAN BE
THE BEGINNING OF THE END

Very small children focus exclusively on themselves. Between the ages of two and three, they begin to test boundaries, which marks the beginning of every parent's worst nightmare: the "terrible twos and threes." They throw food around, throw tantrums on supermarket floors, give their siblings less-than-friendly taps to the head with toy trains, burst into tears at the slightest setback, refuse to go to bed, and offer a whole array of other charming displays.

The conventional parental strategy for dealing with this used to be to resist as best you can, supporting each other as much as possible and praying for some higher power to bring this phase to an end. Eventually, the kids grow out of it and return to more acceptable behavior patterns. A parent's job is simply to manage this challenge as best they can, for as long as it lasts.

The last thing you want to do is reinforce the child's unruly defiance. This is why I find myself a little bemused whenever I see a child prance around in a T-shirt with the word "Princess" printed on it. Or "Boss." Or "I call the shots." Or "Badass." Or "Supermodel." Or "Chick Magnet." Or "Future Reality Star." Or even—I'm not making this up—"Spoiled." Why would you want to draw attention to how spoiled your kid is? Not too long ago, that would have been a source of undying shame for any parent. It was the kind of thing people said about *other* people's children. "So-and-so is really spoiled." It was never a compliment.

I get it. The point of those T-shirts isn't to produce a generation of spoiled children. And it seems evident that many people find a moderate helping of attitude to be quite adorable in a child. What harm could it possibly do? It's not as though the children themselves understand that there's anything strange about it. The target market for those T-shirts is really the parents. And some of the T-shirts are actually quite funny.

However, let's discuss the one that had "Princess" emblazoned across the chest. Let's say your daughter spends her entire childhood being told she is a princess, who ought to be regarded and treated as one . . . At what age exactly do you expect that she will spontaneously conclude that this is not a suggestion that she is actually the long-lost heir to the throne of some far-off land? Or how about this: Assuming your daughter really *is* a princess, does that make you a king or queen? Perhaps all it makes you is a useful and loyal subject, bound to honor the princess's every wish?

WHAT'S FOR DINNER?

A few years ago, I was in the supermarket, wracking my brain and trying to remember what, if anything, was missing from our fridge back home. Next to me was a young father. His three-year-old was crawling around on the floor.

The dad asked his kid, "What should we have for dinner tonight?"

I presumed the question was a rhetorical one, or that he was simply thinking out loud. Suddenly, the boy said, "Hot dogs!" His father gazed at him in disappointment, sighed heavily, and wandered over to the refrigerator with the hot dogs. Whenever I think of this memory, I react the same way as I did at the time: Why on earth is a three-year-old deciding what the family eats for dinner?

My parents, who were kind, friendly, and caring in every imaginable way, would never have dreamed of putting my sister and me in charge of the menu. If we weren't in the mood for dumpling stew, that was tough, and we got dumpling stew all the same. Naturally, this didn't stop us from occasionally wishing that Dad would bring home a nice pork roast for Friday night. But if he didn't, dumpling stew it was.

Twenty years later, I was a parent myself. One of my own specialties is spaghetti Bolognese. While my children were growing up, the whole family used to eat it. Only as an adult did my son, who is a chef today, reveal to me that he had never really liked my Bolognese. That was disappointing to hear, of course, but he didn't seem to have suffered any serious trauma from eating it.

These days, many families cook one, two, or even three different meals for dinner, because of their children's particular wants and preferences. Homes are becoming more like high-end restaurants. Some families seem to think that the idea of everybody eating whatever is served is an outlandish concept.

"Would you like me to cut your sandwich for you? Do you want the crusts removed, or would you like it whole? Tell me how you want me to make it, or if maybe you'd prefer something else? I could make that for you, of course."

"Hold on!" somebody will no doubt interject. "Why shouldn't the kids get to say what they want to eat?"

Of course, they can. What they *want* to eat. But they aren't necessarily experts on what they *should* eat.

According to all available data, seven-year-olds tend not to be up to date on the most recent developments in nutritional science and can't really be expected to know why they should bother eating broccoli. Minerals, vitamins, and antioxidants are not very familiar concepts to them. Perhaps they like ketchup. Ketchup, however, is not a vegetable. The broccoli ends up being left on their plate because they find it hard work to eat.

Mom and Dad are exhausted by the challenges of their days and dreading the prospects of having to argue their way through another dinner. The kids, on the other hand, have nothing better to do. Their minds aren't preoccupied with any plans to read emails or get a load of laundry done before bedtime. They might even be looking forward to a refreshing round of the broccoli versus ketchup wars.

So, you give in. It's only human. I did it, too, although I've since come to believe I was wrong. It seems to me that everybody does their best as parents. However, doing this teaches the children that what they want comes first. Just like narcissists, they're not going to back down. The same arguments can be made about all kinds of things: food, what to wear, when to go to bed, and what to watch on TV. In many families, the kids get to pick everyone's Friday night entertainment. Adults and children alike end up watching Disney movies.

Nowadays, children get involved in family purchases to an extent that would have been unimaginable just twenty years ago. Vacation destinations. Christmas celebrations. What car to own. I'm not making this up. It's becoming increasingly common. Eleven-year-olds hold sway over purchasing decisions involving thousands of dollars.

Naturally, people who give in to their kids in these situations aren't thinking *it would be neat to have a kid who is a narcissist*. But there has to be some limit to what a parent is willing to accept. The question, of course, is where to draw the line.

I'm not going to pretend to know the answer to that. I probably made countless mistakes myself as a parent. All I can do here is indicate some of the risks involved in handing children too much power. Sometimes the responsibilities we give them can be quite significant. Maybe they should just get to be kids for a while?

It seems unlikely that anybody can say for certain what the outcome would be if children were given too much influence or control. It's complicated.

HELICOPTER PARENTS!

The term "helicopter parents" has seen increasing use in the last thirty years or so, and so I thought I'd go over it briefly. It has often been suggested that making things too easy for your children spoils them and leaves them unprepared for life. If a boy becomes a man without ever having faced adversity, how will he cope? When adults continue to behave like children, their behavior is regarded as narcissistic. So, the hypothetical question here is this: Is there any danger that a certain parenting style might exacerbate existing narcissistic dispositions in a child?

One theory suggests that what we ought to do is take care of our children, nurture them, and protect them from obvious dangers—but not at the expense of training them for the challenges in life. They need to be prepared for anything the world throws at them, basically. One small step at a time.

The other approach is to do everything in our power to protect our children; after all, they're small, they're fragile, and they could suffer if we make them face a challenge before they are ready for it. They should be protected from all the ills of the world, for as long as it is possible. Eventually, they are bound to have to make their way in the world and overcome the dangers it involves.

So, which is it? Do we need to hover over our kids, or is that the worst thing we could do to them?

Parents used to be a lot more authoritarian. Traditional values like punctuality, hard work, loyalty, and protecting your family were still quite important. For better and for worse. Grown-ups respected children far less, physical discipline was still a thing, and kids were in danger of becoming withdrawn and inhibited. Kids were supposed to do as they were told, and when conflicts arose parents weren't expected to reason with them. People were generally more confident in their roles as parents, and much more aware of the values they wanted to instill in their children.

Parents today have a more democratic approach. Swedish parents, for example, reason with their children more than parents of any other nationality. Some people call this the intellectualizing approach to parenting. It often involves treating children as though they are far more mature than they actually are.

How many parents have successfully talked their kids into going to bed by lecturing them on five-year-olds and their need for sleep? I couldn't guess. How much good will it do to debate the utility of tying your shoelaces when it's snowing outside and your four-year-old is already jumping up and down in the hall? Hard to say. Who can actually negotiate snack times with kids who know the cupboard is full of treats? No idea.

CULTIVATING BLINDLY

Is it so wrong, then, to give in to your child's wishes and demands? As usual, a research-based consensus has proven elusive here.

For example, a Danish study suggests that children who receive excessive helicoptering at home don't actually fare worse in life, at least not in terms of *subjective well-being*. That makes sense. The children who are best prepared appear to be those who were helicoptered to some degree by their parents but who also had to help out with a lot of chores around the house. A study like this will no doubt be received with a sigh of relief by many, as it offers partial confirmation that helping your kids won't necessarily do them harm.

We should slow down at this point and make sure we've got our concepts straight.

Helping your kids is a given, of course. Any parent who won't help their children is a pretty bad mother or father. But offering a reasonable degree of help isn't quite the same thing as eliminating *all obstacles*. The problem arises when we help our children so much that they never get a chance to learn to take care of themselves. There's always a middle ground between being overprotective and being neglectful. Should you prepare a sandwich for a two-year-old? Probably. At what age should you expect them to make their own sandwiches? Three? Five? Twelve? You have to draw the line *somewhere*.

How do things look towards the end of life? Here, we get the occasional reminder of what it was like to be a kid. In geriatric care, there is a common and pretty healthy philosophy: They say you should never do anything for somebody if they could do it themselves. Why not? Because it robs them of a great deal of their dignity. It disempowers the patient, who may stop trying altogether as a result. It can actually weaken their lust for life. This means, then, that being too helpful can in fact be harmful. Let them handle what they can on their own. Don't deprive them of their right to master their own worlds. When they aren't coping, intervene and give them your support. Of course. But if it's not necessary, it's undignified.

Is there some reason why we should be treating our children differently? Should we allow them to cultivate their confidence as far as possible, by encouraging them to take responsibility for themselves? For what it's worth, I find myself leaning this way.

Now, we're not talking about making five-year-olds get out and change the tires in pouring rain; we're talking about teaching them about cooperation and how to function as members of a family. The slice of society they are familiar with. To some extent we're also actually talking about the fact that your seven-year-old is perfectly capable of making a sandwich. They probably know what the process involves.

Not providing children with the things they need, however, is a sensitive topic, and discussions are prone to get heated. I'll probably get criticized for writing this, but it's only to be expected. However, if you feel provoked by this, you should know that it's actually a good thing that this is ruffling your feathers; that means that you're taking this seriously. But you need to consider the whole picture before you make up your mind.

Some—although far from all—psychologists I know promote the idea that children are equally capable as adults when it comes to knowing what they need. They just don't know it yet—the parents, that is!

Go back and read that sentence one more time.

The kids know what they need as well as their parents do.

How does this attitude make you feel? Perhaps this knowledge is somehow magically preprogrammed in them? If that were actually the case, maybe we would have sent them out to work instead of encouraging them to draw stick figures all day.

THE DANGERS OF RESTAURANT DINING

I'm sure this sounds familiar to you: You've gone to a restaurant with your family. Perhaps it's a special occasion. You're enjoying yourselves; the food is great, and the service is everything you'd expect from an upscale establishment.

There is a couple with a child at another table. This kid—let's say it's a two-year-old—has come to this restaurant to explore! They're running around and making sure to take in all the sights. Soon, they start to yank at things and wander around among the tables, emitting loud exclamations of delight over everything there is to see.

The first shriek of glee startles you, as you weren't expecting to hear that particular sound in a restaurant. Your husband or wife has already scoped the situation out and nods discreetly towards your right. That's where the culprits are seated.

But maybe that horrific yell was a one-off thing. Surely, things are bound to quiet down in a moment. You don't quite believe yourself as you think this, however, and your instincts soon prove correct. The adorable little thing starts running around the tables and hollering again. The parents are so used to this noise that they hardly even react.

Eventually, one of them gets up and herds the escapee back to their table. This marks the beginning of the true mayhem, however: The whole restaurant gets to enjoy the sounds of a violent tantrum followed by a torrent of tears.

If things get really bad, the parent who tried to resolve the situation will be overcome by the ferocity of this assault, and will simply release the child back to the floor. Whereupon the whole scene will repeat itself. Now, imagine the same thing happening repeatedly throughout this child's early years and teens. Nobody is able to deal with this individual. Things simply turn out the way they turn out. Everybody plays along in order to keep things nice and simple.

Narcissistic tendencies have been brought to life and nurtured. This isn't mere speculation on my part; this is exactly how the narcissistic child is going to behave once they're grown up.

TEARS—EVERY PARENT'S NIGHTMARE

Who can stand to see or hear a crying child? Our every instinct screams at us to pick them up, hug them, and tell them that whatever is troubling them will soon go away. However, if a child is never told no, there is a danger that their endearing little requests for treats on Tuesday evenings will evolve into an entitled expectation to be gifted a car in just a few years.

Is it okay to tell your child not to do something that they shouldn't do or that they can't have something they're asking for? Are children ruined for life if they have to endure a single moment of disappointment? Could they actually even learn an important lesson from it? When you tell them they can't drink Coca-Cola with their dinner, the message will get through after a while.

I'm only saying this with such confidence because I've gone to the trouble of looking at the findings of child psychology researchers, rather than relying on mere opinion. There is endless documentation in support of the notion that all this is real. But it can certainly be a touchy subject.

BACK TO THE NIGHTMARE AT THE RESTAURANT

Imagine if the child's mother or father had immediately told them to sit back down as soon as they left their chair? That's how you behave in a restaurant, right? Now, imagine that the child had already learned that there's no point in debating the matter, has grown comfortable with these firmly established boundaries, and is now at ease, free to investigate the contents of their dinner plate.

Some of you are probably amazed that there are people who don't get this. All you have to do is set boundaries for your kid. Make a time investment, at home, over the course of a few months, and then it'll be smooth sailing from that point on. People have been doing it for millennia; why wouldn't it work today?

Other readers might be thinking that there's no way I've ever been in close contact with a two-year-old. What two-year-old can sit still for hours on end? No upbringing, no matter how perfect, can ever defy nature.

Fair enough. But in that case, maybe you should consider waiting to go to a restaurant until you've worked this stuff out?

An American study revealed that around 80 percent of the population felt that children were far too spoiled in general. Amusingly enough, a third of respondents also felt that *their own* children were spoiled. How about that!

As I mentioned earlier, I'm no psychologist. On the other hand, you don't need to be a meteorologist to explain a thunderstorm. What we're still looking for here is an explanation for the increase in narcissism we're witnessing. It has to originate somewhere, after all.

MAYBE PARENTS JUST SUCK

Every generation of parents that ever lived has been given a hard time over something or other that they got horribly wrong. My own grandparents were quite tough and demanding. They've certainly received their share of censure over that. But still, they managed to raise a reasonably functional generation—my parents—that grew up to be far nicer, more agreeable, and much more permissive than my grandparents. That generation, in turn, has been heavily criticized for what they did to their kids. Us. My own generation is even more permissive, sensitive, and inclusive. But only a fool could expect to escape history's judgment. In fifty years, it'll be our turn to be the idiots who didn't get it.

How will my own children be raising my grandchildren? I don't have the faintest idea. Perhaps the next generation will simply leave their kids out in the yard and let nature take its course. They won't have any influence over anything anyway. All they did was have the children—what do they know? Whatever they do, they'll end up being told how wrong it was.

All jokes aside, being a parent has never been a walk in the park. And everybody has their own idea of how it should or shouldn't be done. Maybe that's inevitable when what we're talking about is the most precious thing we have: our children. We didn't bring them into this world just so we could neglect them. The authoritarian parents of old, who felt no obligation to explain anything at all to their kids, have had to make way for a more modern, responsive approach to raising children.

But as we've seen, we can get too much of good things like responsiveness. If you don't fully understand all the different aspects of a certain issue, it makes it difficult for you to make wise decisions about it.

POWER CORRUPTS ABSOLUTELY?

In child psychology, the subject of power is sometimes mentioned, often in combination with the notion of abuses of power.

Naturally, parents hold power over their children. They feed and house them. If you can't exercise power, there's really no way you can be a parent at all. Anything less would simply result in endless negotiations.

And if nobody is allowed to hold power over anybody else, how come we so often see children exercising power over their parents? Are the less competent parties really supposed to hold authority over the more competent ones? Personally, I can't make any sense of it.

It's like asking a new employee at the factory to instruct the CEO and owners on how they should be running the business. He could be a genuine, stand-up guy—he could even smell great! Maybe he's actually up to the task? Now, competence or the lack thereof has nothing to do with the value you assign to a particular person. There's no connection between the two. Everybody has value, of course, but not everybody is capable of doing the same things.

Parental authority should be exercised in an intelligent, empathic way, with the objective of ensuring that the child gets what they need.

THE POWER OF CONSISTENCY

While I'm on the topic of power, I thought I might discuss the ultimate form of power: the power of consistency, which I touched on earlier in this book. As I said then, this involves first laying down the ground rules and then sticking to them. Come thunder, hail, or ice, you are going to remain resolutely committed to your original assertion that the kids are not going to be getting any candy Tuesdays. Naturally, you'll have to consider the details of your decree before announcing it; simply uttering whatever nonsense comes to mind and expecting the kids to obey will only prove futile.

Since most people's behavior is glaringly inconsistent, this means that you'll be giving yourself a very strong card to play in interactions with your kids. Think it over. Give a response. Stick to it. It's so simple that it's almost ridiculous. But heaven knows, it isn't easy!

You also have the authority to do things the children don't get to do. Let's say you snuck yourself a piece of chocolate right before dinner. Your child notices, and demands a piece of chocolate, too— you got one, didn't you? Although you've admittedly made a bit of a mess of the situation, you can still say no. There's no need for any negotiations. You're the adult. You're allowed. Maybe you shouldn't really, but you're still *allowed*. It's always your responsibility. You enjoy different privileges than the children. You get to vote. You get to drive a car. You get to buy alcohol. You get to smoke. You even get to make more children. You're the adult. *You're allowed*.

The idea that children are somehow harmed or traumatized for life by being refused privileges that adults are afforded seems strange to me. I've searched but have not yet found any research to support that idea.

Do we really need to be reflecting on whether it would be abusive of us to fail to give our children the maximum amount of agency and influence we possibly can? This is worth considering. Saying that children, young children in particular, have a limited capacity for understanding situations isn't the same thing as calling them completely useless, or less valuable than adults. Once again, these are entirely separate things.

As I see it, you have to keep your sense of a person's inherent value separate from your intellectual realization that this is an individual, of flesh and blood, who has their own particular blend of strengths and weaknesses.

Stay in control of your parenting. Be the adult. You're entitled to call the shots in your own home. You're entitled to use the simple but oh so useful word "no." It doesn't mean you love your children any less. It might even mean you love them more.

If we adults aren't prepared to set boundaries for how we all cooperate to help society progress, who will? If you think I'm blowing this out of proportion, you could be right. But consider the alternative: Imagine a world in which everybody thinks of themselves as number one. How could that world even function at all?

27

Test Yourself: Are You a Narcissist?

*In each of us there is another
whom we do not know.*

—CARL JUNG

The time has come for us to move on. After my discussion of cultural narcissism, you may have found yourself asking a natural question: *What if I'm a narcissist?*

What if you are? This is a good question, and I should let you know up front that we all possess these traits to some degree—the question is simply to what degree.

But does that make you a *narcissist* per se?

Maybe it does, a little, anyway. I don't suspect for a moment that you're really a narcissist in the clinical sense. It's highly unlikely that you would ever be diagnosed with narcissistic personality disorder. I've already shown you the general criteria for a clinical diagnosis of narcissism. You probably recognized at least one or two of the criteria in yourself, and that can be enough to give some people pause. But just as nobody can deny that they sometimes procrastinate, or get too pre-occupied with something to be able to listen properly, or take the last bit of chocolate when nobody else is around, nobody can truthfully deny that they occasionally exhibit narcissistic behaviors. This is a complex issue.

You're about to take the test that psychologists have been using to identify narcissistic traits for several decades now. This test is probably less than perfect, and it has detractors who claim it isn't fit for its intended purpose. But it *can* help us identify narcissist tendencies in people who wouldn't necessarily be diagnosed as full-on narcissists. In all likelihood, your personality does have a narcissistic element or two—but in order to be diagnosed with narcissism, you'd have to exhibit more of them, and more often. Sometimes you simply have to accept that you're not a saint; the benefit in doing so is that it can help you better appreciate your true potential.

THE TEST

Time to end the speculation and actually take the test! (It begins on the next page.) Choose the option that you identify with the most for each dual choice. If you happen to identify with both options, choose the one you find the most important.

Below are some average scores from studies conducted in the United States.

SAMPLE	SCORE
US University Undergraduates (Raskin and Terry, 1988)	15.6
US Adults (Pinsky and Young, 2009)	15.3
US Celebrities (Pinsky and Young, 2009)	17.8

THE NARCISSIST TEST

I have a natural talent for influencing people.	☐ 1 point
I am not good at influencing people.	☐ 0 point
Modesty doesn't become me.	☐ 1 point
I am essentially a modest person.	☐ 0 point
I would do almost anything on a dare.	☐ 1 point
I tend to be a fairly cautious person.	☐ 0 point
When people compliment me I sometimes get embarrassed.	☐ 0 point
I know that I am good because everybody keeps telling me so.	☐ 1 point
The thought of ruling the world frightens the hell out of me.	☐ 0 point
If I ruled the world it would be a better place.	☐ 1 point
I can usually talk my way out of anything.	☐ 1 point
I try to accept the consequences of my behavior.	☐ 0 point
I prefer to blend in with the crowd.	☐ 0 point
I like to be the center of attention.	☐ 1 point
I will be a success.	☐ 1 point
I am not too concerned about success.	☐ 0 point
I am no better or worse than most people.	☐ 0 point
I think I am a special person.	☐ 1 point
I am not sure if I would make a good leader.	☐ 0 point
I see myself as a good leader.	☐ 1 point
I am assertive.	☐ 1 point
I wish I were more assertive.	☐ 0 point
I like to have authority over other people.	☐ 1 point
I don't mind following orders.	☐ 0 point

The Narcissist Test continued

I find it easy to manipulate people.	☐ 1 point
I don't like it when I find myself manipulating people.	☐ 0 point
I insist upon getting the respect that is due me.	☐ 1 point
I usually get the respect that I deserve.	☐ 0 point
I don't particularly like to show off my body.	☐ 0 point
I like to show off my body.	☐ 1 point
I can read people like a book.	☐ 1 point
People are sometimes hard to understand.	☐ 0 point
If I feel competent I am willing to take responsibility for making decisions.	☐ 0 point
I like to take responsibility for making decisions.	☐ 1 point
I just want to be reasonably happy.	☐ 0 point
I want to amount to something in the eyes of the world.	☐ 1 point
My body is nothing special.	☐ 0 point
I like to look at my body.	☐ 1 point
I try not to be a show-off.	☐ 0 point
I will usually show off if I get the chance.	☐ 1 point
I always know what I am doing.	☐ 1 point
Sometimes I am not sure of what I am doing.	☐ 0 point
I sometimes depend on people to get things done.	☐ 0 point
I rarely depend on anyone else to get things done.	☐ 1 point
Sometimes I tell good stories.	☐ 0 point
Everybody likes to hear my stories.	☐ 1 point
I expect a great deal from other people.	☐ 1 point
I like to do things for other people.	☐ 0 point

The Narcissist Test continued

I will never be satisfied until I get everything that I deserve.	☐ 1 point
I take my satisfactions as they come.	☐ 0 point
Compliments embarrass me.	☐ 0 point
I like to be complimented.	☐ 1 point
I have a strong desire for power.	☐ 1 point
Power for its own sake doesn't interest me.	☐ 0 point
I don't care about new fads and fashions.	☐ 0 point
I like to start new fads and fashions.	☐ 1 point
I like to look at myself in the mirror.	☐ 1 point
I am not particularly interested in looking at myself in the mirror.	☐ 0 point
I really like to be the center of attention.	☐ 1 point
It makes me uncomfortable to be the center of attention.	☐ 0 point
I can live my life in any way I want to.	☐ 1 point
People can't always live their lives in terms of what they want.	☐ 0 point
Being an authority doesn't mean that much to me.	☐ 0 point
People always seem to recognize my authority.	☐ 1 point
I would prefer to be a leader.	☐ 1 point
It makes little difference to me whether I am a leader or not.	☐ 0 point
I am going to be a great person.	☐ 1 point
I hope I am going to be successful.	☐ 0 point
People sometimes believe what I tell them.	☐ 0 point
I can make anybody believe anything I want them to.	☐ 1 point
I get upset when people don't notice how I look when I go out in public.	☐ 1 point
I don't mind blending into the crowd when I go out in public.	☐ 0 point

The Narcissist Test continued	
I am a born leader.	☐ 1 point
Leadership is a quality that takes a long time to develop.	☐ 0 point
I wish somebody would someday write my biography.	☐ 1 point
I don't like people to pry into my life for any reason.	☐ 0 point
I am more capable than other people.	☐ 1 point
There is a lot that I can learn from other people.	☐ 0 point
I am much like everybody else.	☐ 0 point
I am an extraordinary person.	☐ 1 point
	total _____

What's your score? I'm prepared to admit to scoring 14 points, which makes me average, more or less. To qualify as a narcissist, a score of over 25 points is required. If you score 30, you can rest assured that your friends find you to be hard work from time to time. Over 30? Hm. I actually find it hard to believe anybody would ever score over 30, for a very simple reason: I find it hard to believe that a genuine narcissist would actually respond truthfully to these questions.

Again, note that this score is only to be viewed as an indication. Whether you actually are a narcissist or not is a matter that only a qualified psychologist could resolve.

WHAT MIGHT YOU USE THIS INFORMATION FOR?

It can let you know when you're at risk of behaving in ways that might make you unpopular with others. If, on the other hand, you couldn't care less what other people think, you're probably not a narcissist after all.

If your score is higher than you'd like, you might want to spend some time thinking about why this might be.

HOW "WHO YOU ARE" CAN ALTER YOUR EXPERIENCE

Naturally, who you are is going to have a significant impact on how you assimilate the contents of this book. However, it will also influence your interpretations of whether or not there are signs that you're at risk of slipping into narcissistic behavior patterns. Perhaps you know what your colors are; perhaps you don't. If you'd like to learn more about how other people perceive you and how you actually function on a deeper level according to the DISC model, you can download the Surrounded by Idiots app and perform a simplified analysis of yourself (or of anybody you meet).

Having more information about your color can help you interpret the results of the test you just took. Different colors tend to assess the different questionnaire options slightly differently, and this is something that is rarely factored into the design of tests like these.

For instance, take this statement:

I have a natural talent for influencing people.

And the statement that it's supposed to be weighed against:

I am not good at influencing people.

A narcissist wouldn't hesitate for a second before determining that option 1 is clearly the superior one—and go on to choose it for that exact reason. Score a point for narcissism, then. But is influencing other people really a good thing or a bad thing in and of itself? Well, that depends.

If we're talking about negative influence, like manipulating or deceiving others into doing things they don't really want to do, then yes, it's a bad thing. But if we're talking about encouraging people to make positive changes, that's a completely different matter. It could actually help someone turn their life around. They might stop drinking at the weekends, start working out, start treating their significant other better, or whatever it may be. This means, then, that we can't really say that there's anything inherently negative about the ability to influence others.

However, the fact that somebody thinks of themselves as a powerful influencer is still telling.

To take another example:

The thought of ruling the world frightens the hell out of me.

As opposed to:

If I ruled the world, it would be a better place.

Suppose you respond like most people alive today would do and pick option one. Ruling the world ought to be a daunting prospect to most. But if your response was the second option, that the world would be a better place with you at its helm . . . well, score a point for narcissism.

The problem here is that you might actually be right. There definitely are people whom we would prefer to see in charge of the world—and who would make it a better place if they were! However, those most suited for the task are also very likely to turn down the offer to take it on. The greatest leaders, you see, possess a large measure of humility.

If you ask people from different parts of the world who their role models are as leaders, the responses you get will naturally vary from one continent to the next. However, a name that is universally mentioned, a person whom everybody always seems to appreciate, is Nelson Mandela, the former president of South Africa. Would the world be a better place today if he had been more influential during his lifetime? My highly unqualified guess is that *yes, it would*.

The interesting thing, though, is how Mandela would have responded to the offer.

It seems very likely that even Nelson Mandela would have been terrified at the prospect of wielding that much power. This, then, is our challenge: to separate an individual's real abilities from their own assessments of them. A narcissist is always going to say that things would be better if everyone did as they said. Whether they actually have the skills required to lead doesn't factor into it.

My suggestion to you is that you go over all the questions one more time and make sure you answered them accurately. This might even teach you a thing or two about yourself.

NOW, WHAT DOES ALL THIS HAVE TO DO WITH MY COLORS?

Your confidence will vary depending on your color. Reds and Yellows both tend to exhibit very high levels of confidence. They have strong egos, and basically expect to be up to most challenges they come across.

Yellows don't think too much; they trust their intuition. "I'll have fun ruling the world—just think of all the new, important friends I'll make!"

Reds usually don't really care what other people think. But if they really think they might make a difference and help the planet, they'd give it a go. They are risk takers, after all, and they'll figure that they'll manage to deal with any mishaps that occur along the way.

Greens tend to have less faith in their abilities. They would certainly be hesitant to take on a challenge like this. Sometimes there's just no way you could get a Green to admit that they're good at anything at all. Least of all ruling the world.

Blues are self-critical. All they see, wherever they look, including inside themselves, is flaws and imperfections. I doubt they would be prepared to pick option two without doing a lot of serious soul-searching first.

Again: What we're measuring here isn't really their abilities per se, but rather the individual's estimation of themselves and their abilities.

So, what are your colors? Do you feel that they influenced your responses to the questions?

IF YOU STILL THINK YOUR SCORE IS TOO HIGH

Let's say that after giving it some thought, you're still uncomfortable with how high your score is. Maybe you feel that there are things in your life that look like they're headed in the wrong direction and you're not happy with your behavior overall. If this is the case, you're very insightful, and I can only congratulate you for your maturity.

Self-esteem is beneficial for the individual. I discussed that earlier. Nobody wants people to dislike themselves and be unhappy with who they are. But as with so many things, this is only true up to a certain point. The matter of *whether it's possible to like yourself too much* is one that's worth serious consideration. As we saw earlier, you can get too much of a good thing. An excessive focus on the self can cause people to exhibit behaviors along the narcissistic spectrum.

In our society, our focus has shifted gradually from the needs of the collective to the needs of the individual. This may actually date back all the way to the Renaissance. I'd be surprised if we'd seen the worst of it, too. I'm not seeing any signs that the trend is slowing down right now.

QUICK VERSUS LONG-TERM GAINS

Since being a narcissist brings short-term benefits, our own impatience will always encourage us to seek immediate solutions. We want instant gratification. Nobody has the patience to wait for anything anymore. The downsides to narcissistic behavior are never obvious from the start—it can take years before a narcissist is exposed. But by then, it might be too late.

Good habits are hard to cultivate but easy to live with. Bad habits, on the other hand, are easy to cultivate and hard to live with. The thing about bad habits is how often we mistake them for good habits at first. The negative effects don't come about until later. Years later, sometimes.

Why do some people steal supplies from their workplaces? Is it because they can't afford to buy their own screwdrivers or pencils? The stocks run out, and then when my coworkers need a pencil they're all gone! It's a shortsighted, immoral way to behave. But all the same, many do it. Not you, of course, but other people have allegedly done that kind of thing.

Why do people eat too much fast food? It's not because they hold some deep desire to be overweight. The answer is short-term gratification. It can take years before you suddenly realize that your pants no longer fit in the waist. Despite this, we choose pizza over salad a little more often than we ought to.

Some people drink too much. The reason for this is probably not that they've formed a deliberate intention to ruin their lives—it's just that the alcohol gives them relief in the moment. The hangover will be harsh. In theory, you could have made a fool of yourself in front of the whole company. The long-term consequences of drinking too much, as we all know, can actually be far worse than that. And yet many of us consistently allow ourselves one or two drinks more than we should.

Compulsive gamblers exhibit the same disturbing psychological mechanisms. You start out just giving an online casino a try, because you heard about how somebody hit the jackpot and was able to quit their job. So you bet twenty dollars or so. The excitement of playing and the anticipation of winning the jackpot are captivating. Maybe you even win a little at first. This encourages you to make another bet, and before you can spell "debt collector" you're wagering hundreds of dollars every night. Not you, of course! I know you wouldn't do that. *Other* people.

Good habits are hard to cultivate but easy to live with.

Bad habits are easy to cultivate but hard to live with.

It's a similar story with narcissism. It's self-destructive in the same way that gambling, adultery, drinking, and the like are. Think of it as a trap with a time delay—it doesn't spring until much later. The effects of focusing exclusively on yourself and ignoring everyone else might seem to be all positive at first. Taking everything for yourself is the same thing as stealing from others. It's also like stealing from your own future self. This can be pretty hard to pick up on.

Is there something we can do about this? Having to step out of the spotlight isn't going to appeal to everybody, but as long as you're not a clinical narcissist with a full NPD diagnosis, there's still hope for you!

HUMILITY AS A CURE

I can remind myself of the long-term effects of focusing exclusively on myself. True contentment is only awarded to those who are able to refrain from focusing on themselves all the time. Think of the greatest names in history. All the most important people promoted the opposite of narcissism by publicly preaching the virtues of generosity and humility.

Nelson Mandela.

Mother Teresa.

Martin Luther King Jr.

Mahatma Gandhi.

To mention just a few. These people's names are immortal. They and their deeds have forever left their mark on history. But they weren't motivated by some drive to be famous, or even memorable.

This topic connects in specific ways to our nervous system and its neurotransmitters. Serotonin is a neurotransmitter that causes you to experience a sense of pride and elevated status. Whenever you feel important or acknowledged, you receive a dose of serotonin. That's why so many of us value public recognition so highly. It's also necessary, to some extent, for us to feel accepted by our peers.

That's why big award ceremonies are so important. When you graduate from school or win a sports competition or a singing contest, the point of celebrating your success with a public ceremony is that it's enjoyable—both for the winner and for the audience. If serotonin weren't a part of this picture, we could just have sent a letter that read: "Congrats, you won! Just print out a copy of your certificate using your own printer. Oh, and you should probably sing the national anthem, too."

This is the part that hooks the narcissists. It turns them into attention junkies. They constantly crave more of it, even when they know it might annoy other people. They simply can't help themselves.

In our world, things like status and prestige matter a great deal. How do we display our status and prestige? By indulging in excessive materialism. We buy a more expensive car, a more impressive house, better-looking clothes, with all the right accessories and all the right logos on them. That's why the logo is there, on the outside of your bag. Other people are *supposed* to see it. It's not enough for you to know that the bag was made by so-and-so (insert your own favorite brand). The problem, as anyone who's prone to excessive shopping will know, is this: The high doesn't last long. That is because it lacks any kind of connection to other people. You're not forming relationships with the people who are admiring your new belongings. Most of them are just strangers you meet in town, and what they think doesn't really matter to you. So you end up feeling empty inside, and craving more.

Maybe there's another way you could be expressing yourself. A way that could allow you to get what you truly crave: true appreciation from people who genuinely care about you. That would be a humbler attitude.

Maybe the opposite of narcissism is exactly that: humility. Genuine humility is a great source of strength. The ability to view and assess yourself objectively and exaggerate neither the positives nor the negatives. Truthfully.

Correctly, accurately, and precisely.

Humble people are highly appreciated by others. They tend to find themselves surrounded by people who genuinely care about them.

Humility also means being grateful for what you have. Note: There's nothing wrong with wanting more from life. I have a long list of things I'd like to have, do, and experience. But I also constantly remind myself of the things I already own or have already experienced or done. This doesn't make me a better person, but it does help me maintain a realistic outlook on my life, and ensures I always have something to strive for. As I said earlier, very little in life is free.

Practicing humility, being grateful for what you have, and actively helping others can all be effective ways to counteract any narcissistic tendencies.

THE THREE HAPPY DRUGS

Oxytocin is the neurotransmitter that kicks in whenever you experience emotions like love, trust, friendship, and caring. Oxytocin releases can be triggered by a variety of means. One of the simpler ones is physical touch. This is one of the reasons why hugging somebody can feel so good—it can give you a genuine buzz.

Neuroscience has already taught us that we can get a kick out of helping others. Try doing something friendly and helpful for somebody who *has no way to reciprocate*. Make note of how you feel afterwards. I can promise you this: You'll be feeling good—it did feed you a dose of oxytocin, after all! Free of charge! The great advantage to this is that your body is actively encouraging you to repeat behaviors that make you feel good. The more oxytocin you have flowing through your body, the more generous you'll be to your fellow human beings.

Perhaps the question is this: *Why* do you want to feel good?

Self-promotion is one thing. Humility is another. Both of them can produce a high, then.

The most serious risk you'll be running is having an infinite supply of genuine admirers. I imagine you might be able to learn to live with that.

One way of practicing humility is to reconsider your material needs. Do you really need a new car every three years? Do we need to replace all the furniture every five years? Is it necessary to buy a new smartphone every six months? Could you maybe make do with this coat for a little longer?

The images you post of yourself on social media—who are you really doing it for? Is it for yourself? Or is it for somebody else? Does it really detract from your value if you don't receive public acknowledgment from your peers every day? Could you perhaps get by on acknowledgment you receive from the people you actually care about?

I sometimes hear the following quote, but I haven't managed to find out who to credit it to: "We buy things we don't need with money we don't have in order to impress people we don't like."

Many have suggested that mindfulness might serve as a counter-weight to this. Or meditation. At a minimum, they might provide inner contentment. That seems worth a try. Learning to meditate isn't difficult at all. And if it can actually bring us inner peace and help us relax, what do we have to lose?

Imagine if we could feel that great, almost every day, without it costing us anything at all.

28

Being the Change

*Every man is guilty of all the good
he didn't do.*

—VOLTAIRE

Too much? Over the top? Maybe. But I do *want* a reaction from you.
I *want* you to give these matters some thought. Genuinely. You see, I
think this stuff is important. Everyone agrees that narcissism is a bad
thing in the long term. Assuming we really are living in a narcissistic
culture, in a society that makes us act and behave in ways that might
not come entirely naturally to us, is there some way we could reverse
this trend?

In the end, you and I are just like everybody else—we all think
about ourselves more than anything else. It's what we do, and we do
it in a multitude of ways.

Let's suppose you're aware of the risks, and that you realize that
you, too, are vulnerable to the danger of focusing too much on yourself. You've accepted the idea that it's not good for the people around
you in the short term, and that it's even bad for yourself in the longer
term. You've decided not to let yourself get carried away by this narcissistic culture. You want to take a stand for something else instead.

That's my main objective in writing this book: to stir something up in those who read it that might cause them to choose an alternative path. Perhaps you could even do some good here? Of course you could, and I'm sure you can find ways to do it that I've never even considered.

GET INSPIRED—BUT THEN WHAT?

When you listen to an inspirational speaker, you become . . . inspired. You feel a rush of energy, a sense that something big is about to happen. I know plenty of people in the industry, and some of them are unbelievably skilled. You feel like you're on top of the world afterwards (even if you haven't made any progress). The problem with this kind of inspiration is that it is entirely dependent on your going home and making something of it afterwards. If you don't get started that very same day, your buzz will start to fade, and the lecture will soon become just another memory.

Inspiration is a good thing. We need it. But we also need to do the things of our own accord. So, where do we start?

With the most natural thing: yourself.

Instead of exclaiming, "I am the greatest!" when you see your reflection in the mirror every morning, cultivate genuine confidence. You do this by managing things by yourself. Genuine confidence can only be created by successfully achieving things on your own. Why not exploit the way nature has designed us?

The idea here is to start off with something minor—perhaps something you've never tried before but would like to learn. You try things out, learning a bit at a time. When you take a step back, you realize that you've accomplished something you were unable to do a week ago.

You've made progress. *Dopamine* gushes forth. You experience a mild rush.

You tell some other people about it, too. They smile at you, because they feel invigorated by what you're telling them. They congratulate you. *Serotonin* kicks in. You feel proud.

Perhaps you choose to teach your new skill to somebody. You see the happiness and gratitude in their eyes. *Oxytocin* time! You feel even better now.

And, come to think of it, things aren't really that bad, are they? Once you've enjoyed all those waves of brain chemicals, how will you be feeling about yourself? Will you appreciate yourself a little more than you did a month ago?

I can guarantee you this: Your *self-esteem* will be stronger now. Perhaps not by much this first time around. But ever so slightly. You'll be feeling better and more comfortable with yourself, for entirely natural reasons. There's nothing artificial or complicated about this.

You feel better. It's genuine.

Also, learn to accept this: There will be times when you'll feel terrible. It's one of the injustices that come part and parcel with living on this unforgiving planet. Every day can't be wonderful. Nobody is happy all the time. Only a fool would imagine that there's some way to avoid feeling down ever again.

But now you know of a simple way you can change that feeling. Give it time. Apply the procedure, and learn it step by step.

You should be aware that there are risks involved in this. What you want to avoid at all costs is the narcissistic trap of always favoring short-term thinking. *Dopamine* brings short-term rewards. Its effects are powerful, and it can be just as addictive as some hard drugs.

Cocaine, amphetamine, and various opiates have the same effects on the brain as dopamine. They all make you feel absolutely fantastic. However, this feeling only lasts for a short time, after which you'll need to get hold of more of the same drug in order to experience the same effects. Eventually, you'll need a lot more. This is how some drugs can be so addictive and can get people hooked so quickly. Anybody who has tried them will tell you that it doesn't take long to develop an addiction.

However, this reward is a deceptive one, as it doesn't actually do anything to solve any of your problems. Whatever caused you to need that high will still be there afterwards. Basically, the body's rewards system has been hot-wired.

So, how do you go about getting your reward without risking picking up any shortsighted, risky addictions?

If it was easy more people would be doing it. What we know for sure is that most people need a reason to actually do the right thing. They need a purpose in order to see meaning in anything. Without a purpose, you might as well spend all day on the couch at home, playing video games and smoking weed. After all, nothing matters.

ANCIENT WISDOM

At this point, I'm going to take a chance and resort to a very old— and, if we're being honest, slightly clichéd—metaphor. Perhaps you've heard the story of the stonemason in the desert? If you have, please bear with me—and know that this version won't end the same way as the one you've heard before.

The story goes more or less like this: A wanderer is crossing the desert and comes across a man cutting stones. The wanderer asks the stonemason what he's doing. The mason responds, perhaps unsurprisingly, that he is cutting stones. When asked how he feels about his work, the stonemason spits on the ground and exclaims that it is mind-numbingly dull.

The wanderer walks on and comes across another stonemason. Again, the wanderer asks him what he is doing. This stonemason responds that he is making parts to build an amazing cathedral, which will reach high into the sky and be the most incredible building ever seen. When asked how he feels about his work, this man says that he loves it. Just imagine being a part of something that incredible!

The story usually ends somewhere around this point. It is supposed to help people reach the profound insight that stones can be cut for different reasons. However, the true lesson here is slightly obscured. We all grasp the basics of the story: It's more fun to build a beautiful cathedral than to simply cut stones, even if the actual tasks involved are identical.

Why is this, though? Why does it feel more meaningful to cut stones for one reason than for the other?

FINDING DEEPER MEANING

This is where the question of meaning enters the equation. Is there some hidden meaning behind everything? Does it really matter what I do? Am I cutting stones for a paycheck or to create something that's greater than myself? A beautiful cathedral, sure.

But does the cathedral itself mean anything in particular? It represents spirituality, sharing something huge with—potentially—millions of people. Now, a cathedral is a house of worship, and not everybody is religious. But the real point here has to do with taking part in the joint creation of a value that's greater than the sum of its parts. Making a place where people can find faith, or themselves, or whatever they need to manage their lives. However, it's also a place for contemplation, and for concepts and ideas that are perhaps greater than any individual person.

All this makes a cathedral far more than just a beautiful piece of architecture.

Few individuals—narcissists and psychopaths are the exceptions, here—are immune to the feeling that comes from being part of something like that. This time, the neurotransmitter doing the work isn't *dopamine,* but rather *serotonin* and *oxytocin.* These substances are more associated with long-term happiness than anything else.

No meaning. No purpose. No goal. No direction. No reason to get off the couch.

No positive expectations of any kind.

This feeling has been familiar to human beings for millennia. Early on, they may not have known as much about the mechanisms of the brain, but they did know how human beings function on a basic level. It's actually quite remarkable.

That's what makes the story about the stonemasons such an important one. We need meaning, purpose, and a goal. We need direction in our lives. When we have that, we'll suddenly find countless reasons to get off the couch.

This is precisely why long-term unemployment is such a disastrous fate. It instills a sense of hopelessness. It pacifies the individual, and creates the illusion that they can no longer contribute at all. Somebody who has no purpose and performs no function will soon break down.

That's why you're better off taking a low-paying job than persisting in unemployment: It will protect your mind. Credible studies suggest that unemployment is a far worse outcome, even when the economic compensation remains identical. Anybody who decides that there's no point in working since it won't earn them more money than they would get from welfare is living dangerously then, it seems.

SOCIAL MEDIA—AN ALTERNATIVE APPROACH

I'm not sure I can repeat this enough: The Internet is not the real world. On the other hand, the Internet is an excellent tool for spreading narcissism. Narcissists love attention. Narcissists love to show off. They take great pleasure in knowing that all eyes are on them.

They are driven by a deep craving for likes and positive feedback, and they are prepared to go to great lengths to get them.

The image they present of themselves and their lives is often a highly exaggerated one—and they demand recognition for the illusion they've spun, too! The more fully they can deceive people about the true state of things, the more they expect people to cheer.

Influencers present themselves in perfect settings, wearing elegant clothes, with perfect tans, always on the move. They are in the back seat of a limo or driving a Ferrari. If you look closely, you'll start to notice peculiar details.

A common thing on Instagram is posts where you see two cars in the same picture. Not any old lemons, though—perish the thought! On the left, a $300,000 Bentley. Jaw-droppingly elegant, it is a wonder of design. On the right, a $400,000 Rolls-Royce. Simply divine, unattainable. Below the picture, a call to action for the followers: *Which one would you like to own? Which one will you be driving next year?* People post their responses. *I'll take the Bentley! No, no! The Rolls is much nicer! BOTH OF THEM!* somebody shouts in all caps. The air is heavy with daydreams. Others exclaim that they would literally do *anything* to get their hands on a car like that.

WATCH TV OR ENGAGE IN MEANINGFUL ACTIVITY?

In an interview he gave a few years ago, one of Lamborghini's top executives was asked why Lamborghini never advertises on TV. His response? "Our customers don't watch TV." Let that sink in for a moment, and think about what he's actually saying.

In one post, a guy is steering a small yacht towards another much larger and more expensive ship, which has a large open hatch on the side of its hull. The post reads: *While you're watching TV, this guy is parking his boat in his other boat.* I don't know.

Diamonds. Female influencers wear millions of dollars' worth of jewelry on their hands. Often with a pretty nonchalant look on their face. Like they couldn't care less. It's just some old diamonds. They just happened to be valued at something like the lifetime earnings of an average worker.

You often see pictures of houses, too—palaces, really: gaudy and costly enough to be the envy of kings. Some of them look like they have thirty bedrooms. There's an Aston Martin in the driveway. The post often reads something like this: *I'll be living in a house like this in five years.* Or: *Like this if you're the first millionaire your family has produced!*

There are worse examples than this. Far worse. I'm not lying. On several occasions, I've seen Instagram posts of people *literally* bathing in money. Filling their bathtubs with cash. We're talking banknotes here. A table full of stacks of bills. Kilos and kilos of paper. The written post underneath these photos will often say something like: *What's it going to be? Have you decided what you want your lifestyle to be? What are you prepared to do to get it?*

Bizarre? I'd say so.

In one video clip I saw, a guy walks up to his fridge, grabs a fistful of money, and carries it out to the balcony. There, he tosses it over the side, from the tenth floor or so, and the bills spread far and wide. Another guy releases fistfuls of money from the sunroof of his car while he drives down the street at full speed. It's literally raining money.

Are the videos fake? We'll have to hope so. But there's no mistaking the message here: Accumulate money until you have enough to fund any harebrained scheme you can come up with!

Some people make a point of letting everybody know that they're *self-made;* nobody helped them. They did it all themselves, simply by doing their thing. Many of them go on about how they don't care about anything or anybody else, and invest everything into themselves and their own success. And to top it off, they encourage the rest of us to do the same.

"You could just go for it, too! You could have all this cool stuff that I have. You could travel by private jet and sports car. You could stay in five-star hotels and enjoy a life in the sun."

It sounds cool, it oozes confidence, and it's even the kind of thing many of us might actually go for.

Claim your share of the world. Go for it. Do your thing.

But what does that really mean, to *do your thing*?

Apart from the obvious, that is: Since nobody can achieve much of anything on their own, you have to give some thought to what this message is actually supposed to be telling us.

Of course, feeding yourself this kind of thing won't do you any harm as long as you keep in mind that it's all a deceptive illusion, from start to finish. You can always choose to laugh at all the insanity.

At the same time . . . this particular kind of self-centered hyper-narcissism—I can't think of a better word—is actually an indication that all the people who can't make it on TikTok or Instagram but who still want that glamorous lifestyle are going to try to get it, or something like it, some other way.

What might that be, assuming we rule out a life of crime? Well, if you want enough money to buy a new car more often than your neighbor does, travel constantly, and heap plastic toys over your children, your options are basically to either get yourself into a huge amount of debt or spend your money on endless scratch cards or bets on horse races. Relax! I'm not actually recommending this; I'm just making sure you understand what I'm getting at.

HOW TO COUNTERACT HYPERNARCISSISM

You start your own business, work hard for seven years, and reap the rewards of your efforts. Success takes time. It doesn't come overnight. When I started writing this book, Jeff Bezos was the wealthiest human alive. Apparently, as I am finishing it, it is now Elon Musk. Those guys are legitimately loaded. But they didn't achieve that overnight. It took them both more than thirty years to get to where they are today.

You have to work until you're groaning with exhaustion, but if you do, success will be the outcome more often than not. Like financial icon Warren Buffett said when someone asked him why so few people actually follow his investing advice: "Nobody wants to get rich slowly."

Perhaps we should be more cautious about comparing ourselves to others. After all, there's always going to be someone out there who's outdone us. We can't compete with the narcissists. Let them burn themselves out in their struggle to appear to own the most stuff.

If you need a role model, pick a wholesome one. But more than anything, make a point of considering your life in comparison to one year ago. Do things look better now? If so, that's great. Celebrate with a night on the town! If things, unfortunately, seem to have taken a turn for the worse, that's bad. You should immediately sketch out a plan for addressing the situation. Get to work on that, and as soon as it's finished start implementing it! But don't worry too much about comparing yourself to the people you see on Instagram or Facebook.

Remember: The Internet is not the real world. There's a lot of content out there, from bad news to hate speech, bullying, and whatever else that's anything but confidence boosting. I don't want to get too deeply into all that stuff, because it's a real mess.

DIGITAL DETOX

My advice: Turn everything off for a month and see what effect this has on your stress levels.

Ditch Twitter for thirty days. Uninstall the Facebook and Instagram apps for a month. Are you on other platforms, too? Remove them. For thirty days.

Did this idea give you chest pains? Did you suddenly find it a little hard to breathe? That might be a clue, of course—I'm just saying!

Relax. You can always reinstall it all later.

Try it for just *thirty days*. If you live to be eighty, that'll be just one-thousandth of your life. You can do it! It's free. You actually stand to learn a lot from an experiment like this. Thirty days is nothing.

More and more people have started doing this. And all of them, without exception, say the same thing: "I feel so much better. How can this be?"

There is a simple, physiological explanation. The stress hormone *cortisol* is suddenly no longer being frantically pumped into your system. You're finally disengaging from the state of being permanently ready for battle.

You're no longer constantly on alert. You begin to relax, both physically and mentally. You start valuing other activities besides sitting around with your phone. Perhaps you'll start spending more time with your child, or husband, or wife, or parents, or whoever matters to you. Perhaps you'll start exercising. Or reading books. Or calling a friend and engaging in more genuine communication.

Some people are so happy with the results of giving up social media that they never go back. Ever. It's quite remarkable.

I raised the issue of a digital detox during a digital lecture I held in 2020, and it was met with a certain measure of skepticism. The most common reaction was this: "What on earth will I do instead?" Well, what did you do before you got hooked on using that device?

But to return to the subject of narcissistic culture: After denying yourself these options for some time, you'll see the deviance inherent to certain behavior much more clearly. You won't be numbed to it anymore. It'll be more obvious to you that what some people get up to online is actually far from normal.

You may even insert yourself in the situation more actively and say, "That thing you did, my friend, was not okay. Please don't do that anymore."

Suddenly, you'll have made yourself a part of a positive change.

EXHALE

Is it possible for you to figure out how you can find more meaning in your life? Of course. Think deeply about this, and feel free to ask others to help you figure out your true purpose. Not when do you feel good? But rather, what constitutes your meaning? This will bring you a sense of inner peace that you'll never want to let go of.

Perhaps, as I mentioned earlier, mindfulness is an option for you. Or perhaps a skilled CBT therapist might be able to help you. There are many excellent personal coaches who are experts at challenging people to think new, revolutionary thoughts about their lives. This is often time extremely well spent. I wouldn't have been where I am today—which also happens to be where I truly want to be—if one of my coaches hadn't forced me to stop lying to myself.

It felt a little painful at the time, but overall, it was the best piece of advice I've ever received. I'm definitely buying her lunch when I'm done writing this book.

Linda, Part 3: How Can We Help Her?

To confront a person with his own shadow
is to show him his own light.

—CARL JUNG

If the person sitting in the front row of the airplane leans their seat back as far as it will go, the person sitting behind them will have to do the same or end up with a kneeful of coffee. This spreads all the way back until whoever is in the last row has to contend with the problem. This person is seated by the wall and has nowhere to go.

Sometimes I get the feeling that a growing number of us have started pushing our seats back all the way. And, somewhere along the way, we're going to have to address the issue before we lose control completely.

It's time for us to revisit our old friend Linda one last time. I'm sure you haven't forgotten her. Linda with the overly supportive parents, who finally had enough of her behavior and told her that she would have to make her own way in the world from now on. Linda, whose go-to strategies for getting what she wanted from other people included coercion, tears, and arguing. She used these tricks on everyone: her mother, her father, her teacher, and, as in the first example in this book, her boss.

As you may recall, Linda's father ran out of patience in the end, and drew the line: No more bailouts. No more running from responsibility. Time for Linda to act like an adult.

Let's say you and Linda were close friends and she came to you to complain that her father was no longer supporting her. Everything was so unfair. Nothing turned out the way she imagined it would.

Let's suppose you don't actually suspect that Linda is a clinical narcissist (men are actually much more often narcissists than women, probably because they're less empathic overall) who has been diagnosed with NPD, but that you rather see her as a victim of what I've defined here as narcissistic culture. This means that she doesn't really have a narcissistic personality as such; she's simply established a bunch of behavior patterns that one could categorize as narcissistic. We can safely presume that she's never even considered her own behavior this way, and since nobody has actually said anything to her about it in the past, her father's announcement came as something of a shock to her.

Let's say she never even gave it a moment's thought. *Everyone does this!*

It's not Linda's fault that society is the way it is. She never asked to be caught up in something she's not even able to perceive.

But you want to help. And this is what I want to emphasize: We *need* to help one another. I don't want to get all preachy here, but collectively, we do need to get back into the habit of actually having the energy to do things for one another, rather than just for ourselves. Our entire system only got us to where we are today because we based it on mutual interest and cooperation. This is your chance to do some genuine good.

Naturally, I'm only speculating here, but what could you actually do to help Linda, if you had the chance? Assuming you—for reasons we needn't go into—care for Linda, and want the best for her. What should you do? What should you say?

What do you think she would have to do in order to get the problem under control?

What risks are you prepared to take in order to help her truly escape the downward spiral she's caught in?

What would you be prepared to say to her?

One of the most difficult things you can ever attempt is helping somebody who doesn't want to be helped. It's like trying to hug somebody who would prefer a fistfight. In my experience, the prospects of success are practically zero. The psychology here is actually pretty simple: When you give a piece of good, well-meaning advice to somebody, it also contains an implied criticism of whatever their current status quo happens to be. You wouldn't be giving them advice if everything was great, would you? So, that means you're being critical. And even if the person in question claims to be unhappy with their current situation, that doesn't necessarily mean they'll be asking you to reinforce their misgivings and ram some advice down their throat to go with it.

Sometimes you need to just listen. And then listen some more. Without opening your mouth.

Women are better at this than men. Men, as we all know, tend to head straight for the solution: "*Here's what you should do.*" If you, the reader, happen to live with a woman, she'll readily confirm this if you ask her: Sometimes all she wants is for you to listen. Let her describe her experiences for a while, without interrupting.

But then what?

If you're not coming up with any ideas that might help your friend improve their situation? Take Linda, for example. How might you genuinely help her and get her on board with her community?

The most important step is to make sure you know what the

problem really is. It's not Linda's dad who is the problem here, even though Linda may have implied as much.

If you don't understand which problem you're supposed to be solving, you'll never see the need for a solution. You'll have to figure that out first. And so will Linda. She will only refuse to take good advice for as long as the real problem remains invisible to her.

First, identify the problem. That means you have to get Linda to describe her life as she is experiencing it right now. Only once she has accepted that she needs to change will there be any point in explaining how you think she might go about it.

Is this stuff easy?

Not at all.

But I am fully and firmly convinced that we all need to support one another whenever we see somebody struggling. The sooner the better, of course, and it's worth remembering that most of us haven't yet succumbed to the narcissistic currents within our culture. If we are brave enough to address anything that looks like it could potentially lead us astray at the earliest possible moment, we might be able to be more generous with our time and help one another break the pattern.

Is it too late for somebody like Linda?

I don't know. That depends entirely on what will happen over the next few weeks.

Is there a Linda in your life? Do something! Anything. Together, we can all change the course and steer clear of the most difficult problems.

I like that old expression: It takes a village to raise a child.

Thanks for reading all the way to the end.

Be good to one another out there!

Bibliography and Sources

INTRODUCTION

Twenge, Jean M., Ph.D., and W. Keith Campbell, Ph.D. *The Narcissism Epidemic*. New York: Atria Books, 2009.

7. DO I LOVE MYSELF? IT'S COMPLICATED

Campbell, W. K., J. K. Bosson, T. W. Goheen, C. E. Lakey, and M. H. Kernis. "Do Narcissists Dislike Themselves 'Deep Down Inside'?" *Psychological Science* 18 (2007): 227–29.

Gentile, B., and J. M. Twenge. *Birth Cohort Changes in Self-Esteem, 1988–2007*. Unpublished manuscript. Based on B. Gentile, master's thesis, San Diego State University, 2008.

Twenge, J. M., and W. K. Campbell. "Age and Birth Cohort Differences in Self-Esteem: A Cross-Temporal Meta-Analysis." *Personality and Social Psychology Review* 5 (2001): 321–44.

13. HOW ARE NARCISSISTS MADE?

Bronson, Po. "How Not to Talk to Your Kids." *New York*, February 9, 2007. http://nymag.com/news /features/27840/.

Horton, R. S., G. Bleau, and B. Drwecki. "Parenting Narcissus: What Are the Links Between Parenting and Narcissism?" *Journal of Personality* 74. (2006): 345–76.

Miller, J. D., and W. K. Campbell. "Comparing Clinical and Social-Personality Conceptualizations of Narcissism." *Journal of Personality* 76 (2008).

Otway, L. J., and V. L. Vignoles. "Narcissism and Childhood Recollections: A Quantitative Test of Psychoanalytic Predictions." *Personality and Social Psychology Bulletin* 32 (2006): 104–16.

Twenge, J. M., and W. K. Campbell. *Parenting and Narcissism: A Prospective Study*. Unpublished manuscript. Taken from Twenge and Campbell, *The Narcissism Epidemic*.

20. WHEN THE PROBLEM AFFECTS MORE THAN JUST A FEW INDIVIDUALS

Ogden, C. L., C. D. Fryar, M. D. Carroll, and K. M. Flegal. "Mean Body Weight, Height and Body Mass Index, United States 1960–2002." *Advance Data from Vital and Health Statistics* 347, October 27, 2004.

21. EXPRESSIONS OF A NARCISSISTIC CULTURE

Buffardi, L. E., and W. K. Campbell. "Narcissism and Social Networking Websites." *Personality and Social Psychology Bulletin* 34, no. 10 (2008): 1303–1314.

25. SELF-ESTEEM: MORE TROUBLE THAN YOU'RE WORTH

The South Koreans, however, far exceeded the US students' actual performance on math tests: This testing data (from the Trends in International Mathematics and Science Study [TIMSS]) as well as the data from the National Assessment of Educational Progress (NAEP) can be found online on a site run by the US Department of Education. http://nces. ed.gov/index.asp. See, for example, http://nces.ed.gov/timss/results03_ eighth95.asp.

26. NORMALIZING NARCISSISM

Foster, J. D., W. K. Campbell, and J. M. Twenge. "Individual Differences in Narcissism: Inflated Self-Views Across the Lifespan and Around the World." *Journal of Research in Personality* 37: 469–86.

Gibbs, Nancy. "Do Kids Have Too Much Power?" *Time*, August 6, 2001. http://www.time.com /time/covers/1101010806/cover.html.

27. TEST YOURSELF: ARE YOU A NARCISSIST?

https://opeNPDychometrics.org/tests/NPI/.

Raskin, R., and H. Terry. "A Principal-Components Analysis of the Narcissistic Personality Inventory and Further Evidence of Its Construct Validity." *Journal of Personality and Social Psychology* 54, no. 5 (1988): 890–902.

Index